# THE POLITICS OF DUBLIN CORPORATION, 1840–1900

# The Politics of Dublin Corporation, 1840–1900

*From reform to expansion*

JAMES H. MURPHY

FOUR COURTS PRESS

Set in 10.5pt on 13.5pt CaslonPro by
Carrigboy Typesetting Services for
FOUR COURTS PRESS LTD
7 Malpas Street, Dublin 8, Ireland
www.fourcourtspress.ie
*and in North America for*
FOUR COURTS PRESS
c/o IPG, 814 N Franklin St, Chicago, IL 60610.



ISBN 978-1-84682-853-9

A catalogue record for this title is available
from the British Library.

Comhairle Cathrach
Bhaile Átha Cliath
Dublin City Council

Published with the support of Dublin City Council.



Printed in England
by TJ International, Padstow, Cornwall.

*For Jamie O'Connell*

# Contents

# Introduction

THE CITY OF DUBLIN HAD BEEN the capital of the kingdom of Ireland, a subordinate country to the kingdom of England (later Great Britain) but, nonetheless, a kingdom with its own parliament, which periodically met in Dublin, and a court of sorts, under the king's representative, the lord lieutenant, who periodically lived in Dublin. It had lost its status as a capital city with the parliamentary union of Ireland with Great Britain in 1801. Economic slumps and a general decline characterized much of the experience of the city during the nineteenth century. It remained, nonetheless, the residence of a lord lieutenant who lived mostly in a residence in the Phoenix Park on the outskirts of the city and partly at Dublin Castle in the centre of the city, where the first months of each year saw a variety of formal court ceremonies and entertainments that brought a good deal of prosperity to the city's merchants. Dublin Castle was also the centre of the government under the chief secretary, who was a British politician, and of the civil service answerable to the under-secretary. The politics of the first decades of the century were dominated by the efforts of British governments to modernize the country and by a struggle between those who supported the continuing dominant role of the existing landlord class – the Protestant ascendancy – in society and those who wanted that role to give way to one for the rising Catholic classes. Under the leadership of Daniel O'Connell (1775–1847) the latter had attained Catholic emancipation in 1829, enabling Catholics to sit as members of parliament. By the 1840s O'Connell had set his eyes on a goal he was not to attain, the repeal of the union with Britain. Nonetheless, religious and political differences mapped themselves onto politics in Dublin as well as in the rest of the country.

Dublin Corporation was the name for the ancient municipal council of Dublin. It was reformed under the Municipal Corporations (Ireland) Act of 1840 and the power of the trade guilds that had kept it exclusively in Protestant hands was removed. A second, lesser known, reform took place with

I am grateful to DePaul University, Chicago, for grants and research leave, and to Boston College, for the Burns visiting scholarship in Irish studies, which enabled me to undertake research for this book. I am grateful to Ciaran O'Neill of Trinity College Dublin for his advice on this work.

the Dublin Municipal Act of 1850. On the one hand, this act increased the powers to the Corporation, amalgamating into it many of the powers of the semi-autonomous bodies that had controlled aspects of Dublin life, such as the wide streets commission. On the other hand, it had the effect of somewhat restoring the influence of wealthier Protestant Tories, or Conservatives, on the Corporation. Thereafter, the Corporation remained relatively unchanged until the end of the century. Then the municipal franchise, which had tended to be more restrictive than the parliamentary franchise, was widened; and the boundaries of the city of Dublin, which had hitherto been circumscribed by the Royal Canal to the north and the Grand Canal to the south, were expanded to include several of the surrounding townships.[1] These had been formed from the middle of the nineteenth century and had become havens for Protestant Tories anxious to escape the higher taxation in the city and the prevalence there of nationalist power.[2]

Perhaps the only figure from Dublin Victorian civic politics who is in any way remembered is Sir John Gray (1815–75), the promoter of the Vartry water scheme whose statue still adorns O'Connell St. In January 1867 the Corporation debated a proposal to move Hogan's statue of Daniel O'Connell, who had been lord mayor after the initial reform, from the rotunda of the City Hall outside to the front of the building. (This was done though when the statue began to deteriorate it was soon moved back in again.) Speaking in support of the statue motion and with reference to O'Connell's achievement of Catholic emancipation and work with Dublin Corporation, Gray said that O'Connell had 'opened the portals of the constitution to his Catholic fellow-countrymen against whom they were so long closed (cheers). He created that little civic parliament, which would, perhaps, serve hereafter as the model of a parliament for the whole of Ireland. (cheers).' [7/8 Jan. 1867]

This book is the first comprehensive study of the politics of Dublin Corporation between its initial reform in 1840 and its reform at the end of the nineteenth century, when the city's electorate and boundaries changed radically. In undertaking it I had hoped that it would form the final part in a trilogy of books, beginning with *Abject loyalty: nationalism and monarchy in Ireland during the reign of Queen Victoria* (2001) and *Ireland's czar: Gladstonian politics and the lord lieutenancies of the red Earl Spencer, 1868–86* (2014). These two books had traced the ways in which Irish nationalist political culture had

1 The seven townships were Pembroke (1863), Rathmines (1847) and New Kilmainham (1868) immediately to the south of the city; Blackrock (1860) and Kingstown (1828) further to the south; and Clontarf (1869) and Drumcondra (1878) to the immediate north of the city. 2 In the 1830s, Protestants had constituted twenty-seven per cent of the city's population. By 1871, they had already declined to twenty-one per cent and by 1901 to eighteen per cent. Mary E.

been formed within the contours of its interaction with institutions of constitutional affinity, such as the monarchy and lord lieutenancy, between Ireland and Britain. My expectation was that Dublin Corporation, the most important and prestigious deliberative body in Ireland, might prove to be another such, that it might have proven to be the little civic parliament of which Gray spoke. Yet this has not proved to be the case. Gray's notion had only briefly been true. There had been a moment in early 1843 when O'Connell and the then Tory Isaac Butt (1813–79) debated repeal during meetings of the Corporation. But a parliament requires legitimacy to be authoritative and the story of the three decades from the initial reform of Dublin Corporation is of Tory attempts to wrest back their dominance by undermining the notion that a Dublin Corporation, under Catholic nationalist control, was legitimate or authoritative. Thus, later attempts to debate great national and international issues eventually ran into the sands when Tories, who were the minority, simply did not turn up to challenge motions that they could not win and which, in any event, could not effect any change. Dublin Corporation in the nineteenth century was thus to contribute little to the functioning and successful parliamentary culture that developed in the twentieth century in post-independence Ireland.

The political sectarianism in the Corporation is evidence for the continuing relevance of events such as Catholic emancipation and the disestablishment of the Protestant episcopal church (now known as the Church of Ireland) as the official state church. Important in popular history, they have seemed less important to historians. What real difference had Catholic emancipation made to the political power of Catholics? Was not disestablishment of the Church of Ireland just window dressing? Yet these changes were of great importance, albeit mostly for Protestants and their view of themselves in Ireland. The reform of Dublin Corporation in 1840 was Catholic emancipation *après la letter*, coming a decade late to Dublin civic politics. For Protestant Tories it was a challenge to their view of themselves as the dominant community and they spent thirty years resisting its implications. After disestablishment in 1871, whether coincidentally or not, they withdrew from the battlefield of Dublin city to the redoubts of the townships. Sectarianism in nineteenth-century Ireland is often associated with Ulster and in terms of cities, with Belfast. Yet, as Mary Daly wrote in her classic study of nineteenth-century Dublin, 'While sectarian tensions in Dublin were expressed in places such as the City Hall rather than in street rioting as in Belfast, they were nonetheless acrimonious'.[3] The middle of the century in

Daly, *Dublin, the deposed capital: a social and economic history, 1860–1914* (Cork, 1984), p. 122.
3 Daly, *Deposed capital*, p. 17.

particular was associated with religious tension, after the Church of Ireland archbishop of Dublin, William Magee (1766–1831), called for the conversion of Catholics, leading to the so-called 'second reformation' as evangelicals sought to win over the majority population. The latter was itself growing in confidence, in religious terms, in a change that has been termed the devotional revolution, under the later Catholic archbishop of Dublin, Paul Cardinal Cullen (1803–78). Tensions were real in Dublin and there were some celebrated cases such as the controversy surrounding the work in children's homes of the evangelical Ellen Smyly (1815–1901).

After disestablishment there followed a relatively non-political decade for the Corporation until the early 1880s saw the control of Corporation politics subsumed by the nationalist movement under the control of the Irish Parliamentary Party and in the 1890s by its post-Parnellite factions.

Dublin Corporation therefore offered no formative structure for political culture. But Corporation politics was of great importance not only in itself but because of the window it offered onto a myriad of social and economic issues. These included the arrival of the railways; the provision of water and sanitation, of food and markets for produce, of health care and education, and of opportunities for recreation; the problem of crime; the position of industries such as brewing; growing conflict over labour relations; and the development of the middle classes. In tackling these issues the Corporation was facing challenges familiar to other large cities within the United Kingdom. In many ways Dublin was just as much a British city as it was a specifically Irish one.

This book, which presumes some general knowledge of nineteenth-century Irish history on the part of the reader, has a limited aim inasmuch as it seeks principally to offer a narrative of the politics of the Corporation itself as a deliberative assembly. I have decided to use the word Corporation both to refer to Dublin's governing entity and to the council that controlled it. This was a common practice at the time and the context should indicate the usage. It might be argued that it would be better to use the term 'city council' for the assembly but this term sounds too generic and, in any event, under legislation Dublin's was technically a town council.

There is a uniqueness to the history of Dublin in the nineteenth century as it has hitherto been researched. Whereas in most of the writing of Irish history political history has preceded social and economic history, in the case of Dublin social and economic history has dominated and what political history there has been has tended to focus on political movements. This therefore is the first study of the politics of the Corporation in terms of political actors engaging with the issues of their day. It has that limited, but important, aim. It ought to serve as a significant piece in the wider jigsaw that includes Dublin politics more generally, local government in Ireland and in Britain and issues in social and economic history.

Corporation politics was certainly part of the wider politics of Dublin though in a limited way. Indeed, because of the restricted municipal franchise some of that wider politics gained only partial traction within the Corporation. Thus the Corporation was largely a bystander during the years of most intense Fenian activity in the 1860s. Equally, though, the Corporation was open to perspectives that wider Irish politics often ignored. As a large city Dublin often looked to other large cities in Britain and elsewhere in a transnational way over questions of taxation, industry and infrastructure. In addition Corporation politics offered a fascinating insight into the labyrinthine world of local government with its myriad forms of taxation. Central government was in a rudimentary condition when it came to issues of local infrastructure. Indeed, many were against too centralized an approach on local matters. Dublin Corporation had thus to expend time and money both promoting its own legislative agenda at Westminster and defending the city against the agendas of other interest groups.

Written records of the Corporation's proceedings are available in the Dublin city archives. However, they constitute a fairly minimal record, generally confined to recording motions and votes. As its principal source for debates in the Corporation this work refers, therefore, to accounts of council meetings as reported in the *Freeman's Journal* newspaper which published near verbatim versions of meetings of the Corporation during the period and functioned in this regard as a newspaper of record. The *Freeman's Journal* was the mainstream, daily, nationalist newspaper throughout the period covered by this book, being controlled by Sir John Gray and later by his son, Edmund Dwyer Gray (1845–88), until 1891 when it was taken over by the Irish Parliamentary Party. Formally, the Corporation was only required to meet four times a year, on the so-called quarter days. In practice it met weekly, sometimes more than once a week. While some meetings were short, accounts of many meetings often took 10,000 words. The *Freeman's Journal* may thus have published nearly thirty million words in its accounts of the main proceedings of the Corporation over the period covered by this book. Two examples from different periods may illustrate how much more important it is than the official record as a source of information on the workings of the Corporation. In February and March 1843, the Corporation spent three days debating home rule. The reports in the *Freeman's Journal* on 1, 2 and 3 March came to 60,000 words. The length of the official, hand-written record, now in the Dublin city archives, was 800 words. Similarly, in October 1881 there was a debate on granting the freedom of the city to Charles Stewart Parnell. The

*Freeman's Journal* report on 26 October 1881 came to 16,000 words. The official record amounted to 200 words.[4]

These accounts in the *Freeman's Journal* enjoyed widespread confidence in terms of their reliability. At one point the paper was referred to as the Hansard of the Corporation in a reference to the official record of proceedings at Westminster. [8/9 Jan. 1852] Equally, when the account was inaccurate members of the Corporation soon complained about it, though this did not happen very often. [15/16 Oct. 1846] Indeed, the accounts in the *Freeman's Journal* were sometimes used to correct inaccuracies in other papers. Thus in 1848 when one member denied reports that he admitted to lying he referenced the report in the *Freeman's Journal*, 'whose reports are always so accurate', to back him up. [19/20 Dec. 1848]

For the sake of concision references to the accounts in the *Freeman's Journal* are included in square brackets in the text and follow the day month year pattern. Where two initial numbers are given separated by a solidus (commonly called a slash) the first refers to the date of the meeting and the second to the date of the report in the paper. The same broad convention applies when other events or documents are referred to. Occasionally, quotations from the *Freeman's Journal* are journalistic comment rather than reports of proceedings, but this should be clear from the context. The vast majority of quotations from and references to the *Freeman's Journal* in this work therefore are to impartial reports of debates in the Corporation as reported in the newspaper. They do not carry the nationalist editorial agenda of the newspaper.

4 Dublin city archives. City council minute books, 12. C2/A1/12. Dec. 1842 to May 1844. 28 Feb., 1, 2 Mar. 1843, pp 132–7; *Minutes of the municipal council of the city of Dublin from the 1st of January to 31st of December, 1881* (Dublin, 1882). 25 Oct. 1881, pp 379–80.

CHAPTER 1

# Reform, 1839–41

THE PERIOD AFTER THE END of the Napoleonic wars was one of political radicalism in Britain. This was among the reasons for the passing of the 1832 parliamentary reform act that increased the franchise and redrew boundaries. It gave the vote to many middle-class men while granting representation to some hitherto unrepresented urban areas during a period when the industrial revolution was causing the expansion of new towns and cities. Around the same time the removal of the final civil disabilities against Catholics was achieved in the 1829 Catholic emancipation act, that allowed Catholics to sit in parliament, though Jews would have to wait nearly thirty years for a similar reform.

The 1830s were years when reformists looked towards the overhaul of local government both in Britain and Ireland. Reform was achieved in England in 1835. It had been an urgent matter as many new industrial towns and cities had not had real municipal government. But it would be a further five years and five failed attempts before the passing of the Municipal Corporations (Ireland) Act of 1840, which dissolved fifty-eight Irish boroughs and thus reduced the number of Irish boroughs to ten, including Dublin, though Wexford managed to get itself reprieved a few years later.[1] Reform was limited in Ireland, however, due to pressure from Tories against the stirrings of democracy.

Before reform Dublin Corporation was bicameral. It was an arcane body which was oligarchical and to a large extent self-perpetuating, though its offices often had important judicial and administrative functions attached to them. In 1829 James Norris Brewer in his *History of Leinster* attempted to explain how it functioned thus:

> The Corporation of this city consists of twenty-five aldermen, of whom one exercises the office of chief magistrate under the title of lord mayor; ninety-six members of common council; a certain number of sheriff's peers, not exceeding forty-eight; a recorder and other officers. The lord

1 J.R. Hill, *Patriots to Unionists: Dublin civic politics and Irish Protestant patriotism, 1660–1840* (Oxford, 1997), p. 366.

> mayor is annually elected from the court of aldermen; and that court returns the name of the member chosen by themselves for the approbation of the commons. No person chosen lord mayor, sheriff, recorder or town clerk is capable of executing that officer until approved by the lord lieutenant, or other chief governor, and the privy council. The lord mayor, aldermen and two sheriffs, are justices of the peace in the city and liberties of Dublin.
>
> The aldermen are chosen for life, from the sheriff's peers or those who have either served or fined office of sheriff, and are elected by the lord mayor, aldermen and common council. The common council are elected for three years, by and out of the twenty-five guilds, or Corporations, existing in this city. The sheriff's peers are perpetual members of the commons.[2]

The sheriffs – or high sheriffs – and the recorder had a number of administrative and judicial functions. The lord mayor, whose role was more honorific than executive, presided over the aldermen and the two sheriffs over the common council. All those involved in the Corporation were drawn from a group of about 4,000 hereditary voters called freemen.[3]

Other unreformed Irish Corporations had different structural configurations, at least *de facto*. In the city of Cork the common council reflected the professional and mercantile interests of the Protestants of the city, who amounted to one fifth of the population. However, real power lay with an informal Protestant group, the Friendly Club, membership of which was sought after and which ensured access to the Corporation. The senior sheriff for each year was almost always the club's president, for example. In reaction Catholics and reform-minded Protestants congregated around the city's chamber of commerce. By contrast, in mid-century Dublin, as we shall see later, the chamber of commerce often reflected a hostility to the reformed Corporation.[4]

After reform Dublin Corporation would consist of one chamber. Hitherto the dominance of the guilds and freemen meant that the Corporation had been in Protestant hands.[5] And even after reform large numbers of new freeman voters continued to be recognized, albeit only for the purposes of the separate parliamentary franchise rather than the municipal franchise.[6] Now,

2 James Norris Brewer, *History of Leinster* (London, 1829), p. 53. The city of London has maintained a similar structure of governance down to the present day. 3 Virginia Crossman, *Local government in nineteenth-century Ireland* (Belfast, 1994), pp 77–8. 4 Henry Alan Jefferies (ed.), *Cork: historical perspectives* (Dublin, 2004), pp 159–63. 5 Hill, *Patriots*, p. 368. 6 Daly, *Deposed capital*, p. 204, writes that the new municipal franchise was 'a straightforward property

however, all eligible male voters could vote in Corporation elections via a restrictive property qualification which consisted in a £10 property franchise. There were fifteen electoral divisions called wards, nine on the south and six on the north side of the city, with an alderman and three councillors being elected for each ward. The term alderman took on a new meaning but retained the sense it supposedly had under the old Corporation of denoting a more senior member. The aldermen were now those who had initially headed the vote and whose positions thereafter became a separate category with the privilege of longer terms in office. Every three years half the aldermen would face reelection, whereas one-third of councillors (one in each ward) would face reelection every year. This gave councillors a term of three years but aldermen a term of six years. Voters, or burgesses as they were called, had to occupy a house or live within seven miles of the city and be separately rated. This excluded those living in houses under £8 valuation as they were not separately rated. They also had to be living at the same address for at least three years. Members of the Corporation had to be burgesses, living within seven miles of the city, having property in the city to the value of £1,000 or the rated occupier of a property to the value of £25.[7]

Party politics in Dublin replicated that of the United Kingdom, with Tories, who would later be called Conservatives and, later still, Unionists, against Whigs, who would later merge with other groups to become Liberals. In general and in the Irish context it is true to say that the Tories were strong supporters of Protestant ascendancy, the dominance of the Protestant upper and middle classes in society. Whigs/Liberals tended to be a more amorphous though less sectarian group, whose porous boundaries could shade into Irish nationalism. They would eventually be displaced by assertive nationalism in the 1880s.

Faced with the likelihood of municipal reform in the late 1830s members of the Tory-dominated Corporation had been confronted with a choice of diehard opposition or openness to compromise in the hope of getting the best possible terms. Opposition, led by the young lawyer Isaac Butt, was the choice

franchise'; whereas Crossman, *Local government*, p. 78, writes that the freemen 'retained their municipal vote' in the new system. Subsequent controversy over freemen, however, occurs only in connection with the parliamentary context, so it would appear that freemen retained their vote in the parliamentary but not the municipal franchise. In November 1853, for example, John Reynolds called for the abolition of 'a body of parliamentary voters know as "freemen", now amounting in number to about four thousand, the great majority of whom are non-resident.' [1/2 Nov. 1853] 7 Daly, *Deposed capital*, pp 203–4; Ruth McManus and Lisa-Marie Griffin (eds), *Leaders of the city: Dublin's first citizens, 1500–1950* (Dublin, 2013), p. 109; Stefanie Jones, 'Dublin reformed: the transformation of the municipal governance of a Victorian city, 1840 – 1860', 2 vols (PhD, TCD, 2001), 1, p. 19.

of most and the Corporation petitioned parliament against change, with Butt delivering an address to the House of Lords on the matter.[8] A number of Irish Tories in the Commons were open to compromise. They were led by Frederick Shaw (1799–1876), an ally of the once and future Tory prime minister, Sir Robert Peel (1788–1850). Shaw was also recorder in Dublin, a judicial position that had been the gift of the Corporation. He was now unpopular among Dublin Tories. At a Dublin dinner in October 1839 Shaw was branded as a traitor and the following week a motion of no confidence in him was passed in the Corporation. It was also suggested that he had been feathering his own nest as the post of recorder was retained in the legislation [8/10 Oct. 1839; 18/19 Oct. 1839; 3 Aug. 1840]

In January of the following year the terms of the proposed legislation were denounced in extreme terms. Whig governments had certainly been trying in recent years to establish what they saw as a more impartial form of government in Ireland, to the detriment of the Protestant ascendancy so prized by Irish Tories. O'Connell had repeal of the act of union in his sights. Anxious Tories were bound to see municipal reform in sinister terms. Thomas James Quinton believed that the legislation showed 'that her majesty's ministers thought it unnecessary to preserve Protestantism in Ireland any longer.' If passed the Corporation would 'become exclusively papist'. It would be better for them to 'fall to the ground altogether' than to be 'transferred from the hands of the Protestants to those of popish demagogues.' [27/28 Jan. 1840] Quinton, a former sheriff, went on to publish a letter to the Protestants of Ireland in which he equated municipal reform with the end of Protestant ascendancy. There would instead be a 'Popish ascendancy'. 'All the time-honoured emblems of the victories of our forefathers must be trampled into the dust … we must cower before the believers in absurdity and error.' [6 Feb. 1840] It led to a meeting of Protestants at the Mansion House on 13 February, to coincide with debate on the bill in the Commons, at which one speaker presented the reform as threatening the integrity of the empire. 'It would also give increased means to the revolutionary and anti-Protestant party to get possession of the Protestant institutions of the country, which were intended for the better union of this country with Great Britain, and which they are so anxious to get into their possession in order to overthrow them and thereby to bring in a dismemberment of the empire.' [13/14 Feb. 1840]

There were of course also more personal reasons to oppose reform. Members of the existing establishment, including Corporation officials who anticipated losing their jobs, began to break ranks as reform seemed inevitable.

8 Hill, *Patriots*, p. 372.

A petition for compensation was presented to the House of Lords on behalf of the Dublin sword bearer who was reported to have twenty children. [16/27 Mar. 1840] Junior aldermen had paid money as part of the process that would one day lead them to the office of lord mayor and were interested in proposals to compensate them. [17 Feb. 1840] Alderman Drummond came in for particular criticism for having had discussions with Daniel O'Connell about the matter. [3/4 Mar. 1840]

All of this led to difficulty with electing a lord mayor for 1841. On 1 May 1840, one of the quarter days, the board of aldermen, which had been more moderate on reform, and the members of the common council, who had been more resistant, met separately at the city Assembly House to elect a lord mayor and high sheriffs for the following year. At 115 the turnout for the commons was large and it was determined to punish those who had temporized over reform. When Drummond was nominated for lord mayor he was defeated by sixty-three black beans to fifty-one white beans. A message was sent to the aldermen 'requiring the latter to send down the name of another alderman in place of that of Mr Drummond'. The next candidate turned out to be even less acceptable, attracting eighty-nine black beans and only three white beans. The following candidate did even worse, receiving only one white bean to eighty-nine black beans. Four further candidates were also rejected, the last gaining no white beans. Finally, at midnight the aldmermen nominated Sir John Kingston James who was elected by sixty-two white beans to eighteen black beans. [1/2 May 1840]

As it turned out Drummond had been foolish to have spoken to O'Connell on behalf of the junior aldermen as he had stood every chance of becoming lord mayor for the last year of the old system, though the fact that the law's implementation would be effectively delayed by a year did not become clear until August. [7/10 Aug. 1840] Nonetheless, he was tarred with mercenary intentions by one of the speakers against him who said that a quarter of a century before, O'Connell had been looking for a copy of *Bertram*, a play by the Revd Charles Robert Maturin (1782–1824), as proof of the immorality of established church clergymen. Drummond had apparently come forward with a copy but had been disgusted when O'Connell had refused to pay him the £5 he had promised. Drummond's opponent concluded: 'I would not now come forward to tell this story of Alderman Drummond, if it were not that the motive which induced him to offer his book for sale at thirty-five years of age is his ruling passion still (cheers).' [1/4 May 1840]

Meanwhile, as it became clear that the Tories, such as the Duke of Wellington (1769–1852) and Lord Lyndhurst (1772–1863), were prepared to countenance some form of reform speakers in the Corporation continued to lament its consequences. Irish Protestants, one member believed, had only agreed to the union with Great Britain 'under the pledge of being protected and their principles maintained in the government of the state.' Municipal reform would lead to repeal of the union. Protestants would say: 'we have lost our mercantile prospects forty years ago as a nation – we have lost our resident nobility and gentry – we are a nation of workers – a nation of hewers of wood and drawers of water – we have been deceived in all the professions made to us by an English government.' He concluded by somewhat daringly threatening that municipal reform would increase Protestant support for repeal: 'it might have the dangerous effect of enlisting ourselves under the banners of repeal.' [17/18 May 1840] But Quinton warned against rushing down this route. 'There is no necessity for haste; we can form associations of our own, in which we can discuss the question of repealing statutes on a still larger and better scale than that now contemplated. We can reserve for such occasions our opinions respecting the repeal of the legislative union upon which, if we once pledge ourselves to join Mr O'Connell's gang, we should indeed be ever after deprived of the power of seeking the restoration of other rights which have been so unjustly taken from us (hear, hear and cheers).' [21/22 Aug. 1840]

One member despaired of appeals to reason. 'If anything could have been done for the preservation of the Corporation, it would have been by the truly talented and all-powerful address of Professor Butt, before the House of Lords.' Now was the time for retribution. 'It was quite clear that they owed the present change to the treachery of their friends, rather than to anything else … No man should leave that room without having come to the determination of not supporting anyone who had given his support to this bill.' [10/11 Aug. 1840]

Indeed, acrimony was to become the note as the old Corporation entered its final term. At that banquet that followed James's inauguration as lord mayor there were anti-Catholic speeches and the aldermen were booed, though one MP spoke in favour of the Tories not having opposed the bill in parliament. [30 Sept./2 Oct. 1840] Members of the Corporation began to eye its property, though a move to sell off the state carriage was successfully blocked in the courts. [22 Jan. 1841]

Under the new act Dublin's deliberative body was to be formally known as the town council. As has been noted, the city was to be divided into fifteen wards with fifteen aldermen and forty-five councillors. [26 Aug. 1840] In order to qualify to vote electors had to show that they had paid their local taxes including those levied under the poor law rate, grand jury cess, wide streets cess, police tax, paving and lighting tax, parish cess and pipewater rent. [1 Dec. 1840; 11 May 1841] These taxes, most levied on the basis of property, were paid to a variety of bodies that had been established at different points in time to provide particular services. Eventually most of them would be integrated into the work of the Corporation itself and they will receive attention later on in this work. The functions of some of them were self-explanatory; others less so. The poor law rate supported the work of recently-established poor law unions that maintained workhouses for the poor. The north and south Dublin poor law unions had been established in 1839. Cess was an antique name for a tax. The grand jury was an older form of local government, dominated by the ascendancy, that provided for certain public works.

The electoral roll could be altered by the court of revision which had to take into account reports from tax collectors for the various taxes. Dublin city came within the operation of the act on 10 April 1841 and an election was set for 21 October. 'Every man of full age who, previous to the first day of August next, shall have resided within the borough for six calendar months previous, occupying a house or other tenement of the yearly value of £10, and rated for poor tax, shall be a burgess.' [22 Apr. 1841] The burgess list was initially to be the responsibility of church wardens, reflective of a time when the parishes of the established church had a role in civil government, though this responsibility was soon transferred to the collectors of the poor law rates. [26 Apr. 1841]

The forthcoming Dublin municipal election presented Dublin Liberals with a great opportunity, as Catholics would now form a significant part of the municipal electorate. Equally, it provided Dublin Liberals with the challenge of possibly being overwhelmed by candidates, claiming to be Liberals but pledged to support Daniel O'Connell and his Repeal Association. The latter body intersected deeply with Dublin Liberal politics. O'Connell had established the association in 1830 and was to increase his popular agitation for repeal in the early 1840s. He had established an alliance with the Whigs for cooperation in parliament in the 1835 Lichfield House compact. He lead a group of around thirty MPs in parliament and saw municipal reform as an opportunity to establish a base in Dublin Corporation which historically was one of the most prestigious local authorities in the United Kingdom, with ceremonial precedence and petitioning access to the monarch. As early as 8 August 1840, just before the news broke that the elections were not to be for another year, O'Connell, who was then MP for Dublin City, had called a meeting in the Corn Exchange in Burgh Quay, Dublin, next door to Conciliation Hall, the headquarters of the Repeal Association, about agreeing candidates for the forthcoming election. 'I am quite convinced that I will find sufficient disinterested patriotism amongst my constituents to prevent any dissension in the ranks of the Liberal electors.' He was sanguine even about the sort of Protestants who might be returned under the new system. 'We shall have the best class of the Protestant mercantile men in the city composing a portion of the common council, many of whom will be elected by the Liberal rate payers.' [8/10 Aug. 1840] The general election of July 1841 was to see the return of the Conservatives to power under Sir Robert Peel at Westminster and to Dublin Conservatives playing down their internal disputes for the sake of a common front against O'Connell.

At the general election O'Connell's repeal party won twenty seats (almost all those they had contested) but it still represented only a fifth of the Irish seats in parliament. Perhaps Dublin might in microcosm offer him a more visible political platform. As the Dublin municipal election approached O'Connell was very active in the city. On 19 August he attended five Liberal nomination meetings: at 11 a.m. at Bentley's shop on Capel St for Linen Hall ward; at 12 p.m. at the Corn Exchange for St Patrick's ward; at 2 p.m. at the Apollo Saloon, Grafton St, for the St Andrew's ward; at 3 p.m. at St Patrick's Seminary, Arran Quay, for St Paul's ward, where he was himself nominated; and, finally, at 4 p.m., at 13 Linenhall St for the Four Courts ward. The only meeting he missed that day was that at 3 p.m. in the Corn Exchange for College ward. [19/20 Aug. 1841] On 24 August he chaired a meeting at the Corn Exchange at which nominations were finalized for eight wards. He imposed strict discipline. Foreseeing legal challenges he required each person nominated to subscribe £50. Each ward was to appoint counsel to attend the revising court. [24/25 Aug. 1841] The revising court met continuously in October in the weeks leading up to the election. On 21 October, O'Connell held a meeting for Liberal candidates. He warned against Tory tricks. They might rush in towards the end of the day and 'thus wrest out of our hands a ward which we had reckoned on as our own … The man who is not on the spot at nine o'clock in the morning is a traitor to the cause – the man who does not vote for the whole ticket is a traitor to the cause.' [21/22 Oct. 1841]

The election on 25 October saw all the sixty seats in the new Corporation in contention. It was a triumph for O'Connell with forty-seven Liberals elected (including O'Connell twice) and thirteen Tories. Liberals won all the seats in twelve wards. Thirty-six of the Liberals were also Repealers.[9] The Tories won all the seats in two wards. They took three seats in another ward and two in a final ward. Tories gained the poll-topping alderman position in all four wards in which they took seats, indicating that their strength was located in particular parts of the south side of the city.

Of the Tories returned one was described as a baronet, two as gentlemen, one as an architect, three as barristers, one as a solicitor and five as merchants.

9 Hill, *Patriots*, p. 381.

Of the Liberals the profession of one member was not recorded. Daniel O'Connell was described as a member of parliament in Linen Hall and Four Courts wards where he was elected (he chose to sit for the latter). In addition there was one baronet, three gentlemen, two attorneys-at-law, one barrister, one doctor of medicine, one banker, one newspaper proprietor, thirteen merchants, one silk merchant, one feather merchant, one hide merchant, one grocer and wine merchant, two timber merchants, two tobacconists, two distillers, two builders, one mail coach proprietor, one printer and bookseller, one ironmonger, one factor, one tallow chandler, one miller, one farmer, one baker and one iron founder. [25/26 Oct. 1841; 28 Oct. 1841] Undoubtedly, the social composition of the Tories was a higher one than that of the Liberals, though there was a broad social stretch among the latter. The social composition of the membership of the Corporation would change greatly during the course of the century, with publicans becoming a significant group by the end.

Meanwhile the old Corporation was living out its last days and was descending into internecine vindictiveness. There was considerable ire directed against one alderman for participating in the ceremonies to mark the arrival of the new lord lieutenant. 'On yesterday he was to be seen in the procession of the new lord lieutenant – laughing, smiling, and exhibiting himself as in the best possible spirits on the occasion.' One member said 'that he belonged more to the Romanist than the Protestant party, as he had been instrumental in passing the new Corporation bill' while another believed he 'was a Jesuitical jobber, and would die one.' [16/18 Sept. 1841] They agreed money to paint the statue of William III on College Green, which the *Freeman's Journal*, in its editorial comment, described as being '[t]he dying kick of the old Corporation of Dublin' [15/16 Oct. 1841] Just after the election rumours that the outgoing lord mayor was not going to surrender the Mansion House led to a pro-reform crowd gathering outside the residence which only dispersed when an incoming councillor 'reminded them of the duty of evincing, by their forbearance and good temper, that they were superior to any unworthy ebullition of party exultations. It should be the boast of the people to prove themselves nobler and more generous than their opponents had been, and thus to convince all men of their fitness to discharge the duties of self-rule.' [27/28 Oct. 1841] The fitness of Catholics to rule Dublin would be a continuing implicit point of contention over the next thirty years.

In the aftermath of the election O'Connell was anxious to ensure that all the Repealers and Liberals elected would be able to take office. Forty of the new members were Catholics, one Tory, all but two of the Repealers and five of the Whigs (non-repeal Liberals).[10] To ensure that there would be no challenges O'Connell arranged for Catholic members to take the emancipation oath, prescribed under the 1829 Catholic emancipation act, before two magistrates, in the lead up to the first meeting of the new Corporation, though it was not entirely clear that this was necessary. O'Connell was already anticipating taking on the role of lord mayor. He had a special set of robes made and was keen to give the impression that the dignity of the position would put him above politics. 'He (Alderman O'Connell) would, of course, never think of visiting Lord De Grey [1781–1859, the new Tory lord lieutenant] as Daniel O'Connell, nor in his capacity of member of parliament for Cork or Meath. He did not feel inclined to pay any marked compliment to a man who kept giggling and gibbing at the theatre the other night, amid scenes of the most uproarious Tory tumult, instead of preserving that dignity of mien and manner which became his lofty position; but in his (Mr O'Connell's) capacity of lord mayor of Dublin he was bound, as representative of the city, to pay as much honour and respect as possible to the representative of the crown (loud cheers).' [29/30 Oct. 1841; 30 Oct./1 Nov. 1841] It was part of O'Connell's plan to make the most of the role of lord mayor in terms of dignity and national prestige. Again, this would be a continuing reason why nationalists would prize control of the Corporation throughout the century.

The date on which the new Corporation met was 1 November 1841. The *Freeman's Journal*, in its editorial comment, was keen to present it as a first exercise in self-government, a sign that for O'Connell and his supporters the new Corporation might, indeed, become the civic parliament to which Gray was later to refer:

> On this day the city of Dublin, by it chosen representatives, enters on the business of self-rule. Today, for the first time since the revolution [1688], will the Irish people see a council composed of Irishmen – chosen by Irishmen without respect of religious creed or sectarian opinions – sit to administer the affairs of the metropolis, free and uncontrolled by any alien power, and subject to no influence save that of the burgesses whom it represents. [1 Nov. 1841]

O'Connell was duly elected Lord Mayor and the following day the paper was ecstatic:

10 Hill, *Patriots*, p. 381.

> The darling object of the citizens of Dublin – the proudest hope of the people of Ireland, has at length been accomplished, in the selection of their great and mighty leader to fill the highest civic office which his grateful country could confer upon him. It was, indeed, in every sense of the word, a great day for Ireland! It was a day distinguished by the great principles of civil and religious liberty, after the lapse of centuries, during which persecution and penal enactments threw a gloomy horror over the land. [2 Nov. 1841]

Consonant with his desire to mollify Protestant worries O'Connell had himself nominated for lord mayor by two Protestant Liberals, John Arabin and the wealthy distiller, George Roe. He asserted that as lord mayor he would be above religion and even repeal politics. 'I pledge myself to this that in my capacity of lord mayor no one shall be able to discover from my conduct what are my politics, or, of what shade are the religious tenets I hold (cheers).' Sir Edward Burroughs, who stood against him as candidate for lord mayor, disagreed. O'Connell's 'political life has most assuredly not been such as to afford promise that his conduct while in office will be calculated to spread tranquillity and contentment through this distracted land, or to promote the peaceable union of all classes'. [1/2 Nov. 1841]

O'Connell's behaviour as lord mayor was thus an open question. The Tory John Tandy Boyce echoed this and for the first time enunciated what was to become a constant Tory criticism down the years of nationalist politics on the Corporation, namely that it would be bad for the prosperity of the city:

> The agitation of the repeal question is opposed to that amity of feeling and reciprocity of kind sentiments which ought to subsist between the two countries; it is calculated to distract our social existence, and is deeply injurious to trade and our commercial interests, by promoting such a state of things as prevents what most we need – the arrival amongst us of capitalists and men of enterprise. [1/2 Nov. 1841]

O'Connell portrayed himself as a reformer with an uphill task ahead of him. 'There is no city of which I have ever heard where the burthens on the citizens are so great – where the taxation is so enormous, and yet where, I grieve to say, so much of poverty and distress exists.' He denounced the current practice whereby the lord mayor's court was held at the Mansion House, thereby giving 'private hearings' on public matters.[11] He would hold the court weekly in the

11 The lord mayor's court and the court of conscience were municipal courts that dealt with minor matters, usually matters of debt. Both courts had had the power to detain defendants at the city Marshalsea but this power had been rescinded under the recent municipal reform.

Green St courthouse. He also raised what would be a long-standing issue concerning the admitting of freemen to the parliamentary franchise. He then donned the velvet robe and cocked hat of his new office and proceeded to address the crowd outside the Assembly House, resiling somewhat from the non-political pledge he had made within:

> Oh! What a great day that was for old Ireland, when the lord mayor of Dublin was a Repealer. It was only a foretaste of what they might expect for their country, when she should enjoy their own independent and protective legislature (loud cheers). [1/2 Nov. 1841]

Within a few days O'Connell had attended a solemn Mass of thanksgiving at the Catholic pro-cathedral in Marlborough St and the lord lieutenant's first levee. [7/8 Nov. 1841; 17/18 Nov. 1841] But then it was to be down to work, as he told the Corporation: 'There was an Augean stable to be cleaned, and he thought they should commence the work as soon as possible.' [5/6 Nov. 1841] This prelude to the working of the new Corporation had raised expectations but had also signalled what would be matters of ongoing political contention, such as the capacity of Catholic nationalists to govern and the damage a focus on nationalist politics might do on the progress of the city.

CHAPTER 2

# O'Connell: lord mayor to the repeal year, 1841–3

THE ISSUE OF O'CONNELL'S CONTROL over the new Corporation came to the fore right from the beginning. In theory he had an overwhelming majority, though many of those elected as Liberals, whether Whigs or Repealers, were independent-minded persons of some eminence, at least in their own minds, in their professions. Even some of his supporters on the Corporation raised the question as to whether the Corporation should vote by secret ballot, thus allowing them greater independence from him. Prominent among them was the merchant Ignatius Callaghan. He objected to a speech O'Connell had made at his repeal headquarters, Conciliation Hall on Burgh Quay, naming others he thought would make good lord mayors. This was tantamount to O'Connell giving instructions as to his successors. Callaghan thanked O'Connell 'for bringing him out of a state of slavery to the station in which he was placed by wholesome agitation; but they would not enjoy the advantages of the liberty he had achieved for them if they were to be fettered or restrained by undue influence.' Callaghan was abused and accused of jobbing for supporting the ballot. O'Connell was certainly having none of it and put him down forcefully. 'They came into that room voluntarily and were they to shrink from letting their constituents know what they did, because of an imaginary bugbear said to exist in his overweening influence (hear, hear)?' [8/9 Dec. 1841] The furious electors in Callaghan's ward were not pleased either. 'When Mr Callaghan sought their votes he did so on the ground of being a friend and supporter of Mr O'Connell's principles and upon that alone he was returned.' They expressed 'indignation, not to be described' though some did not want the criticism to be too severe lest 'it might go abroad that they were endeavouring to stifle the free expression of public opinion and that they were only sending their representatives to the common council as their slaves.' Eventually, they agreed a motion '[t]hat with feelings of disgust and contempt we treat the vile effort to brand upon the liberator the imputation of unworthy motives.' [14/15 Dec. 1841] O'Connell told the Repeal Association that Callaghan had wanted the ballot because he wished his son appointed junior counsel for the Corporation and knew O'Connell preferred another and that he wanted to be a director of the Hibernian bank but knew O'Connell, who had three votes there, preferred someone else. [28/29 Dec. 1841]

Another early issue concerned the new Corporation's insertion into other existing structures in Dublin. Some of the powers of the Corporation and, more specifically, of the lord mayor, consisted in having a role in the running of various bodies in Dublin. As will be seen, the lord mayor had oversight of the city markets. As well as being an issue of responsibility these powers offered an opportunity for patronage and thus a means of securing political support. The ballast board had controlled the city docks since 1787. Among the members of the board had been the lord mayor and the city's two high sheriffs (representing the common council), during their terms of office, and three aldermen elected for life by the court of aldermen. This arrangement did not map easily onto the new Corporation. The sheriffs had been removed from the Corporation and the ballast board now refused to accept two councillors, in lieu of them. This development was to the delight of one Tory councillor, John Mackay, who cheered the news, increasing O'Connell's irritation. [15/16 Dec. 1841] The old Corporation had appointed the sheriffs for Dublin but this role had been transferred to the lord lieutenant until the power of nominating sheriffs for appointment by the lord lieutenant was restored to the Corporation in the mid-1870s. There was additional annoyance that the lord lieutenant rather than the Corporation now had the power of appointing magistrates for Dublin. [11/13 May 1844]

Shortly thereafter O'Connell resisted Tory requests that the Corporation issue an address of welcome to Lord de Grey on his appointment as Tory lord lieutenant. 'He never knew any man less suited for the high office he held than Lord de Grey.' O'Connell was reminded of a pledge he had made not to introduce party politics into the proceedings of the Corporation. The question was as to which side was doing it in this instance: those who wanted the address and claimed it was to the lord lieutenant as the Queen's representative, or, those who rejected the address on the grounds that the lord lieutenant was also the representative of the government. O'Connell was in no doubt it was the former and launched into an attack on the Tories that Sir Edward Borough described as 'one of the most furious tirades on politics he had ever heard.' [22/23 Dec. 1841] Meanwhile, the last lord mayor under the old system, Sir John Kingston James, who had also been city treasurer, was proving reluctant to hand over the Corporation account books. He claimed he no longer had them and was dismissed. [16/17 Feb. 1842; 1/2 Apr. 1842]

The early months of 1842 saw O'Connell return to politics in London, albeit with the new authority of the lord mayor of Dublin, which enabled him to gain access to Queen Victoria (1819–1901) to present addresses on occasions such as the birth of the Prince of Wales (1841–1910) and her escape from an assassination attempt. The Queen was intrigued to see O'Connell and left detailed descriptions of the several occasions on which he appeared before her as lord mayor to deliver an address from Dublin. The king and queen of the Belgians asked to be present for one of them. O'Connell was, after all, a statesman of international standing. The office of lord mayor, time consuming as it was, gave him for a period a correlative official position to match his popular stature.[1]

At the same time O'Connell began to refocus on repeal, as he told a London audience: 'my hopes, my cares, my anxieties – all are for repeal, and for repeal alone.' [21 Feb. 1842] George Roe, a Protestant Liberal, acted as lord mayor *locum tenens* while O'Connell was away. Some of O'Connell's supporters used the occasion to remove an official O'Connell did not want in office, albeit in too naively open a fashion. John Reilly proposed the removal of the high constable, who was believed to have supported the election of William Gregory (1816–92) as Conservative MP for Dublin. 'Councillor Reilly observed that his reason for pressing it on that day was that he heard the lord mayor express a wish at the last meeting of the assembly, from motives of delicacy, that it should be disposed of in his absence. He thought every deference should be paid to his lordship's convenience and that every member of the assembly, even those who differed with him in political opinions, would agree that that courtesy was due to the lord mayor.' Some held that O'Connell had surely promised to be politically impartial but Michael Staunton set them right: 'on the contrary, on the last day he [O'Connell] emphatically declared that the council ought to be served by persons of his own confidence – of course alluding to those professing the same political opinions'. The high constable was duly removed. [1/2 Mar. 1842] New appointments to other offices such as law agents and sword bearer followed. James Finn replaced Sir John Kingston James as city treasurer, though the latter was pursued over alleged irregularities in the accounts for some time. [23/24 Aug. 1842; 1/2 Feb. 1843]

In August, O'Connell announced that he would not accept a second term as lord mayor, as he wanted to focus on the campaign for repeal of the act of union, though he would use a debate on repeal in the Corporation in early 1843 as an impetus for his popular campaigning in the 'monster meetings' of that year.[2] There then arose for the first time a debate on the salary for the

1 James H. Murphy, *Abject loyalty: nationalism and monarchy in Ireland during the reign of Queen Victoria* (Washington, 2001), pp 22–3. 2 Patrick M. Geoghegan, 'The impact of O'Connell, 1815–50' in James Kelly (ed.), *The Cambridge history of Ireland, iii (1730–1888)* (Cambridge, 2018), pp 102–27: p. 120.

office. Mackay proposed it be set at £1,000 though it was pointed out that under the old Corporation the lord mayor had received £3,500. [16/17 Aug. 1842] This was always a good way of attacking the incumbent though O'Connell laughed when it was reported that Mackay had told the Conservative Association that the Liberals on the Corporation were 'the dupes and slaves of the greatest tyrant that ever lived' and that, except for the Tories, the Corporation would have paid O'Connell a salary of £5,000. Mackay apologized. [20/22 Aug. 1842; 23/24 Aug. 1842]

Mackay had been trying to rally the Tories in the hope of electoral advance but when the first reelections under the new system took place in October, with one councillor's position in each ward being up for reelection, there were two Liberal gains and Mackay was one of the Tories who lost his seat. In another ward two Liberals stood against each other until O'Connell arrived 'and strongly remonstrated' with one of them who then withdrew in favour of the other. [25/26 Oct. 1842] On 1 November George Roe, the Protestant Liberal and wealthy distillery owner, assumed office as lord mayor. As a sign of the changed times it was announced that portraits from the old regime in the City Assembly House, including that of John Giffard (1745–1819), who had coined the phrase Protestant ascendancy, would be removed and one of O'Connell installed.

William McCullagh (1813–94, later known as William Torrens McCullagh Torrens) was a Liberal barrister and councillor, whose career would eventually take him to Westminster representing an English seat. He paid tribute to O'Connell's efforts to ensure that the election had gone well, by presiding over the revision court in order to refresh the burgess roll. 'He chose the first year because it was the difficult one. There was no risk or toil which he did not cheerfully share; and thus we have seen him at nearly the termination of this our primary stage endure fatigues such as no man but himself would have done, for the sake of leading us safe over what seemed an insurmountable obstacle.' He also addressed Roe on the issue of his religion. 'Having chosen a Catholic in the first instance, he [O'Connell] has shown that he can be thoroughly just, and now we have chosen you, my lord mayor, from amongst Liberal Protestants, that you may, in like manner, evince equal impartiality, fearlessness, and justice (cheers).' An understanding would eventually grow that there had been an agreement for an alternating in the position of lord mayor. It was always a nebulous concept. In later decades it was understood to mean an alteration between Liberals and Conservatives. Its first iteration here, however, suggested a religious alternating.

As for O'Connell, he complained that he had not been offered a baronetcy, as the lord mayor of London had been and as was traditional on the birth of an heir to the throne, though of course he would have refused it. At a reception in the Mansion House that evening a spirit of inter-party amity seemed to break out. For the Tories Isaac Butt 'trusted that after the generous manner in which that assembly had received his humble name that the unjust sentiments of both parties would be at an end and that they would cease to suffer party spirit to blind them to the virtue which, they might believe him, both parties possessed (hear, hear). They were, on both sides, Irishmen who felt warmly for their country, and … they would find on both sides much of honesty, of patriotism, and of independence (cheers).' [1/2 Nov. 1842] Amity soon evaporated at the Corporation, however, over a proposal to award the freedom of the city – even though that right had been removed by the recent reform – to British generals who had recently been involved in the first opium war (1839–42) in China and the first Anglo-Afghan war (1839–42). The former sought to enforce the sale of opium to China to counter a trade imbalance disadvantaging Britain. The latter was an unsuccessful British attempt to exert a controlling influence in Afghanistan. The proposal occasioned an anti-colonial backlash from some Liberals, one of whom wondered why the honour was to be given. 'Was it for having succeeded in the desire to poison the inhabitants of China, by drugging them with opium, or, was it for the invasion of the kingdom of Afghanistan (hear)?' Another member said that the army had been engaged in 'an unjust case' and he felt that they should not seek to sanction 'shedding the blood of an unoffending people for glory's sake'. [29/30 Nov. 1842]

On the domestic front the next officials to go were the town clerks on grounds of inefficiency. [8/9 Nov. 1842] William Ford, the new town clerk, reported that the Corporation muniments, or archives, were in a state of confusion and seemed to have been so since they were carried over in carts to their current location in Green Street when the old Tholsel, a civic building, had been demolished in 1820. [15/16 Nov. 1842]

The financing of the city was one of the major concerns of the new Corporation. The old Corporation was thought to have had a debt of £300,000. Annual income came to £29,000 from tolls, rent on city estates (£15,400) and the pipewater estate (£12,200).[3] However, £25,900 was owed yearly in charges, including interest on the debentures of the old Corporation.[4] The complexity of the new municipal voting process cost £7,000 in printing costs so at an early stage the new Corporation sought a loan of £15,000 from the government, which was refused. [9/10 Aug. 1842] An extra short-term tax, the borough rate, was levied at the rate of 3*d.* in the pound on property

3 Water was under the control of the Corporation, whereas the paving and lighting and wide streets commissions were independent. 4 Jones, 'Dublin reformed', 1, p. 34.

valuation, on 30 September 1842. It raised £6,949 of an expected £8,639. O'Connell, with some exaggeration, blamed the financial position on Sir John Kingston James. He claimed that the old Corporation had had debts of £400,000 but that no one knew where the bonds were. It was also claimed that James had been charging the Corporation with £300 a year interest for a sum of £6,000 'which he alleged he had lent to the city; but they had in vain demanded from the books any entry to show he had lodged that sum to the credit of the city. He had been, in fact, a creditor of the Corporation as well as treasurer.' [20/22 Aug. 1842; 30 Sept./1 Oct. 1842; 1/2 July 1847] This was certainly seen as a conflict of interests.

Because some of the services in the city were provided by bodies independent of the Corporation, the taxes the citizens had to pay were much greater than those gathered by the Corporation alone. O'Connell claimed Dublin was the most taxed city in the empire. 'They had to pay the poor rate, the police tax, the paving tax, the watering tax, the grand jury cess, the parish cess, the wide-street tax, the pipe-water rent, the ministers' money, the cholera tax, the Fitzwilliam-square tax, the Merrion-square tax, the Stephen's-green tax, the Rutland-square tax, the north and south quay-wall tax, and some other taxes.' These taxes had separate systems of collection and he claimed that the salaries involved took up between seventeen per cent and thirty per cent of the money collected. [15/16 Nov. 1842] In December the Corporation addressed a letter to the lord lieutenant calling for a reform of city taxation which raised the point that the antiquated valuation system meant that 'the highest rate is chargeable on the localities fast sinking into decay.' The grand jury, the commissioners of paving and lighting and the wide streets commissioners were independent bodies and their members were not accountable to any form of electorate. Ministers' money, a tax for the benefit of the clergy of the established church, was raised at a higher rate in smaller parishes and other taxes were dependent on it: 'they are liable by a valuation made many years ago of the holdings of Dublin rated for ministers money and any valuation founded on such a principle could not be equal, for that valuation was made not only with reference to the value of holdings, but also with reference to the amount to be received by the clergyman for his support.' In poor St Audeon's parish some houses had to pay £53 whereas in wealthy Fitzwilliam Square houses had to pay £27. The Corporation proposed that the independent bodies be merged into the Corporation:

> The town councillors reside among the people, know the wants they feel, and the comforts they should enjoy in common; they are men of business and are responsible; taxation by them would be founded by its

necessity and the ability, which would be well known to them, to pay; besides, from the amalgamation of all the boards, one staff would discharge the duties of the several paid officers of the several boards. [20/21 Dec. 1842]

The Conservatives on the Corporation were supportive of some of the proposals but were wary of others. The Tory Edward Hudson 'did not see why it [taxation] should be placed in the hands of the council, when the majority had evinced such political predilections, and even dismissed the officers of the Corporation for political purposes (cries of no, no).' The new Corporation was supposedly not politically worthy to be trusted with the responsibility of dealing with the greater expenditure that greater access to taxation would bring. Thus began the campaign for and against further reform of the Corporation that would not be completed until the beginning of the next decade, with greater efficiency and fear of politicization being the principal arguments on either side. [10/11 Jan. 1843]

Initially, there was bad news when the government proposed a pawnbrokers bill that would have reduced the rental from the Corporation estate by the one eighth of it that came through fees paid by pawnbrokers to the city marshal, though little money in practice came to the Corporation from the fees because of the entitlement of the marshal. [17 Mar. 1843; 20 Mar. 1843] On the other hand the Corporation moved to reduce its costs by abolishing some of the offices that had been held under it, such as the now superfluous clerk of the sheriffs and commons, and replaced other office holders with new holders at reduced salaries. [18/19 Apr. 1843] It also moved to increase its revenues by identifying £8,000 from the income of the pipe-water committee that could be used for Corporation purposes. Meanwhile, prominent Tories, such as the law adviser to the lord lieutenant and a judge of the court of exchequer, were reported to have refused to pay the borough rate, allegedly at the instigation of Tory members of the Corporation, though overall its collection was progressing well. Eventually legal action had to be taken against the law adviser, though the judge soon paid up. [6/7 June 1843; 13/14 June 1843; 11/12 July 1843; 18/19 July 1843; 21/22 Nov. 1843] The year 1843 ended with a debate on whether better interest rates could be obtained by consolidating all the Corporation debts. [27/28 Dec. 1843]

Utilities were also an important concern of the Corporation, not only during these years but throughout the century. There had been firms supplying gas for lighting in Dublin since 1825. By 1843 the Alliance Gas company was already established as the supplier of gas with a contract until 1846 in spite the views of many that gas ought to be supplied directly by the Corporation, or, at least, that there should be more competition. [26/27 Sept. 1843; 4/5 Oct. 1843; 1/2 Aug. 1844; 21 Aug. 1844; 26 Aug. 1844] In Belfast the streets had since 1800 been under the jurisdiction of the police commissioners. As will be seen later, improvement commissioners, such as police commissioners, were often created as a means of modernizing local services throughout the United Kingdom more generally with remits beyond what today would be considered the province of law enforcement.[5]

Matters were often more complicated in Dublin. Thus the provision of water, or pipewater as it was referred to, was the direct responsibility of the Corporation and would later be a major issue that preoccupied it after the midpoint of the century. In 1786, however, Dublin's paving and lighting commissioners had obtained the right to provide public water fountains with a supply from the water mains, of which sixty-nine were still in various forms of operation by 1832. In return they were to pay an annual fee of £150 to the Corporation, which they were chafing at by the early 1840s on the grounds that the water pressure was weak. [26 Aug. 1842; 26/27 Aug. 1842] The Corporation had its own pipewater committee, though it was often in conflict concerning the awarding of contracts. [6/7 Mar. 1844; 21/22 Mar. 1844; 7/8 May 1844; 12/13 Nov. 1844]

O'Connell designated 1843 as the 'repeal year' as a means of putting pressure on the government and began to hold his mass meetings, 'monster meetings', throughout the country to keep up the pressure, though the government's response was a solemn declaration in parliament by the Tory leaders there, the Duke of Wellington and the prime minister, Sir Robert Peel, against repeal.[6] The major event of 1843 on the Corporation was undoubtedly the debate on repeal on 28 February and 1 and 2 March, designed to be part of O'Connell's campaigning strategy. It was a dramatic debate with O'Connell clashing with the Tory Isaac Butt. Perhaps it was an event that came nearest to approximating Dublin Corporation functioning as a civic parliament, though its true purpose was to stir up public opinion as, of course, no resolution of Dublin Corporation carried any weight with effecting repeal. There was some initial Tory truculence about having the debate at all. Butt thought it was an improper topic for discussion but Michael Staunton, the newspaper proprietor and Liberal member, replied that 'I think we are a body appointed for the express purpose of administering public affairs; and that there is no question interesting to us as citizens or inhabitants of this country that can be an unfit subject for consideration and discussion in this assembly

5 Francis J. Cullen, 'Local government and the management of urban space: a comparative study of Belfast and Dublin, 1830–1922' (PhD, Maynooth University, 2005), pp 10–11. 6 Murphy, *Abject loyalty*, pp 36–7.

(hear, hear).' The old Corporation had discussed the union. O'Connell used his charm to mollify Butt, at whose convenience the motion would be debated: 'no person can admire his talents more than I do.' [21/22 Feb. 1843]

There was considerable public interest on the day of the debate with the streets outside the Assembly House crowded with people and with O'Connell cheered from the public gallery as he entered the chamber, to the chagrin of the lord mayor, George Roe, who thought the debate a bad idea. The motion was formally that the Corporation send a petition to parliament in favour of repeal. O'Connell began his four-hour speech by noting that the old Corporation had petitioned three times against repeal. The first half of his speech was about economics but the second half touched on matters concerning Dublin, referring to the decline in numbers employed in the woollen and cotton trades in the city, from 61,074 in 1800 to 14,446 in 1843, as well as to the deleterious effects the loss of Dublin's capital status had had on people of financial standing living there and providing a stimulus to the city's economy. Butt's response was to have the matter dropped before further debate and used an argument that Tories, knowing that they were likely to be in a permanent minority on the Corporation from then on, would deploy for many years in the hope of having the most influence. The Corporation should be run simply for the civic good and partisan politics should be excluded. He proposed that as the debate would be calculated to 'prevent all cordial co-operation between persons of different political opinions and to prevent this body from exercising its municipal function for the good of the citizens at large, this assembly repudiated in the strongest manner the introduction of the question and that, therefore, the consideration of the question be adjourned *sine die*.' [28 Feb./1 Mar. 1843]

Butt's point was amplified on the second day of the debate by the Tory Robert Guinness and found an echo with the Sackville St mail coach proprietor and non-repeal Liberal Peter Purcell. 'I feel with Mr Guinness that the continuance of the repeal agitation would deprive us of the co-operation of the Protestants of Ireland … if we are to gain anything for Ireland it is only by unity of feeling we can succeed. It is not by introducing any question, here or elsewhere, that will create angry discussion.' [1/2 Mar. 1843] The following day John Reilly challenged this view, albeit on limited grounds. Among the members of the Corporation John L. Arabin was a Protestant and Robert McClelland a Presbyterian and they both supported repeal. Thomas Symes pushed the anti-repeal side with a flourish towards the end of the debate: 'whatever doubt he had in his mind previous to this discussion, as to the expediency of repeal, this debate convinced him that the carrying of it would be the destruction of the empire (cheers).' Replying to what had been said

O'Connell repeated the facile line that repeal could win cross community support. '[H]ere we stand together, Protestant, Presbyterian and Catholic, the evidence of our social condition – the evidence or our total unanimity ... Yes, bigotry has vanished from the land and intolerance, persecution, and oppression, its hateful attendants, have also disappeared from amongst us.' [2/3 Mar. 1843]

The Corporation debate was a significant moment in the growing momentum for O'Connell's repeal year, as has been noted.[7] Within the Corporation it was a significant moment particularly for non-repeal Liberals. George Roe said he would not have agreed to become lord mayor had he known the topic was going to be debated. He mordantly noted that the choices open to non-repeal Liberals, as O'Connell's dominance grew, were limited and referred to three options that had been put forward in one of the speeches in the debate: become a Tory; become a Repealer; or, retire from politics. When it came to the vote on O'Connell's resolution and Butt's counter motion the figures were equal and opposite in each case. Of the sixty members of the Corporation four were absent, forty-one members voted for repeal and fifteen against. Four Liberals voted against including Roe, Purcell and Symes, meaning that the Liberal party was overwhelmingly now the repeal party. [2/3 Mar. 1843] O'Connell was to present the petition to parliament himself as neither Roe nor the Dublin MPs were willing to do so. [22/23 Mar. 1843]

After the vote and in an indication of the emotions surrounding the debate O'Connell 'proceeded to a front window in the Assembly House and implored of the vast multitude not to offer any violence to the gentlemen who were in the minority upon his motion.' [2/3 Mar. 1843] The *Freeman's Journal* editorial thought that the whole debate had been testimony to the readiness of Ireland for self-government:

> How often has it been asserted that if we had a resident parliament the whole time of that assembly would be occupied in aimless declamation – the patience and good sense of the country outraged by violent personalities, while common sense and sound political discussion would be overwhelmed by the ambitious biddings of every tiny demagogue for popularity. We should have, said the Tories and their organs, such men in the Irish parliament as we have in the town council; their proceedings would be a burlesque upon legislation. We know not what manner of men would or will compose our parliament; but this we know, there are many member of our town council who would do

7 Patrick Geoghegan, *Liberator: the life and death of Daniel O'Connell, 1830–1847* (Dublin, 2010), pp 121–30.

> honour to any assemblage of gentlemen and legislators. We point with national pride to the discussion in the Corporation and we say, where is the deliberative body whose debates have been conducted under the excitement with such admirable calmness and whose addresses have been delivered with such admirable attention to every quality which could add interest and dignity to the matter they discussed? … Let us hear no more, then, of the conduct to be anticipated in an Irish parliament – let our revilers, in this, as in all their other accusations, stand rebuked by the evidence of facts. [3 Mar. 1843]

In the aftermath of the debate, however, not everything was sweetness and light. Peter Purcell, who had been associated with the agricultural society, complained that he had come in for considerable public criticism. He had never hidden the fact that he was anti-repeal and had stood for the Corporation because he had believed O'Connell's 'public declaration that no distinction should be made between persons on account of their political feelings upon the question of repeal.' He appeared obliquely to refer to O'Connell when he quoted one alderman who had said 'that he would feed the people and let Peter Purcell feed the pigs (laughter) … There were a thousand persons daily fed and clad through his agency, and it was therefore not right for the learned alderman to say' this. [14/15 Mar. 1843]

Equally the Corporation was soon to find itself in difficulty, albeit of a more sensational kind. At its 1 May quarter day meeting the lord mayor announced the city treasurer, James Finn, appointed under the new Corporation, had absconded with some of the Corporation's money. [1/2 May 1843] He was pursued to Liverpool by the city's accountant, Sir Drury Jones Dickinson, but he had gone to the United States where it appears he was never apprehended, in spite of being tracked there on behalf of the Corporation. He owed the Corporation £3,3701. [3/4 May 1843; 5/6 July 1843; 1/2 Aug. 1843; 6/7 Sept. 1843]

The aftermath in Dublin was more unseemly, however, and called into question O'Connellite protestations of non-political cooperation. In the immediate wake of the disappearance of Finn, Robert Guinness, a Tory member of the Corporation and founder of Guinness Mahon bank, had volunteered personally to meet all immediate expenses if there was a cash flow problem. On 3 May the Corporation moved quickly to appoint a new city treasurer. Denis Costigan of Rathmines applied for the job and Guinness was nominated by John Tandy Boyce. In a vote Guinness was elected to the office by twenty-three votes to twenty-one. He then resigned from the Corporation to take up the position, promising that he would use his own financial staff to work for the Corporation. [3/4 May 1843] But this was far from the end of the matter. Costigan took legal opinion, which held that votes for Guinness had been invalid because he was a member of the Corporation when he was elected (he should have resigned before the election). Several weeks of conflicting legal opinion and argument in the Corporation followed. It was soon accepted that Guinness's election had been invalid but Costigan's argument that therefore he had been elected was not accepted. Some proposed that Guinness resign and, now not being a member of the Corporation, be immediately reelected. Costigan was against a new election. He would withdraw if Guinness also withdrew. Guinness duly resigned but by then it was becoming clear that some of those who had supported him were changing sides. [9/10 May 1843; 10/11 May 1843; 17/18 May 1843] Isaac Butt alleged that Costigan's supporters had been lobbying against Guinness. 'He saw that Mr Guinness's election was lost and, indeed, he was not sorry for it, for it would have caused him grief to think that any friend of his was a servant to a Corporation that could act in such a manner (hear, hear, and disorder).' The whole matter was becoming bitterly politicized and was made more so when one member said that the recent declarations by Sir Robert Peel and the Duke of Wellington in parliament against repeal meant that he could no longer support Guinness.[8] [17/18 May 1843]

McCullagh, who had tellingly been absent on the repeal vote and who was to resign from the Corporation the following year, was disgusted by the behaviour of the Repealers. '[H]e could not have imagined it possible that that party, in unison with whom he had so long acted and whose interests he had invariably endeavoured to promote, could have brought themselves to adopt such a course as they had that day pursued.' A new vote was held with twenty-five votes for Costigan and twenty for Guinness. Butt and another Tory thereafter resigned from their seats on Corporation committees. The entire debacle may in part have been the result of a sense of humiliation on the part of the Repealers/Liberals after the person they had appointed to the post of treasurer had absconded and that Guinness, whom they no doubt perceived as a representative of the old order, had had the impertinence of attempting to come to the rescue of the Corporation.

The nomination of the next lord mayor occurred around the same time. Timothy O'Brien was proposed by Robert McClelland, the Presbyterian Repealer, and by Sir John Power, a Liberal who was absent from the repeal vote. James Fagan was proposed by McCullagh. It was apparently an intra-Liberal affair. The Tory Joseph Boyce wanted to know where they stood on

**8** Murphy, *Abject loyalty*, pp 36–7.

repeal. 'Alderman Boyce only wanted to count the Repealers in that house that he might measure the strength of the cause there.' When one member said he would only vote for a Repealer O'Brien immediately said he supported repeal whereas Fagan replied that though he had voted for repeal in the recent vote he would be neutral as lord mayor, just like O'Connell. O'Brien won the vote by twenty-nine votes to twenty-three, with the Tories voting for Fagan. On 1 December O'Brien was formally elected, being proposed by O'Connell, who had stayed away from the nomination meeting. [1/2 Dec. 1843]

As O'Connell's campaigning and 'monster meetings' during the repeal year of 1843 gathered pace so several matters to do with national politics were brought before the Corporation. On 23 May a resolution condemning the arms bill, a security measure proposed by Peel to counter the perceived threat to public order of the repeal meetings, was passed and on 6 June a resolution on 'the state of Ireland' was tabled, calling for more resources for Ireland and critical of the government. [23/24 May 1843; 6/7 June 1843] As was the custom the petition on the arms bill was presented to parliament by Edward Grogan (1802–91), one of the MPs for Dublin. At the time both Dublin MPs were Tories and there was annoyance that Grogan had merely laid it on the table in the Commons without drawing attention to it. The promoters of the petition on 'the state of Ireland' wanted to have the more sympathetic MP, William Smith O'Brien (1803–64), present their petition. This led to some comments on the futility of petitioning parliament at all. One member remarked that '[t]he grievances and oppressions of Ireland were only subjects for merriment and ridicule in parliament.' And, as if to reinforce the point in an assembly where some members had a retail interest, he added, in a parody of such attitudes, that '[t]he Irish grocers petitioned repeatedly, and used every possible exertion to obtain justice but all to no purpose.' John Reilly, nonetheless, believed that desisting would not serve the cause of repeal. 'The people of Ireland had long been treated with contempt in the House of Commons; but still it was the temple of the constitution and they were not to refuse to knock at the door to demand their rights and liberties. If they were refused admittance, or, if their expostulations were disregarded, they would be only furnishing themselves with another argument to prove the necessity for a parliament of their own (hear, hear).' [5/6 July 1843]

O'Connell planned a meeting for Clontarf on the outskirts of north Dublin for 8 October 1843. When it was banned by the government, O'Connell, ever afraid of violence, backed down. Thereafter the repeal campaign petered out. O'Connell has sometimes been blamed for his decision, allowing momentum to be lost. However, it was likely that this would have happened in any event in face of the government's implacable refusal of repeal.

The immediate aftermath of the Clontarf banning brought O'Connell to the Corporation with a motion, passed by thirty-eight votes to ten, condemning the banning as an insult to the capacity of the lord mayor and Corporation to keep the peace. [20/21 Aug. 1843] When the annual partial Corporation election took place in November only five wards were contested by what were then known as Repealers and Tories/Conservatives. The most telling result was the further marginalization of non-repeal Liberals with the replacement of Thomas Symes, the non-repeal Liberal who had stepped down, admittedly at the last minute, in Merrion Ward by a Tory. The new mood was encapsulated with the criticism of George Roe for a toast at his last banquet as lord mayor when he linked O'Connell's name with others including Butt. [18/19 Dec. 1843; 20 Dec. 1843]

CHAPTER 3

# O'Connell's last years, 1844–7

IN THE AFTERMATH OF Clontarf O'Connell was arrested, convicted and imprisoned for conspiracy at a trial that was widely regarded as unfair. After a few months the conviction was overturned by the House of Lords and he was released. O'Connell's last years – he died in 1847 – also saw the rise of the Young Ireland group of radical nationalists who both supported repeal but also challenged O'Connell's dominant position. Finally, the great Irish potato Famine began in 1845, though its worst effects would not become apparent until 1847, after the death of O'Connell.

In Dublin Corporation these years were preoccupied with trying to make financial savings. In April 1844 a tontine investment scheme was launched by the Corporation. In August there were proposals to have the Corporation meet in the Mansion House, thus avoiding the £130 cost of the Assembly Building, and to sell Green St courthouse. In October several bank loans were renegotiated at reduced rates of interest, in spite of obstacles allegedly placed in the way by the treasury in London. [ 11/12 Apr. 1844; 1/2 Aug. 1844; 8/9 Oct. 1844] Controversy over attempts to raise money by selling or letting Corporation property led to a motion being tabled in November to the effect

> [t]hat inasmuch as the property of the Corporation of Dublin has deteriorated in value and a want of confidence is getting into the public mind against that body, in consequence of some aldermen and town councillors bidding for the property at auction; that, as guardians of the public property, the aldermen, town councillors or any person holding any place or situation under them shall not in future become purchasers of the aforesaid Corporation property and that no lease be granted to them. [1/2 Nov. 1844]

Yet when it was debated the motion was lost. Some did not like the Corporation being seen to be critical of itself. Others maintained that letting was a matter of public competition, though the proposer maintained that people were deterred from bidding when they learned that councillors were themselves interested. [10/11 Dec. 1844]

In August 1845 it was announced that the Corporation defecit was £5,800. It occasioned interventions by two newish members of the Corporation who would play prominent roles in its proceedings over the next quarter century. John Reynolds (1794–1868), an associate of O'Connell's earlier banking endeavours, a maverick and a repeal member of the Corporation since July that year, claimed that there was in fact a surplus of £6,000 that the Corporation was concealing. He was taken to task for this claim by another new member, the then Dr John Gray (1815–75), owner of the *Freeman's Journal*, who had become a member the previous November. [20/21 Aug. 1845] Two days later Reynolds claimed that the surplus was £3,959 and was once again criticized by Gray. [22/23 Aug. 1845] Behind Reynolds's assertions was a plan to present himself as an opponent of the imposition of a second borough rate. At the end of the previous year the lord mayor, Timothy O'Brien, had been praised for not supporting the imposition of a borough rate though he modestly attributed it to a reduction in interest rates. [23/24 Dec. 1844] Reynolds claimed that nothing could 'justify the infliction of a borough rate on the principle that the Corporation owed debts which they had no assets to meet.' [23/25 Aug. 1845]

The Tory *Evening Packet* newspaper lost no time in exploiting the situation. If Reynolds was right then a question had to be asked concerning the members of the Corporation as to 'what design could men have who would act as these men are represented to have acted – what but the most base and vile plunder?' [26/27 Aug. 1845] Reynolds was soon backtracking. 'I found fault with the mode of making out the accounts with a view to the levying of a borough rate but I do not impute to the men that made them out any intention of deceiving the public. They take one view of the mode of making them out and I take another view and I believe I am certainly correct.' [27/28 Aug. 1845] Nonetheless, thirteen days of debate took place over the issue in late August and early September during which Reynolds spoke for nearly twenty hours. Gray believed that debate was necessary because '[t]he Corporation was on its trial – its integrity was impeached and he trusted the council would never consent to leave the public presence till a verdict was recorded.' [29/30 Aug. 1845] On 4 September the debate concluded with Reynolds on the losing side. [3/4 Sept. 1945] Nonetheless, the issue of a borough rate had not been settled and it took the presence of O'Connell, now largely absent from Corporation affairs, to get it passed. Speaking on 1 November he referred to the thirteen-day debate as 'the most unfortunate that ever occurred in any body' by people without patriotism who had attacked 'a popular representative body.' A borough rate was necessary 'and I myself will take the odium of being the person to propose it.' As for his view of Reynolds's accusation: 'I again unhesitatingly assert that there never was a fouler or falser assertion made by any one than to say that no necessity existed for the borough rate.' [1/3 Nov. 1845]

A month later O'Connell and Reynolds directly clashed. Reynolds enunciated the numerous taxes the citizens of Dublin had to pay to O'Connell's irritation. 'Don't we know every tittle of these things – they are as familiar to us as the A, B, C, of the primer and it is only keeping us from real business to persevere in these statement (hear, hear).' He had a similar reaction to the hour-long speech Reynolds went on to make. 'We have now been taken up for an hour with the most preposterous inanity, in repeating things that were already before the house over and over again and upon which we have acted and for which he really suggests no remedy.' [3/4 Dec. 1845] Three weeks later O'Connell had a committee set up to look into the Corporation's debts and to make recommendations over a borough rate. At the same meeting the Famine, which was in its first stages, was mentioned, though it was not a topic that would much preoccupy the Corporation in its debates over the next few years. [23/24 Nov. 1845]

The committee's report was accepted in January 1846 by twenty-nine votes to nine. The borough rate was said to be necessary because ordinary expenditure over income was £1,000 and there was an accumulated debt of £14,000. Reynolds vowed that 'he would use all the efforts in his power to parallelize the effort which was then being made to play an unnecessary tax on his fellow-citizens.' [14/15 Jan. 1846; 20/21 Jan. 1846] He, however, was forced to agree with O'Connell that most of those who had supported him were Tories, though this was 'his misfortune, not his fault.' [23/24 Jan. 1846] He knew that O'Connell wanted to return to London. 'For his part he (Mr Reynolds) wished the honourable and learned alderman was safe there at present.' To this O'Connell humorously replied, 'It is well for me that he could not send me on a longer journey (laughter).' [21/22 Jan. 1846] Nonetheless, O'Connell was detained in Dublin trying to get the borough rate passed against Reynolds's opposition through five days of debate at the Corporation. 'If I had not the deepest sense of the necessity of rescuing the Corporation from the hands of Mr Reynolds I would not have devoted it [his time] to such a purpose.' He had urgent business in parliament but 'I am here baited by Mr Reynolds'. He had never been calumniated so much by anyone who says 'he is of my party'. He gathered Reynolds and the Tories together for joint attack. 'Is there a gentleman on that side who ever did a single act to advance the claim of equal rights of his Roman Catholic countrymen … how can Mr Reynolds complain of being taunted when he is found amongst the consistent enemies of the civil rights of those for whom I stood in the brunt of the battle? (cheers).' [24/26 Jan. 1846] The borough rate was passed by thirty-six votes to ten.

O'Connell was to show himself ruthless in crushing dissent from non-repeal Liberals, as will be seen later in this chapter in the case of Peter Purcell. None of them had ever challenged or criticized him in the way Reynolds now was. Yet, perhaps surprisingly, instead of crushing Reynolds O'Connell successfully co-opted him and within six months O'Connell and Reynolds were cooperating in opposing some of the provisions of a new wide streets bill in parliament and publicly praising each other's contributions. [11/12 Aug. 1846]

As for Reynolds he turned his attention to the much more manageable task of rationalizing the collection of Dublin taxes, something that was effected within a few years with the appointment of a collector general. Having researched the matter he reported that the taxation of Dublin, much of which of course did not come the Corporation's way, amounted to £201,000. In round figures it was accounted for as follows [1/2 Oct. 1846]:

| | |
|---|---|
| Paving, lighting and cleansing | £40,000 |
| Police tax, pawnbrokers' licenses, carriage rents etc. | £34,000 |
| Grand jury cess | £30,000 |
| Pipewater | £14,000 |
| Wide streets | £7,000 |
| Ministers' money | £10,000 |
| Poor-rate | £40,000 |
| Parish cess | £12,000 |
| Borough rate | £8,000 |
| Poddle river, Stephen's-green and sundry small taxes | £6,000 |

The following year he was to claim that whereas the first borough rate, agreed in 1843, had come to £8,639 of which £6,949 had been collected and £1,682 uncollected, the second one amounted to £6,942 of which £3,089 had been collected and £3,853 not, making it much less successful. [1/2 July 1847] A year after that, however, the town clerk, from a presumably more impartial stance, reported that the borough rate had come to £6,000, of which £4,000 had been collected. [8/7 July 1848]

Non-financial politics also continued during these years. The year 1844 began with the innovation, which would become established practice from then on, of the changeover in the lord mayorality occurring on 1 January, with George Roe succeeded by Timothy O'Brien. Roe's departing speech made reference to the forthcoming 'state trials' of O'Connell and others for conspiracy that would result in his imprisonment but later release on appeal. Roe lamented their very existence: 'will they tend to allay the angry feelings of our country (hear)? Or, to restore to her peace and prosperity (no, no)?' [1/2 Jan. 1844] Just over a week later Roe proposed that the trials be suspended and the Queen petitioned to have parliament investigate the economic condition of Ireland instead. In the hardening of political lines between Repealers and Tories Isaac Butt dismissed the idea effectively as irenic Whig nonsense: 'never in any deliberative assembly had he listened to a speech more vague in its import, nor to any which contained so little information of explanation relative to the subject and motion which the speaker had in view in bringing forward his resolution.' He also cannily attempted to drive a wedge between Roe and the Repealers, saying that a parliamentary investigation would necessarily involve the suspension of the campaign for repeal. This tactic seems to have worked as Michael Staunton, a Repealer, immediately launched into an attack on Roe: 'He is no Repealer. He is not of the religion of the mass of the people. He did all in his power to prevent the great discussion of the last year.' Then again Dr Henry Maunsell (1806–79), a Tory member and owner of the *Dublin Evening Mail*, tried to detach Roe from whatever support he was receiving from Repealers on the grounds that the latter had a more radical view of the state trials than Roe: 'It was plain that Alderman Roe had never meant to assert … that the traversers had committed no crime and that the prosecution was a vindictive attempt to punish them for holding certain opinions; but it was also plain that the motion before them was so interpreted by gentlemen on the other side of the house – and in fact, it bore that interpretation (hear, hear).' For all that, however, Roe's motion was carried by thirty-five votes to seven. [9/10 Jan. 1844] When the petition was presented to the Queen in early February she blandly replied that she would not interfere with a competent tribunal of justice. [5 Feb. 1844]

The difficulty for Whiggism amid political polarization was illustrated on 10 January at a public meeting in the Royal Exchange, under the new lord mayor, to discuss how best to thank Roe for his time as lord mayor. When Daniel O'Connell spoke he had the unusual experience of being hissed by the supporters of the Revd Tresham Dames Gregg (1800–91). Gregg was a Protestant controversialist and supporter of the ascendancy who had engaged with a Catholic priest in a nine-day disputation in the Rotundo in Dublin in

1838. Gregg himself spoke denouncing Roe. He claimed 'that there were two sections of people in this country and that a neutral party, such as Mr Roe, should not be approved of by the citizens of Dublin (loud hisses and partial cheers).' He went on to condemn Roe for visiting Catholic 'chapels'. [10/11 Jan. 1844]

With O'Connell's conviction and later incarceration on 30 May Repealers used Dublin Corporation and other municipal bodies they controlled throughout the country as vehicles for public protest. Not for the last time the constitutional prestige and ceremonial dignity of the Corporation were to be used by nationalists to further their aims. Dublin Corporation was called together on 6 June by the lord mayor to ask the Queen and parliament to vindicate the constitution and have O'Connell released. Though he might have supported an appeal for clemency, which of course implied an acceptance of guilt, Butt said he could not support this motion. 'He would say without hesitation that the address, not intended as an appeal to mercy, but, founded on such untrue motives, was a libel on the administration of justice in Ireland (cheers).' The motion was passed by forty votes to six, with some Tories, perhaps fearful of the public mood, having stayed away. [6/7 June 1844] A week later the Corporations of Dublin, Cork, Limerick, Waterford, Kilkenny, Drogheda, Galway, Clonmel and Sligo gathered at O'Connell's house on Merrion Square to process to his place of imprisonment in Richmond prison, a couple of miles away on the north side of the city, in protest at not being allowed to see him. Somewhat bizarrely, the proceedings were led by the mayor of Cork, as the lord mayor of Dublin had been allowed to see O'Connell before the clamp down on visits. [13/14 June 1844; 17 June 1844]

In July, John Arabin, a Liberal Protestant, was nominated by the Corporation as lord mayor for the following year, though some felt that he was 'almost a stranger to Dublin.'[1] There was alarm, however, at the news that Roe was now planning to resign from the Corporation, having been put under pressure from his electors in St James's ward to support the recent motions over O'Connell. A proposed delegation to ask him to stay did not take place and Roe told his electors that the repeal issue meant he could no longer remain on the Corporation. [1/2 July 1844; 11/12 July 1844; 15/16 Aug. 1844] Roe spoke at the lord mayor's dinner at the end of the year about what had happened, though in a typically gracious manner. 'He was a mercantile man

1 In the early part of 1846, the year after his tenure as lord mayor, Arabin was involved in a legal scandal in which it was claimed that he had seduced a young girl in 1812, had had several children with her and had gone on to seduce one of his daughters by her in 1842, resulting in the birth of a child in 1843. The charge was later withdrawn and Arabin seems to have been vindicated, being appointed a stipendiary magistrate. [2 Mar. 1846; 4/5 Mar. 1846; 10 June 1846;

and he gloried in it (cheers). He was proud to belong to the trading community of Great Britain, as there was no higher character he would wish to possess and he would not change it for any other title (hear and cheers).' As lord mayor he had tried to bring parties together. He was not now in the Corporation. 'He regretted that, in obedience to the dictates of his conscience, he had to retire from the Corporation.' He looked forward to the time when the issue that had caused his departure would be over and 'they would all meet together in friendship again.' [23/24 Dec. 1844]

O'Connell was released in September, processing in triumph through the city,[2] and in the jubilant moment that succeeded it Maunsell brought forward what he considered to be a conciliatory idea which was widely welcomed though it did not receive much support. Asserting that 'I never recollect a period when less of party bitterness and more general good humour prevailed in Ireland,' he proposed that parliament and the Queen's court should convene in Dublin at least once in every three years. He presented this as to the advantage of Protestants who needed to be proactive rather than simply protective of their final bulwarks, the established church and Trinity College. 'To my Protestant brethren I would then say – make your terms before the breach of your bulwarks become indefensible.' His was 'a demand that before further legislation shall be engaged to our ruin legislators shall see Ireland, Protestant as well as Roman Catholic Ireland, with their own eyes.' [25/26 Sept. 1844]

But by November the mood had soured once again, particularly for the remaining non-repeal Liberals, whose most prominent representative, with the departure of Roe, was now Peter Purcell, a mail coach contractor.[3] Purcell had been open about his opposition to repeal at the time of Roe's resignation. He appears to have adopted an active policy against Repealers rather than waiting for them to come to him. In the run up to the annual municipal elections in November 1844 he was accused of having tried to disenfranchise Repealers in the Post Office ward at the municipal revision court. This provoked O'Connell's ire and he campaigned in the ward for Purcell's repeal opponent Michael Staunton who beat Purcell by 182 votes to 123. [11/12 July 1844; 31 Oct./1 Nov. 1844; 26 Nov. 1844] The Tory alderman Robert H. Kinahan was later to characterize this as an exclusionary policy on O'Connell's part. 'After the first election of members for the new Corporation they had a great many good men returned who did not go the whole extent on many subjects to which the honourable gentleman went and they had been put out of the body in consequence of their refusing to do so. One of them was a most excellent

9 July 1846; 29 Sept. 1846] **2** Murphy, *Abject loyalty*, pp 45–6. **3** David Dickson, *Dublin: the making of a capital city* (London, 2014), p. 320.

gentleman – Mr Peter Purcell – who was an ornament to the country.' [23/24 Jan. 1846]

The early part of 1845 was dominated by moves, which came to nothing, to abolish the court of conscience that dealt with local financial disputes in Dublin. It was unpopular because plaintiffs had to pay fees to be heard before it. However, it had a role in the patronage of the Corporation as former lord mayors were generally appointed to preside over it. [15/16 Jan. 1845; 1/2 Oct. 1845] There were also rumours that Queen Victoria would visit Dublin. [29/30 Apr. 1845] A visit would have come at a difficult time for O'Connell as Sir Robert Peel was in the midst of introducing a series of measures to mollify Irish Catholic opinion that had the effect of creating divisions within Irish nationalism between O'Connell and the Young Irelanders over the degree to which nationalism was to be secular or religious. These measures were the Charitable Bequests Act, that sought to facilitate donations to religious causes; the Maynooth grant, that increased the government subsidy to the Irish Catholic seminary; and, most controversially, the proposal to establish a number of nondenominational 'provincial' colleges in Ireland, dubbed 'godless colleges' by their enemies and eventually named Queen's Colleges, after the monarch.[4] O'Connell had previously said that a royal visit would be treated as apolitical but had now changed his mind and on 28 April the Repeal Association passed a resolution about bringing Ireland's grievances before the monarch. In the Corporation, Edward Hudson believed that if that were the case '[a]ll the elements of political commotion would then be called into play on both sides and instead of there being unity of feeling there would be nothing but strife, rancour and dissension.' O'Connell retorted that it was all the fault of the turn of politics at Westminster:

> [T]he impression which remains on my mind, after an attentive perusal of what is reported to have taken place in the House of Commons since our last day of meeting is this, that if a plot or design to drive us from the unanimity of being neutral on the question of repeal during the Queen's visit, as we had intended to be, had been deliberately entered into by the statesmen of the day, I care not whether Whigs or Tories … it could not have been carried into operation more skillfully or more successfully than it has by the declarations that have been recently made in parliament (hear, hear). It looks like management. It appears to me to have been a plan deliberately carried out to prevent us from combining to show our loyalty to our Sovereign in a spirit of complete harmony and in the absence of all discussion upon exciting topics.

4 Murphy, *Abject loyalty*, pp 47–50.

Subsequent discussion focused on the more pedestrian discussion – though no doubt very important to those affected – on whether a visit would bring extra money into Dublin. In spite of the dissension the lord mayor formally asked the Queen to visit Dublin at the end of May, though it would be four more years until a visit actually took place.[5] [29/30 Apr. 1845; 23 May 1845] The reason for the delay was mostly due to the great Famine which began in the autumn of 1845.

References to the Famine are infrequent in the proceedings of the Corporation during the following years though oddly its beginnings did register alarm and a brief intense attention from the Corporation. It held a special meeting on 21 October 1845 to address the issue of the failure of the potato crop due to disease. John Arabin, the lord mayor, 'had inspected the potato crop on his own lands a day or two ago and he found that the disease had spread through them in a very alarming manner.' From the beginning it was clear that urban Dublin would see itself as something of a bystander:

> Very possibly it would not be in the power of that council to do more than to call the attention of the government and of the public to the matter but even this might be attended by beneficial results; and besides it was not impossible that in the course of the discussion some information of an important and interesting character might be elicited.

They would appoint an information gathering committee. Some members were reassuring. One alderman who was a corn merchant said his contacts down the country were telling him that accounts of the failure of the crop were exaggerated. Even if a quarter of the crop was gone 'there would still be quite a sufficient quantity for the sustenance of the poor who use potatoes.' He went on to touch on what would become one of the most controversial aspects of the response to the Famine, the continuing export of other food. Even if the whole crop failed 'there were ample means to prevent the export of corn from this country, which might be required for the sustenance of the people.' It was John Reynolds who raised once more the issue of the possible national role for the Corporation in such a crisis. 'The subject was one of the greatest importance, involving the supply of between eight and nine millions of people with food; and that council, being the only substitute they had for a national parliament, it was their duty to act deliberately in the matter.' At the same time, and as if in contradiction to what he had just said, he was one of those who thought alarm could only be damaging at that stage. 'It had been

5 Murphy, *Abject loyalty*, pp 50–5.

suggested out of doors that the distilleries might be stopped but he saw no good that could result of false alarms on the country – there would be a tightness in the money market and railway speculation which would give employment to so many thousands would be checked. He thought they should steer a middle course and 'not make their body auxiliary to the alarmists.' [21/22 Oct. 1845] Undoubtedly, Reynolds's position reflected the ambivalence of a Corporation whose members and electors came from the more prosperous sections of urban society. They might have felt concern over the possibility of mass starvation of poor people in the countryside but they also had an eye to their own economic position. Whiskey distilling was after all a major Dublin industry. The Famine gave the Corporation the opportunity to become the civic parliament, substituting for a national parliament, a place where famine relief policy and practice might have been scrutinized. Its moral authority might have made a difference in a way in which it could not have done later when it came to debating more conventional political issues. But the Corporation did not rise to the occasion. Thus one of the reasons why the Corporation failed as national forum was because its interests – urban, professional, mercantile – were out of alignment with rural, agricultural Ireland.

O'Connell himself raised the issue of the Famine in the Corporation but not in terms of summoning it to be a civic parliament, in spite of rhetorical appearances to the contrary. The Corporation met again a week after Reynolds's speech, this time with O'Connell present. He was certainly not shy about sounding the alarm. '[T]here never has been a meeting of this Corporation of one half the importance of the present … The lives of all the Queen's subjects are at stake – the lives of the poor who have no other subsistence but the potato – the lives of the rich who are threatened to be attacked by the contagion of disease.' He went on to propose a series of measures including export controls, a tax on absentee landlords, the importation of Indian corn and soup kitchens, while claiming that he was putting aside the politics of repeal for what he characterized as 'a visitation from providence … one of those mysterious dispensations from on high which we tremble before but cannot account for.' [28/29 Oct. 1845] The reference to the rich being prone to famine disease should be noted. He clearly knew his audience. Yet he was using the occasion to address a United Kingdom audience and not really to rally a Dublin response. In spite of his rhetorical passion, the Corporation did little to respond to the growing crisis.

Debate about the continuing need for municipal reform was a further important thread throughout these years. As has been noted the reformed Corporation's powers were limited. It could collect tolls, levy a borough rate, oversee the city's markets and manage pipewater distribution. However, scavenging (the removal of human waste) and paving and lighting were supervised by the paving commissioners, whose work was paid for by the rates. There were three commissioners and they coveted the Corporation's control over water. Street planning was controlled by the wide streets commissioners (established in 1757), who were appointed for life, and policing was under the policing commissioners. All these bodies were appointed by the lord lieutenant, who now also appointed the sheriffs and local magistrates.[6] In addition there were the poor law commissioners and the north and south Dublin poor law unions (established in 1838 under the poor law act), the still Protestant-dominated grand jury (responsible for a variety of hospitals, jails and courthouses) and the ballast board (of twenty-two mostly self-appointed members that controlled the port of Dublin).[7] [27/28 Nov. 1846] The Dublin reform struggle was to see how many of these might be absorbed by a potentially strengthened Corporation. In the years 1843 and 1844 there were various attempts to rationalize the collecting of Dublin taxes. [15 Apr. 1843; 11/12 Apr. 1844] The struggle for reform was sometimes presented in terms either of the desire for equality between the ways in which Corporations in Ireland and Britain operated, or, in terms of the restoration of the ancient rights of Irish Corporations. [16/17 Apr. 1844] In May 1844 the Corporation petitioned parliament for a restoration of powers. [11/13 May 1844]

John Reynolds began to emerge as a combatant on the side of Dublin Corporation. These were to be the years when he made perhaps his most positive contribution with his energies directed outwards, for a time, on behalf of the Corporation rather than inwards against it, though he would soon revert to internecine dispute. His argument for extending Corporation powers, made in May 1846, referred not to ancient powers or British equivalence but to equality within Ireland itself. 'I would be for making the lord mayor of Dublin, in his official capacity, fully as powerful, and, consequently, as useful, as the mayor of Belfast.' [2/4 May 1846] He saw his work not only in terms of promoting the powers of the Corporation but also in terms of opposing attempts to extend the powers of its rivals, as in the case of the wide streets bill of that year. It was for his opposition to this measure that O'Connell was to praise him. [8/9 May 1846; 22/23 May 1846; 11/12 Aug. 1846] In July the Corporation went on the attack with a petition for a municipal amendment bill that would give the Corporation control over the police, the paving and lighting and the ballast boards. [25/27 July 1846] It also wished to take over

6 Jones, 'Dublin reformed', 1, p. 19. Jacinta Prunty, *Dublin slums, 1800–1922: a study of urban geography* (Dublin, 1998), p. 68. 7 Jones, 'Dublin reformed', 1, pp 69–120.

the work of the wide streets commissioners and to have the ability to appoint the two city sheriffs, the recorder and the police magistrates. [1/2 Oct. 1846]

It was a bid for maximum increased control. Interestingly, the Tories who might have been expected to oppose it outright indicated that they might be willing to compromise in return for a *quid pro quo*. That consisted effectively in increased representation for them based on ward valuation: the richer the ward the larger the number of representatives ought to be, they argued, and richer people tended to be Tories. Thus, St Stephen's ward on the south side was valued at £79,270, whereas St Paul's ward, on the poorer north side, was valued at £17,933.[8] This was the case made by Isaac Butt, though John Reynolds tried to refute his arguments using statistics and Dr John Gray said that that had not been the ancient way of the Corporation, which had relied on the freemen vote. [20/21 Oct. 1846; 21/22 Oct. 1846] Though the Tory argument was not taken up at the time, this exchange laid down the terms of the debate for the next few years.

In November 1846, a Dublin improvement bill, extending the powers of the Corporation, was introduced in parliament. It was supported by the Whig government but quickly met with widespread Protestant and Tory opposition in Dublin. Reynolds reprobated the scaremongering of those opposed to the bill, who claimed, he said, that 'if we got the power to manage the local taxation of the city, that power would be abused; and … that our power of taxation would be unlimited.' [1/2 Dec. 1846]

Earlier the next year Reynolds advanced an ingenious argument to the effect that the new Corporation had not been to the disadvantage of Protestants. Dublin had a population of about 240,000, of whom 180,000 were Catholic and 62,000 Protestant. Of the sixty members of the Corporation forty-eight were Catholics and twelve Protestants. Of Corporation salaried officials and pensioners, the twenty-two salaried persons were all Protestant and twenty-five of the pensioners were Protestants, the remaining eighteen being Catholics. Thus £5,367 went to Protestants and only £2,485 to Catholics. It was not an uncontested position, however, with others arguing that all the Corporation offices were then in fact filled by Catholics. [26/27 Jan. 1847]

Official inquiries into municipal reform were held in Dublin and Rathmines in early 1847, by two British officials.[9] In the Corporation Reynolds pressed hard for Corporation control over the powers of the paving and lighting, wide streets, grand jury and ballast bodies. Joseph Boyce was equally adamant that Tories 'would never consent to the Corporation getting the increased privileges they sought while the representation was so unequal.'

**8** Jones, 'Dublin reformed', i, p. 138. **9** Jones, 'Dublin reformed', i, pp 122–45.

There was talk of compacts between O'Connell and the Tories about balancing representation that each side accused the other side of breaking. The argument then turned to the relative valuation of different wards with one Tory being perhaps ill advised to state that '[w]e desire property, intelligence and respectability to be the qualifications.' [1/2 Feb. 1847] Reverting to type the ill-disciplined Reynolds managed to alienate some of those on his own side by accusing them of wanting an end to the Corporation so that they might hold paid office under a government commission that might replace it. [9/10 Mar. 1847]

The Corporation then dispatched Reynolds and some others to London to monitor the progress of the bill. [9/10 Mar. 1847] When the official report was published it was a disappointment. It 'proved what they had to expect from Englishmen. Everything detrimental had been put down and everything favourable had been withheld.' [23/24 Mar. 1847] Nonetheless, the Whig government in London pressed on with its support for reform. Returning to Dublin in April Reynolds attacked the vested interests opposed to the bill, albeit in an extreme manner that suggested that the battle might be about to be lost. The Hibernian Gas company had contracts with the paving board, costing the people of Dublin £20,000 a year, he claimed. 'Those gas abuses and robberies were going on for twenty years and never were dragged to light till this Corporation came forward to protect the citizens. What did the chamber of commerce ever do for the citizens in this or any other matter?' He reprobated those who tried to give the bill 'a political and sectarian aspect.' He concluded by condemning the Bank of Ireland's opposition to the bill. [13/14 Apr. 1847]

The Dublin chamber of commerce was a powerful body with a particular agenda, often close to that of the Tories, which would clash with the Corporation to an increasing degree in the middle of the century. Reynolds's mention of sectarianism was a reference to Tresham Gregg who had had placards placed around Dublin on the issue. In turn Reynolds's criticism of Gregg brought down on him the ire of the Young Ireland newspaper, the *Nation*, which accused Reynolds himself of stirring up sectarianism. The *Nation* had also accused the Corporation of not demanding enough new powers. Reynolds's answer to this was that they had, for the time being, reduced their demands for control of the police, the ballast board and appointing sheriffs, as the government's more limited measure was better than nothing. As ever he was not muted in his criticism, accusing the paper of siding with what was at least perceived to be a Tory-supporting body. 'I charge the writer in the *Nation* with supporting the chamber of commerce against us and doing so wilfully.' He also took to task the editor of the paper, Charles

Gavan Duffy (1816–1903), for poor attendance at the Corporation, of which he was a member. [1/3 May 1847] Duffy responded to a use of the word 'lie' by Reynolds in connection with him with hauteur. 'He had learned that Mr Reynolds's conduct on former occasions was such as debarred him from being treated as a gentleman … He did not consider that he could hold any communication with him as a gentleman.' [8/11 May 1847] All was in vain, however, as the bill was lost in the Commons at second reading in early May, by 108 votes to 120. [8/10 May 1847] Indeed, there was some anxiety that a threat might come from a private bill to extend the powers of the Rathmines township. [1/2 July 1847]

More trouble for reform of the Corporation loomed in December 1847 when a solicitor called Frederick Jackson promoted his own radical solution to Dublin's financial challenges, under the idea of the three-man commission. It proposed consolidating Dublin's debts – the pipewater debt of £75,000 and the wide streets' debt of £70,000 – and purchasing its utilities – both canals for £850,000, the two gas works for £440,000 and the water works for £200,000. This came to £1,635,000. The interest on this at five per cent would come to £81,750 a year. Together with all the other taxes this would amount to £285,150 a year. It was far too radical a measure to be taken seriously, however. [14/15 Dec. 1847] The year ended with the Corporation considering the method of rating in the city though it quickly turned once more to the effects of rating on the composition of the Corporation. Tories asserted that the then present system, under which they claimed the more highly rated and thus more heavily taxed citizens were under-represented on the Corporation, was unsustainable. Pushing back against the notion of an extension of powers of the Corporation, as it was now constituted, they considered that 'a board of commissioners appointed by the government and responsible to the government would more fully possess the public confidence and more efficiently economically administer such taxation than a municipal body formed on such a basis and such principles' as the present Corporation. [21/22 Dec. 1847] The failed bill of 1847 had at least given clarity to and galvanized Tory demands for a greater say in Dublin civic politics. For many Tories the Corporation needed a new reform, or, to be abolished altogether and replaced by management by expert administrators.

One voice absent from the debate on reform in 1847 was that of Daniel O'Connell. The failure of the 1843 repeal year, the mollifying legislation brought in by Peel's government in the mid-1840s, the splintering of the repeal movement with the rise of Young Ireland, the beginnings of the Famine and, finally, his own failing health had all left him a diminished figure. On 1 December 1846 he appeared at a meeting of the Corporation to announce that early the next year he would ask the Corporation to debate and then to petition for repeal. Perhaps a little cruelly the Tory Robert Kinahan asked what had happened to the petition the Corporation had made for repeal in 1843. He believed that a further rehash of the arguments would be futile. O'Connell disagreed, believing that '[e]very day points out some new and considerable mischief as the consequential result of that measure. New men will come forward; new thoughts, new expressions, new suggestions will be called forth, so that I anticipate the most favourable results from the forthcoming discussion.' [1/2 Dec. 1846] Instead of renewing the campaign for repeal, however, O'Connell set out for Rome in the new year. He died in Genoa on 15 May 1847 and was buried in Dublin with great ceremony and enormous public mourning on 5 August. With O'Connell gone the most prominent nationalist member of the Corporation was now John Reynolds.

CHAPTER 4

# Reynolds: reform and ruination, 1847–50

THE LATE 1840s WITNESSED the growing horror of the Famine. Though affected Dublin was not at the centre of the storm. In the early 1850s, after the death of O'Connell, the dispersal of the Young Ireland movement, following a brief, abortive rising in 1848, and in the aftermath of the Famine, Irish politics tended to deemphasize repeal and to focus on issues such as the rights of tenant farmers and the grievances of the Catholic Church. Irish MPs at Westminster pursued a policy of independent opposition in support of these causes. The Irish Tenant League was founded in 1850. In 1851 an 'Irish brigade' of Catholic Liberal MPs was formed in parliament and a Catholic Defence Association in Ireland at a time when the Liberal government was seen to be pursuing anti-Catholic policies. Eventually, an Independent Irish Party emerged though it had imploded by the middle of the decade.[1]

John Reynolds's career peaked in the late 1840s and early 1850s. He was lord mayor of Dublin in 1850. In August 1847, he was elected as repeal MP for Dublin City, joining the 'Irish brigade', before losing his seat in the April 1852 election.[2] The Conservatives had been successful during the 1840s in the Dublin parliamentary elections, mostly due to the fact of the continuing presence of freemen voters, a relic of the days of the unreformed Corporation. In 1847, these still amounted to one-third of the electorate of 19,562. They were mostly Conservative voters, though O'Connell as lord mayor had admitted 1,400 new freemen who were mostly Whig Protestants. Two-thirds of the £10 householder voters were Catholics. In the mid-1840s the British Conservative Party had divided over the repeal of the protectionist corn laws, a measure in part designed to mitigate the effects of the Irish Famine, with a free-trade minority under Sir Robert Peel splitting from a protectionist majority. It was such divisions that allowed anti-Conservatives to succeed and Reynolds to be elected. The two sitting Conservative MPs had been Sir Edward Grogan and William Gregory. Reynolds unseated the latter at the election.[3]

1 Douglas Kanter, 'Post-famine politics, 1850–1879' in Kelly (ed.), *The Cambridge history of Ireland*; iii, *1730–1888* (Cambridge, 2018), pp 688–715: pp 693–703. 2 Bridget Hourican, 'Reynolds, John' in James McGuire and James Quinn (eds), *Dictionary of Irish biography*; 9, *Patterson to Stag* (Cambridge, 2009), pp 458–9. 3 J.R. Hill, 'The 1847 general election in

In 1848, the Corporation promoted another reform bill in the Commons. This time it proposed the absorption of all boards into the Corporation with the exception of the ballast board and police commissioners. The Dublin Metropolitan Police was a distinct force from the Irish Constabulary. Ironically, the government was for security reasons always reluctant to place the police, particularly in the capital, under civic jurisdiction, whereas in Britain police commissioners had proved themselves to be one of the instruments of improvement in local government.

A new inquiry was commissioned into this latest bill and Jackson's bill for the replacement of the Corporation with a commission. In the Corporation the latter was clearly being used by the Tories as a bargaining counter against the majority's plans for the Corporation as embodied in its bill. [15/16 Feb. 1848] However, Reynolds, as now also an MP, used procedural measures in the Commons to prevent Jackson's bill's progress. As a result, as he triumphantly informed the Corporation, 'There was then no bill before the house but that of the Corporation.' [28/29 Mar. 1848]

This time the surveyors appointed to inquire into the bills were Irish – a barrister and an engineer. Their report, issued in May 1848, was less negative about the Corporation than the last one had been, though it criticized the way the Corporation bill was framed. It was also quite critical of the paving board, which had been praised the last time. With prospects apparently favourable for reform the Corporation even accepted the idea of a committee of three commissioners effectively to run the city's utilities, albeit under the authority of the Corporation. However, the Court of Queen's Bench ruled that the Corporation could not use the borough fund or pipewater money to promote the bill. The Corporation also found itself at odds with the government over its support for the new French republic that had been formed after recent revolution. These factors sealed the fate of its bill.[4] As on the previous occasion the defeat was accompanied by the appearance of another bill that the Corporation found unhelpful. This one sought to extend the powers of Dublin's police commissioners to have control over the city's markets, a move that was comprehensible in the context of the use of police commissioners in British cities. [2/3 Aug. 1848; 7/8 Aug. 1848] The idea of the necessity of redrafting the ward boundaries to advantage Tories was also gaining ground, however. Hudson bluntly told the Corporation that if the ward boundaries were not redrafted the Tories would prevent the Corporation from gaining new powers. [1/2 Jan. 1849]

Dublin city' in Alan Blackstock and Eoin Magennis (eds), *Politics and political culture in Britain and Ireland, 1750–1850* (Belfast, 2007), pp 41–6: pp 44, 52–3, 58. 4 Jones, 'Dublin reformed', 1, pp 145–69.

The year ended with a very angry meeting of the Corporation during which Reynolds was accused of scuppering the possibility of compromise. One member said the choice was coming down to allowing more Tories to be members or dissolving the Corporation as some Tories were proposing. This would mean 'to brand the Liberal members as being incapable after seven years' experience of discharging their duty (hear, hear).' Reynolds replied that 'he was anxious to make large concessions to the Conservative Party for peace sake; but he would never consent to anything that would interfere with the elective franchise, or swamp the popular party (hear, hear).' Yet his challenger had put his finger on the political issue of these years: without O'Connell, could O'Connell's reformed Corporation survive and thrive, particularly with John Reynolds at the helm? [21/22 Dec. 1848]

The pressure for concession from the non-Tory side increased in 1849, with the continuing suggestion that without concession the Corporation might face suppression. Either poorer wards could be amalgamated and richer ones subdivided or, as the Tory Richard Walker suggested, wards valued under £50,000 could return three members and those above £50,000 six. A Corporation committee was appointed and proposed that one ward, St Stephen's, have six seats, six wards – Merrion, St Andrew's, Linen Hall, St George's, Post Office and Custom House – have five each and the rest – College, Castle, St Patrick's, St Audeon's, St Catherine's, St James's, St Paul's and Four Courts – have three each. This proposal pleased no one. The Tories objected that the valuation levels varied widely. Reynolds said he wanted to quit but would stay because 'an attempt was made to annihilate that Corporation'. Legal proceedings were being taken against him to recover the expenses paid to him for official trips to London and he claimed to have been told that they might be dropped if he remained quiet. The matter was resolved when he successfully persuaded the Corporation to vote to ask the government to bring in a reform bill. [8/9 Jan. 1849; 15/16 Jan. 1849; 22/23 Jan. 1849]

By early February William Ford, the Dublin town clerk, had overseen the introduction of two Corporation bills at Westminster, a Dublin improvement bill and a waterworks bill. But he was soon reporting what he considered as vexatious measures to undermine the Corporation, including a suit in the court of Chancery brought by the attorney general at the behest of Jackson (who was still promoting his measures) concerning the use of pipewater rent. In requesting greater funds, the Corporation's London law agent described it as 'a suit affecting your very existence and involving an enormous expenditure of time and money'. At a meeting of the Corporation itself Reynolds accused Hudson of 'playing the game of the bitterest opponents of the Corporation.' [30 Jan./1 Feb. 1849; 1/2 Feb. 1849] March saw confused attempts at negotiation between the Corporation and the government with a delegation going to London while others negotiated with the under-secretary in Dublin. Meanwhile the boards whose existence was threatened by reform tried to create their own common front. The government toughened its position by asserting that there would have to be consensus in Dublin about reform, thus strengthening the hand of the Dublin Tories. On 10 March, Reynolds wrote from London that the Corporation bills and that of Jackson were to be withdrawn and a government bill introduced. The existing Corporation would be dissolved and government commissioners would remodel the wards. There would be a new Corporation modelled on English legislation concerning franchise, qualification and rates. As of 1 January 1851 the public boards (wide streets, paving and lighting, grand jury) would be dissolved and their powers transferred to the new body. He and others in Dublin feared that all this would mean a new government-controlled Corporation. [6/7 Mar. 1849; 13/14 Mar. 1849] At a later meeting between the Corporation's London delegation and the government agent the issue of the much-desired consolidation of tax collection was addressed. A central board for the collection of taxes and a post of collector general were to be established which would be answerable to the government. To the concern of the delegation it seemed that an increase in the remit of the Corporation would not now be only accompanied by an increase in Dublin Tory power and also by greater accountability to the government. [20/21 Apr. 1849]

Reynolds believed the new arrangement would mean that Dublin citizens would have to pay eight taxes before they could be registered as burgesses.[5] It was a triple blow. It would 'seriously injure the present Corporation ... it would have the effect of destroying the popular franchise, giving power to the minority ... and placing additional patronage at the disposal of the government.' [15/16 June 1849; 2/3 July 1849] Yet when the legislation, by then encompassing three bills, became law in August the Corporation's agent, writing from London, and no doubt aware that the lobby effort had cost the Corporation £6,000, attempted to present it in the most positive light. 'Not only the principles but the details of the first bill, produced by the Corporation in 1847, but even more than they have ever asked for have been granted.' On November 1850 a new franchise would come into effect that would increase the number of burgesses by rating premises not individuals. Importantly, given

5 The taxes were paving and lighting; watering streets; grand jury or county cess; pipewater rent; wide streets tax; police tax; borough rate; and poor rate. Minister's money, which will be discussed later, was not included. Burgesses would have to have been rated occupiers of premises not below £10 for two years and eight months, as opposed to the existing period of one year. [7 June 1849] This meant that the number of burgesses ranged between 5,000 and 6,000 for several decades.

the concern about it, the collector general's role would be to collect rates and not determine their use. The paving board and wide streets commission were to be abolished and the grand jury deprived of tax-raising power. It was all, the Corporation's agent believed, a triumph for Reynolds. The Corporation was in his debt 'for the ability he had displayed both in the committee on these bills and in the house and, above all, for the firmness and the address with which he has upheld, to the utmost attainable extent, the principles uniformly professed by the council upon the great questions of municipal reform and improvement.' [14/15 Aug. 1849] At the same time the *quid pro quo* for the Tories was also granted. Two officials were appointed by the government to redivide the wards and created fifteen renamed wards taking account both of property value and population.[6] The net effect was to give greater representation to the wealthier. Thus poorer western wards such as Arran Quay and Usher's Quay had almost twice the number of properties each as more prosperous wards such as Fitzwilliam and South City.[7] There was also concern among nationalists that the largely Tory chamber of commerce was exercising a lot of influence and that the process of revising the burgess roll had been taken away from the lord mayor. [15/16 Oct. 1850]

In practice John Reynolds's years of ascendancy in the Corporation, the late 1840s and early 1850s, and accession to and tenure of the lord mayoralty were not untroubled ones. By 1847 the enthusiasm that had marked the early days of the new Corporation was gone, just as O'Connell himself was gone and repeal seemed a dead letter. Attendance at meetings of the Corporation was low and sometimes there was not even a quorum, indicative of a general state of demoralization. The year 1847 began with desultory attempts to address the worsening Famine. These, however, were ones which were not unmindful of the economic interests of the Dublin merchant classes from which many councillors came. The contradictions were apparent whereby a body beholden to commercial interests was attempting to address a situation whose resolution might disadvantage those interests. Timothy O'Brien, a former and future lord mayor, member of parliament and Dublin merchant, proposed an address to parliament:

> [He] thought it was their duty, as the first Corporation in the country, to make some manifestation with reference to the Famine and pestilence prevailing in Ireland – to let them know that the people were

Dickson, *Dublin*, p. 341. **6** Jones, 'Dublin reformed', i, pp 169–92. **7** J.H. Martin, 'The social geography of mid-nineteenth-century Dublin city' in W.J. Smith and Kevin Whelan (eds), *Common ground: essays on the historical geography of Ireland, presented to T. Jones Hughes MA MRIA* (Cork, 1988), pp 173–88.

> dying and pestilence prevailing in Ireland – to let them know that the people were dying by thousands from starvation – a fact not to be denied (hear). The mortality in one churchyard alone in the present month was double what it was in the month of June last. In one churchyard alone in Dublin 1,546 interments had taken place within the last two months. If these facts were put prominently before the people of England, they would have the most effective results. [12/13 Jan. 1847]

The following meeting was marked with useless grumbling. Charles Gavan Duffy said they should tell the government directly that it 'had not done its duty … he felt bound to state that, in his opinion, the government were censurable (cries of here).' Another member thought that the prime minister 'should be impeached and put upon his trial.' Reynolds, reluctant to burn bridges with the new Liberal government, disagreed, believing that 'since the hideous calamity with which the country was afflicted had developed itself in its full extent, the present ministry had done more for Ireland than any former government.' He blamed the Irish landlord class. But when it came to action O'Brien thought the government was right not to interfere with trade as it would have caused a panic. [21/22 Jan. 1847] All of this amounted to a failure of the idea that Dublin Corporation might act as Ireland's civic parliament.

The lord mayor was formally elected on 1 December in the year before assuming office but in order to give him time to prepare for office a practice had developed whereby he was nominated in July by a vote in the Corporation. The Repealer Jeremiah Dunne was nominated at the beginning of July. His opponents were the Tory Kinahan and his fellow Repealer Reynolds. The Young Irelander Gavan Duffy wanted neither repeal candidate:

> I do think the time has arrived when a Tory – a member of that party of which Alderman Kinahan is a distinguished member, should be chosen as chief magistrate of this city (cheers). I say so because I think it would be serviceable for the repeal of the union. We Repealers profess to unite all Irishmen in the struggle for nationality. We profess to do so totally apart from party politics or religious consideration on the ground that this nation is entitled to rule itself – that the men of this nation, whatever their politics or creed, are entitled to rule themselves.

Reynolds's candidacy was treated with a certain amount of derision with one member opining that because Reynolds had so far failed to deliver municipal reform 'he was considered unworthy of confidence (loud laughter).' As for

Reynolds himself, he felt betrayed as he had been confident of the support of the Repealers. While working for reform of the Corporation in London he had been assured of this. The failure of reform was due to treachery: 'he was only beaten by the treachery of several of the Irish representatives and the treachery of men in that council who pretended to be favourable to the bill but were cutting its throat privately (cries of name, name).' As for the lord mayoralty, he had sought and been given assurances of support. Some had pledged to him who were absent that day or who were present but going to vote against him. On the first vote Dunne received twenty-three votes, Reynolds twelve and Kinahan eleven. With Kinahan eliminated and the Tories not voting, Dunne was elected by twenty-four votes to Reynolds's twelve. Ever the statistician Reynolds claimed that twenty-seven had promised to vote for him, of whom eleven had kept their promise, eight had attended and voted for Dunne and eight had stayed away. At this point matters became heated. When Reynolds appeared to accuse what he believed to be a group of members supportive of Young Ireland of being against him, Dr Gray pointed out that Dunne was an O'Connellite and 'at that moment one of the treasurers of the Old Ireland Repeal Association and it was most unjust to insinuate that he had been returned by Young Ireland influence (hear, hear).' The meeting ended with Reynolds claiming he had been physically threatened by another councillor. [1/2 July 1847]

By convention the lord mayor and Corporation took part in the ceremonial entry of a new lord lieutenant to Dublin. The declining confidence of the repeal movement – though it gained seats at the 1847 election – was noticeable in the debate over the address to the incoming Whig lord lieutenant Lord Clarendon (1800–70) in July 1847. There was a diffidence about pressing too firmly for repeal. In the end stronger references to repeal were inserted in the address, at the behest of Dr Gray, even though Reynolds had cautioned against it. The latter, now casting his ambitions on a wider political area, made a plea for the Corporation to live up to the sometimes hoped for, but hardly ever achieved, role of a substitute Irish parliament: 'He thought that the council ought to express the opinion of the people; that in fact it ought to be a sort of a halfway house between the government of England and the Irish people and that it should be looked upon as a kind of substitute for that parliament of which they had been robbed (hear, hear and cheers).' [13/14 July 1847]

Reynolds's election to parliament in the summer of 1847 led, if anything, to a deterioration in his ability to control his temper. In September he read out a letter to the members of the Corporation from a group of individuals who had wanted to organize a public dinner to celebrate his election but who claimed to have been denied the use of the king's room at the Mansion House by the lord mayor. When the lord mayor denied the use of the room was in his power Reynolds shouted 'you shall not stigmatize the writers of that letter as fabricators with impunity' and threatened legal action. [10/11 Sept. 1847] His growing capacity for feeling slighted – whether such slights were real or imagined – may have been one of the reasons why he increasingly became the real target of attempts to injure him politically. It may also have been because with O'Connell gone, Dublin Tories could dare to attack leading nationalists and because, with the tide of reform running in their favour, it was in their interests to make the Corporation seem as ruinous as possible. Provoking Reynolds was an easy way to do this. Shortly after his election to parliament William Gregory, whom he had defeated, sought information into Reynolds's tax status with a view to challenging the election. [20/21 Aug. 1847] This would set a precedent for later attempts to unseat Reynolds from the Corporation when he was lord mayor. In November there was a confrontation over the fact that the Tory member, Edward Hudson, had succeeded in getting the courts to limit the money the Corporation could use to pay the expenses of those, including Reynolds, who had spent time in London promoting the recent failed reform bill. Reynolds also objected to the reading of a letter from the Corporation's London law agents, causing one member to remark, 'Oh, he is a most complete dictator here (laughter).' [17/18 Nov. 1847] Reynolds may have had a capacity for losing his temper but he was not feared.

The following year began with the lord mayor forgetting to make a toast to the memory of O'Connell at the important civic banquet at which the leaders of Dublin society could meet each other and the lord lieutenant. [18/19 Jan. 1848] Then there was the surprising revival by the Dublin Tories of the idea of parliament sitting in Dublin every three years. [8/9 Jan. 1848] Undoubtedly, though, the most arresting news of the early part of the year was that of the revolution which inaugurated the second French republic and was to have wide repercussions through Europe. It, and the brief Young Ireland rebellion in Ireland in the summer, would dominate the mood of the Corporation.

In March Kinahan attempted to resist the passing of a Corporation address of congratulations to the French people on the grounds, *pace* the civic parliament argument, that the Corporation ought only to consider matters relating to Dublin. 'The motion was foreign to the nature of the body, which was intended for the benefit of their fellow citizens, and they should not go into matters that were never contemplated to be introduced into such an assembly.' [7/8 Mar. 1848] But an address was adopted and the possibility that the French revolution might have implications for Dublin and a Corporation even narrowly focused on the needs of the citizens of the city soon raised itself in nervous references to the fear that the St Patrick's Day parades might lead to rioting. [14/15 Mar. 1848] As for the address to the French people, the lord mayor, Jeremiah Dunne, was diffident about delivering it in person and decided that it would be illegal for him to go to a foreign country to present an address. [28/29 Mar. 1848; 4/5 Apr. 1848] It was thus a Young Ireland delegation that was to visit Paris, though Reynolds later caustically noted that the new French government had promised them no help. [26/27 Apr. 1848]

In April there was high anxiety among the Dublin merchant and professional classes about the possibility of some kind of outbreak of unrest in the city and this was reflected by their representatives on the Corporation. A special meeting was held on 26 April to consider 'the state of alarm and excitement in which the city is placed, to the detriment of all trade, and to adopt such measures as shall restore public confidence.' There had been a run on the banks and there was talk about the city being 'sacked'. As he had done when the early stages of the Famine were being discussed Reynolds advised that a low-key reaction would better suit business interests. If they were not careful, people abroad 'would look upon that city as in a state of open insurrection; and what was the result of it, that the merchants, traders and labouring men, were robbed of their daily support in consequence of these proceedings.' He proposed that a committee be established into the supposed unrest. [26/27 Apr. 1848] There was continuing annoyance in the Corporation over the next few weeks at its apparent exclusion by the government from consultation on or information about the security situation. [1/2 May 1848]

Yet political tensions rose further in August, after the brief, abortive Young Ireland rebellion. The Tory Richard Walker tried to tarnish, as he saw it, the Repealers on the Corporation by association with Young Ireland. In reply Timothy O'Brien tried to deflect the criticism with a reference to commercial self-interest. 'They had as great a stake in the country and as much property to protect.' A more somber mood prevailed in early October when the Corporation met to consider supporting a plea for mercy for William Smith O'Brien who had been sentenced to death as a result of his part in the uprising. 'I feel exceedingly melancholy and oppressed in spirit,' said Reynolds, 'at being called upon to discharge this duty, which I feel is a duty imposed on me not only as an individual citizen but as the representative of my fellow citizens.' [16/17 Oct. 1848] The initiative was seized by the Tories at the end of the year, however, when they proposed an address to the lord lieutenant, supportive of his actions in suppressing rebellion. Kinahan recalled the earlier address to the French Republic which could now be seen as disloyal. 'Who could have censured his excellency had he, following a celebrated example in history, sent a party of soldiers to take away your lordship's mace – "that empty bauble" – and dismiss the assembly to make room for loyal men.' He bitterly recalled that when an outbreak was thought possible in the city the Corporation had wanted the troops withdrawn. In his mind his proposed address to the lord lieutenant would force the Corporation to make a choice: 'they must either approve the constitutional and bloodless triumph obtained by the lord lieutenant over conspiracy and rebellion or avow themselves of that rebel party.' The best the Repealers could muster by way of response was that discussing the matter would prejudice the case of the Young Irelander and Corporation member Charles Gavan Duffy who was then facing trial. In the end, and *pace* Kinahan's polarized view a compromise address, crafted by O'Brien, was delivered to the lord lieutenant which spoke of Irish grievances but began by thanking him for restoring order. [12/13 Dec. 1848; 24/26 Dec. 1848]

The use of formal addresses as missiles in party politics occurred again in the summer of 1849 with the visit of Queen Victoria to Dublin.[8] In contemplating an address to the Queen some, though aware of the general popular welcome for the visit, wanted it to address the Famine, which was now in its latter stages. One member believed it ought to be highlighted though he 'wished to make a distinction between the Queen and her ministers who had allowed the people of Ireland to perish of starvation without making an effort to preserve their lives.' Others wanted the address to include a plea for clemency for those who had been convicted after the 1848 rebellion. Then there were others who disparaged any idea of calling for an illumination of the city – the placing of candles in windows – to celebrate the visit. As for the Tories, they proposed the rescinding of the French address before agreeing anything, though Reynolds responded to this by proposing an address of congratulations to the Hungarian leader Kossuth for resisting the Austrians. Then the Tories suggested that the Corporation adjourn until after the visit in order to avoid any address being agreed that mentioned either the Famine or prisoners. In the end an inevitable compromise address of welcome was constructed that did make some mention of famine and disease. [6/7 July 1849; 23/24 July 1849; 1/2 Aug. 1849; 8/9 Aug. 1849; 14/15 Aug. 1849] After the visit had taken place the motion to rescind the French address was put to the vote with only five Tories supporting it. Meanwhile, attention turned to whether the Corporation was liable for the expense of the official reception of the Queen on her arrival. [10/11 Sept. 1849]

The following year the Queen became an issue for the Corporation once more following an assassination attempt on 27 June. In the aftermath of the

8 Murphy, *Abject loyalty*, pp 78–87, 89–97.

trials and transportations that followed the brief 1848 rebellion the mood in parts of the Corporation was hostile to sympathy for her. At a public meeting Charles Gavan Duffy had apparently said that while William 'Smith O'Brien was in Maria Island [Van Diemen's Land (Tasmania), whither he had been sentenced to transportation] they [the Whig government] shall not dare to bring the Queen of England into this island.' A motion condemning this statement met with opposition: 'the name of self-sacrificing Gavan Duffy should hereafter be the watchword of national independence, the synonym of unselfish disinterested patriotism.' Opponents of the vote then staged a walk out. [16/17 July 1850]

The first Tory attempt to unseat a prominent Repealer on the Corporation occurred during the annual November elections when the Tory James Lambert beat Dunne, the sitting lord mayor, in St Andrew's ward by 122 to 108 votes. But Dunne was returned for St Patrick's ward on the retirement of Arabin. There was a brief four-day period, however, when Dunne was not allowed to sit as a member of the Corporation. [25/27 Nov. 1848; 28/29 Nov. 1848; 1/2 Dec. 1848] In August 1848 – a month late – Timothy O'Brien was nominated as lord mayor, beating Kinahan by twenty-nine votes to nine. It was perhaps a sign of the jaded state of nationalist politics that he had only recently been lord mayor and had been nominated because no one else acceptable could be found. [1/2 Aug. 1848] Another sign was a discussion early in 1849 about moving the meeting of the Corporation from Tuesdays, which was inconvenient because it was the market day, to Mondays, which had been the day on which the Repeal Association met in Conciliation Hall. Hudson said he didn't object 'as the Repeal Association had descended into the tomb of all the Capulets (laughter).' This provoked an angry, if somewhat plaintive, response from one Repealer. 'The poverty of the country has prevented us from agitating for it [repeal] lately with such vigour as we were wont to do; but now that we are commencing a new year we will begin again.' [1/2 Jan. 1849]

By June Reynolds had announced that he would put himself forward for lord mayor for the following year. Kinahan had apparently told him that he would not stand as the Tory candidate, not that this won him any gratitude from Reynolds. The latter asserted that he would never vote for someone who 'when members of the Young Ireland party were about the be placed upon their trial, came forward in that house and proposed a slavish, factious address to the viceroy, for the purpose of prejudging the case of those men and putting a rope about their necks while their destiny was trembling in the balance.' This provoked expressions of support for Kinahan from the Liberal side and sneering references to Reynolds in fact being a Whig, though he preferred to call himself a Liberal and Repealer. [1/2 June 1849] There may have been some expectation of support across the house for Kinahan. Certainly, the mood of the Corporation deteriorated after that. On 26 June it was supposed to meet at 1 p.m. to discuss reform, specifically the Dublin improvement bill. Yet there was no quorum by 2:30 p.m. 'owing to the refusal of several [Tory] members who were standing outside in the lobby to come into the council rooms.' One member inveighed against 'the fact that the gentlemen whom the Liberal members thought would cooperate with them in getting an improvement bill were not keeping their promise (hear, hear). Several of those gentlemen were standing outside, yet they refused to come into the room so as to form a house.' [26/27 June 1849] When it came to it Reynolds was easily elected, by thirty votes to thirteen for Kinahan, albeit in a house where only just over two-thirds of the members had turned up to vote. [2/3 July 1849]

It was not long though until efforts began to unseat Reynolds as a member of the Corporation and thus render him ineligible to be lord mayor. In August a 'very dirty specimen of a Dublin porter, named Christopher Murphy, appeared before the [revision] court unshaved, unwashed and ragged' to try to prove Reynolds should not be a burgess. [14/15 Aug. 1849] By November, as a result of this, Reynolds had been given notice that he had been removed from the burgess roll because of an affidavit by a number of individuals. The Tories on the Corporation at once began to argue that he was thus not a member of the Corporation and could not be the next lord mayor. On 1 December he was, nonetheless, elected lord mayor by thirty-five votes to six. The Tories argued not only that he was ineligible but that he would be unsuitable. He was 'a person liable to the imputation of mean or disreputable conduct in his political capacity and in his political character.' [11/14 Nov. 1849; 1/2 Dec. 1849]

Around the same time the annual partial municipal election had led to the election of one new councillor who unusually seemed more interested in the plight of the country than in party politics:

> I see by the papers of this morning that no less than 14,000 persons are in a state of starvation in the Kilrush union and the artisans and the poor of Dublin are nearly as badly off, while £72,000 per annum of quit and crown rents are taken from the impoverished people of this country to beautify the squares and streets of London. Will you assist me in doing your upmost to have this sum appropriated for the benefit of the poor of this city and point to the best plan to be taken for so desirable an object? [12/13 Dec. 1849]

Of course his plea was completely ignored as Reynolds launched an attack on the town clerk, indicative of Reynolds's capacity to put petty squabbles ahead of important concerns. He accused him of multiple jobbing as he also worked as a lawyer and land agent:

> A few days since he had occasion to call at the town clerk's office to get some returns; he went there between twelve and one o'clock in the day and found it locked. He was told that the town clerk was earning his guinea at a meeting of the gas directors' company and that his clerk was out doing some of the town clerk's duty; and when he spoke of that young gentleman, he did not question that he was giving perfect and entire satisfaction in the discharge of those duties for which he received from Mr Ford some seventy or eighty pounds a year. [20/21 Dec. 1849]

Others believed that there was, as ever, a personal element in Reynolds's attack as he had been in dispute with Ford over their involvement in the Hibernian bank. [21/22 Dec. 1849] Reynolds had been a shareholder in the bank, which was founded in 1825 by Catholic merchants at a time when the banking system was overwhelmingly Protestant. Yet he had cut his links with it in 1834 and gone to work for O'Connell's National bank. Others defended Ford, saying that his organization and efficiency had saved the Corporation a lot of money. An accusation that 'Mr Reynolds had a personal and a bad motive in bringing forward this motion (hear)' doubly infuriated Reynolds, not only because it impugned his motives but because he was not addressed as councillor. [27/28 Dec. 1849] The Tory Hudson said that the motion against Ford 'came with peculiar bad grace from Mr Reynolds' who in any event was also double jobbing as a member of the Corporation and an MP. He hinted that an additional reason for Reynolds's animus against Ford may have been because Ford had not subscribed to the fund to defray Reynolds's election expenses. 'I say it never was asserted that the town clerk was an overpaid officer until he refused to give money for the member for Dublin (hear, hear and much confusion and interruption).' Reynolds denied this. He was 'the best abused man in Ireland' and had been 'visited with vituperation.' The mood was certainly against him, however. One member 'hoped the vote which would be passed this day would be a lesson to him [Reynolds] to curb the ire of his tongue, or, if he did not do so, he would soon find himself disgracefully hurled from the elevated positon in which chance had placed him.' The vote went thirty-seven to nothing against the motion. A relieved Ford had the last word: 'Thirty-seven was the exact number of votes I had when I was first elected (cheers).' [21/22 Dec. 1849]

As Reynolds assumed office as lord mayor in January legal proceedings against his being a burgess continued. In an editorial the *Freeman's Journal* wondered why the Tories were doing this. If he was removed as a burgess or elector, it would require further legal proceedings to remove him as a member of the Corporation and as lord mayor. [15 Jan. 1850] When at the end of the month the Court of Queen's Bench ordered his removal from the roll of burgesses the paper was sympathetic towards him: 'we cannot but look on the lord mayor as a persecuted man.' [30 Jan. 1850] John O'Connell (1810–58), 'the young liberator,' wrote a letter which was read at a public meeting in Reynolds's support. [4/5 Feb. 1850]

The Corporation met on 1 February with Reynolds installing two policemen in the chamber to support his continuance in office by physical force if necessary. When Walker demanded that he leave the chair 'which you have no right to occupy' Reynolds read an opinion from the attorney general to the effect that he was still legally in office and followed it up with an address from five aldermen and twenty councillors who were supporting him politically. The Liberal strategy was to refer the issue for further legal advice, thus delaying any action. This did not please Hudson: 'I believe you have as much right to be called the Duke of Northumberland or the Duke of Wellington as you have to be called lord mayor of Dublin.' Reynolds then had a motion passed that neither Hudson nor Walker 'be not heard' until they addressed him by his correct titles. Hudson lost his temper and started 'striking the table with great vehemence.' [1/2 Feb. 1850]

At the next meeting when Walker refused to remove his hat the tipstaff did it for him. Competing legal opinions were read on whether Reynolds was still lord mayor. Reynolds took it to a further level by raising the perhaps ever present but unstated issue of religion, accusing another Tory of 'unrelenting bigotry against his creed.' 'Another row then took place and in a few minutes the lord mayor's footman … was observed struggling with some town councillors and addressing them in violent and menacing language.' Reynolds asserted that 'he would not abandon his high office or shrink like a coward before the persecution of his enemies.' Hudson retorted that Reynolds wanted 'to occupy the position of a public martyr.' [5/6 Feb. 1850] The Conservative *Dublin Evening Mail* was anxious to scotch this line, true or otherwise. 'Mr John Reynolds, in the same breath in which he heaps the grossest abuse upon his greatest enemies – those who, as he says, kneel before the same altar as himself – declares that he is the victim of Protestant persecution … [However, T]he desire to remove from the city of Dublin the disgrace of his chief magistracy is not traceable to any feeling, political or religious.'[9]

Things had calmed down a week later to the extent that Hudson referred to Reynolds as lord mayor. [12/13 Feb. 1850] But early in March he had

9 *Dublin Evening Mail*, 13 February 1850.

adopted a new line against Reynolds, arguing that he had abandoned his duties as lord mayor due to long absences, including attendance at parliament. 'It was a monstrous thing to leave the city without a chief magistrate.' When he pressed the matter to a vote, however, it was defeated. Many felt that it was unfair on Reynolds who was, indeed, absent at the time in parliament. [5/6 Mar. 1850; 19/20 Mar. 1850]

Reynolds was back the following month and at the earliest pretext summoned a police inspector to his side at the chair. [9/10 Apr. 1850] However, a conditional order was issued by the Court of Queen's Bench requiring an election for lord mayor. Reynolds was still maintaining his political support on the Corporation, from most though not all Liberal, and it decided to challenge the ruling. [29/30 Apr. 1850] After a mandamus order was issued on 30 May the Tories attempted to enforce the order at a meeting on 7 June. Fourteen members declared a Tory member elected lord mayor. 'They are holding an illegal meeting and I won't allow them to continue,' announced Reynolds. He called in the police though 'Alderman Kinahan [was] still continuing to occupy the chair at the end of the table, being surrounded by members who acted with him and who were engaged in signing documents:'

REYNOLDS: I again ask you in what capacity you are sitting there?
KINAHAN: I am advised to answer no question to a person who is not a member of the town council.

Kinahan was removed by the police. [7/8 June 1850]

The decorum of the Corporation continued to decline. In August, Reynolds had a row with an alderman, which quickly went to ludicrous extremes, as Reynolds's remaining authority drained away. Reynolds said, 'I arrest you in the name of the Queen and I shall bring you to the police-office (great excitement).' To this the alderman replied, 'Ah do so and see if I don't make you pay for it. Here I am; I won't stir; arrest me now (confusion)'. [27/28 Aug. 1850] When Reynolds had a disagreement with a member at a later meeting the latter sneered, 'Now, I suppose, you will send for the police.' [15/16 Oct. 1850]

The low ebb which Dublin Corporation reached under Reynolds when it had the luxury of a large majority of Repealers and Liberals might be compared with the situation in Belfast. Unburdened by arcane structures from the past, Belfast, after municipal reform, managed to improve the markets, widen streets and regulate housing. On the other hand, no Liberal was elected to Belfast city council until 1855, due in part to the efforts of the town clerk.

Things were to change in the mid-1850s, however, when a financial scandal drove the town clerk from office and held Conservative members responsible for misappropriating large sums of money. When the matter was settled by arbitration half the seats were offered unopposed to the Liberals and a Liberal mayor was elected in 1861, though the Liberals proved unable to take advantage of the opportunity in the longer term.[10]

There were three major reforms of the Corporation in the nineteenth century, in 1840–1, 1849–50 and 1898–1901. The first reformed the franchise, admitting Catholics. The second changed boundaries and increased the powers of the Corporation by merging many of the hitherto independent boards into it. The third increased the franchise and greatly increased the boundaries of the city. Of the three, the first is the one most remembered. The third is associated with the beginnings of the abolition of the townships. The second reform, however, is forgotten. This is surely because, though it marked a new beginning, it also marked an ending, the ending of the nine years of the O'Connellite Corporation. Though the Corporation in those years had some achievements in the area of controlling expenditure under difficult circumstances, the period ended in shame and disgrace, due in large part to the behavior of the unpredictable John Reynolds. His year in office as lord mayor had something of the same feel of wanton recklessness about it as did the last years of the unreformed Corporation a decade earlier. Reynolds provided Tories with a golden opportunity to demonstrate that Irish Catholic nationalists were incapable of self-rule. In the Corporation of the second reform another battle would be fought, but this time over the issue of water.

**10** Stephen A. Royle, 'Workshop of the empire, 1820–1914' in S.J. Connolly (ed.), *Belfast 400: people, place and history* (Liverpool, 2012), pp 199–236: p. 227.

CHAPTER 5

# A second new Corporation, 1851–3

THE CONTINUING AND DEEP politicization of local government not only in Dublin but throughout Ireland in the nineteenth century along lines of religion, class and national identity was in contrast with the experience in Britain where, to a degree, and depending on the particular location, party politics was set aside in the cause of what was known as improvement. It was no accident that the generic name for bills to make significant changes in Dublin and elsewhere – and in the absence of centralized legislation numerous such bills were required – was improvement bills.

In Britain, there was a social energy to build up cities that was less evident in Ireland. Where the structures of local government, in terms of town or city councils, were initially missing in early nineteenth-century Britain, as they often were due to the rapid expansion of new industrial cities, attempts were made to use what bodies were to hand, such as police commissioners, for the purposes of local improvement and where possible to make them locally accountable. In 1824, for example, the police commissioners in Manchester, which at the time had no Corporation, set up a gas company. Pressure for improvement also came from the government, which was to legislate from mid-century onwards on matters of public health but put the onus on local implementation. In England, the Liberals were the beneficiaries of elections when municipal reform established new or reformed councils. In expanding northern industrial cities such as Leeds, Liverpool, Leicester, Nottingham, Manchester, Birmingham, Salford and Bradford Liberals took council seats over Tories at a rate of six to one. Many of these cities had large religious nonconformist populations and municipal reform had the effect of drawing in hitherto-excluded minorities and thus enhanced the social and political cohesion of the country.[1]

Birmingham was a highly politicized city and a centre of early and mid-century radicalism in the chartist movement. By the end of the century though, and under the guidance of Joseph Chamberlain (1836–1914), who was one of a series of dominant, charismatic figures in the history of city, Birmingham was moving in a decidedly more Conservative direction. It was

1 Derek Fraser, *Urban politics in Victorian England: the structure of politics in Victorian cities* (Leicester, 1976), pp 90–101, 124.

hailed above all as 'a business city, run by businessmen, on business principles.'[2] Meanwhile, in Scotland, the participation of the middle classes in numerous nation-wide voluntary bodies, coupled with reforms to local government, led to the development of a stable civil society that was effectively self-governing and forestalled a nationalism that might have demanded domestic self-government, as it did in Ireland.[3]

Leeds may serve as a comparator with Dublin in terms of the balance sheet of achievement. There the implementation of health acts led to a fall in mortality levels from the 1870s. However, the council did not begin to tackle slum clearance until the 1890s, whereas Liverpool had begun to do so much earlier following an 1866 act of parliament. On the other hand Leeds created a system of sewers, something Dublin did not achieve on a satisfactory basis for another half century. One of the surprising features of British Victorian cities was their resort to public ownership, in an era of economic *laissez-faire*. Leeds acquired the waterworks in 1852. Ironically, the water supply had long been in the public domain in Dublin. Dublin's gas company remained a powerful, independent entity that towards the end of the century sought to expand into electricity supply. By contrast Leeds council acquired its two gas companies in 1870, followed by the trams in 1894 and the electricity supply in 1898.[4]

These comparisons with Britain can help explain the opportunity that the second and now forgotten reform of the Corporation presented for Dublin Tories. They returned with an enhanced presence. They spoke of their coming contribution in terms of professional skill in the cause of improvement and they urged the Corporation to eschew matters of party politics, at least as defined by them. Had they stuck to this line it might have created a culture in the Corporation that would have been conducive to their continuing role. However, debate about the one great improvement project of the Corporation, the Vartry water supply scheme, degenerated into sectional bickering. The competing Tory desire to see the Corporation fail proved too strong a temptation to resist, at a time when the remaining position of the ascendancy seemed to be under threat, in the lead up to the disestablishment of the Irish church.

By contrast in Cork there was something of an alliance between Protestants and Catholics on the Corporation and elsewhere in mid-century. This was in part due to the fact that the Protestant population was diminishing and

2 Roger Ward, *City-state and nation: Birmingham's political history,* c.*1830–1940* (Chichester, 2005), pp 1–40, 108–27, 148. 3 Graeme Morton, *Unionist-nationalism: governing urban Scotland, 1830–1860* (East Lothian, 1999), pp 44–7, 130–32. 4 B.J. Barber, 'Aspects of municipal government, 1835–1914' in Derek Fraser (ed.), *A history of modern Leeds* (Manchester,

Catholics were dominant in various trades and professions. Though Protestants continued to be prominent at the higher levels of social activity, such as the Royal Cork Yacht Club, the Catholic and Protestant middle classes sometimes combined to resists working-class unrest and to promote projects such as the Great Southern and Western Railway.[5]

There were elections for all members and aldermen in the fifteen new wards in Dublin in November 1850, meaning that the Corporation taking office in January 1851 was a completely new body. The election was dominated by an external issue, the proposal by the Whig government to abolish the lord lieutenancy as a means of further integrating Ireland into the United Kingdom, with almost all candidates pledged to resist it, because of the detrimental effect it might have on the economy of Dublin, whose tradesmen relied on the custom generated by viceregal ceremonial and social occasions called levees and drawing rooms.[6] What may now be referred to as the 'old' Corporation voted to oppose the measure in March 1850. Reynolds was furious that the chamber of commerce, which he described as a 'mischievous body', led by its secretary, Francis Codd (*c.*1808–67), had obtained a meeting with the lord lieutenant and tried to negotiate for compensation for the city in return for acceptance of abolition. [28/29 Mar. 1850] In the end nothing came of the abolition move though Codd and the chamber of commerce would loom large in the life of the Corporation in the years ahead, as they were to loom large in Reynolds's imagination.

When the election took place thirty-five Liberals were returned, twenty-two Conservatives and three members of undetermined allegiance. Conservative numbers had almost doubled, which was not a surprise given the new division of wards. What was of note was that Conservatives were to be found in quite a few of the wards. Only six wards returned four Liberal members, Wood Quay, Merchant's Quay, Trinity, North City, Inns Quay and Arran Quay. Two wards returned all Conservatives, Fitzwilliam and South Dock. In two wards there were three Conservatives and one Liberal, Rotundo and North Dock. In the latter, one of O'Connell's sons was defeated. Only in Usher's Quay were there three Liberals to one Conservative. The latter was Benjamin Lee Guinness (1798–1868) who headed the poll. No doubt the reason why a Conservative could head the poll in a Liberal ward in an era of open voting was because his brewery was located there. His election, along with those of several others, marked the reengagement with civic politics of the leading merchants of the city. In three wards there were two Conservatives

1980), pp 301–26. 5 Ellis Stack, 'Victorian Cork' in Henry Alan Jefferies (ed.), *Cork: historical perspectives* (Dublin, 2004), pp 172–91: pp 184–6. 6 Murphy, *Abject loyalty*, pp 101–8.

with two Liberals or, in one case, one Liberal and one 'uncertain', Royal Exchange, South City and Mansion House. In the final ward, Mountjoy, there were two 'uncertains' with one Liberal and one Conservative. There were nine wards south of the river and six wards north of the river. Seven of the twenty-two Conservative seats were in the generally poorer north side. In addition to Guinness other elections of note were those of Francis Codd and George Roe, who returned to the Corporation. Codd, a Catholic merchant, was, as we have seen, secretary of the chamber of commerce, which in some ways acted as a rival centre of influence to the Corporation. Thirty-two of the members of the new Corporation were Protestants and twenty-eight Catholics. Fourteen were bank or railway directors or members of the chamber of commerce, signalling the interest of big business in the new Corporation.[7] [26 Nov. 1850]

Around fourteen Liberals who had previously sat on the Corporation were returned, including John Reynolds, MP, though he came a poor third in the poll in Inns Quay. At least nine former Tories were returned, including one who had been on the Corporation before the 1841 reform. They included formidable political performers such as Edward Hudson, Robert Kinahan and Joseph Boyce, putting the Tories in a strong potential position in relation to experience as well as numbers. Nonetheless, with almost two-thirds of the members newly elected the Corporation was in more than one sense a new body. [26 Nov. 1850]

Though a majority of the elected Liberals in 1850 may still have called themselves Repealers and a minority Whigs the Corporation was entering a period of thirty years when nationalist politics would be more muted in its debates. Only in the 1880s would the Irish Parliamentary Party decide to take it over. There were three ways in which Conservatives saw themselves. Initially, some Conservatives thought that the second reform would restore them to their natural place as leaders of the city. Many felt a genuine sense of public service. For others there was an openness to a bipartisan approach to governing the city by setting party politics aside and working with Liberals for the common good and for the improvement of the city. This might certainly have been the best approach for maintaining influence, for in spite of increased strength they would still always be in a minority. Finally, some Conservatives still wanted to see the Corporation fail. The next few decades would see these approaches wax and wane among Tories.

The Corporation would eventually move to the Royal Exchange on Dame St, which would be renamed City Hall. It had been meeting at the City

7 Dickson, *Dublin*, p. 341; Daly, *Deposed capital*, p. 204; Jones, 'Dublin reformed', 1, p. 193. Jones says that in the1850s there was a balance between Catholics and Protestants but after 1860 it was mostly Catholic.

Assembly House, on South William St, after the old Tholsel had fallen into a state of dilapidation. The new location was inaugurated with a special banquet on 30 September 1852. [30 Sept./1 Oct. 1852] On 2 December 1850, however, the newly elected members met in the old City Assembly Rooms. In a bipartisan gesture Roe proposed Benjamin Lee Guinness as lord mayor for 1851 and he was duly elected. A bipartisan tradition of alternating between Liberal and Conservative lord mayors would develop, though some claimed it was between Catholics and Protestants. Many came to believe that party political issues should not be raised, a move more to the benefit of Tories than Liberals or nationalists. The idea of a civic parliament was set aside. The inauguration of the new lord mayor was marred to a degree when a number of members objected to the vote of thanks to the previous lord mayor, John Reynolds. [1/2 Jan. 1851]

With its increased powers and with an eye to the new mood of efficiency and improvement the new Corporation would do much of its work by committees. Three major committees were quickly established: committee number one, covering wide streets, paving, lighting and cleansing; committee number two, covering pipewater, city estates, grand jury, law and leases; and committee number three, covering finance. [13/14 Jan. 1851] The new arrangements did not suit everyone and the two city counsels soon resigned on the grounds that the new committees were seeking legal advice elsewhere. [18/19 June 1851]

The new powers inherited from defunct boards coincided with an increase in legal responsibility for health and sanitation issues over the next few years, due to legislation from Westminster. Thus there were powers to employ an inspector of nuisances, who was duly appointed in April 1851, and a medical office of health, though the latter was not appointed until 1864.[8] In April 1851 Parke Neville was named as city engineer. [7/8 Apr. 1851]

The changeover to the new Corporation had involved cost, both the cost of the Corporation pursuing reform at Westminster, which amounted to £6,000, and the cost of compensation for fifteen or so former employees, such as the pipewater tax collectors, which came to £1,500. [7/8 July 1851] This perhaps explains the public controversy that arose and that told on members

8 Jones, 'Dublin reformed', 1, pp 193, 204, 258; Prunty, *Dublin slums*, p. 69. The next decades would see the passing of quite a number of health and medical acts which fell to the Corporation to implement. Cholera and other epidemics continued to pose significant health challenges for Dublin during these decades. In 1862, Dr Charles Cameron was appointed public analyst to implement the 1860 Adulteration of Food Act. In 1864, Dr Edward Mapother became the first medical officer of health to the Corporation. In 1866, a sanitary act was passed at the height of a cholera epidemic.

of the Corporation when they proposed to increase the lord mayor's salary from £1,000 to £2,500 in the summer of 1851. Support for the increase was led by Francis Codd. Opinion was strongly divided with members frequently referring to public opinion on the matter and the hostile response they obviously feared. Guinness, as lord mayor, supported the raise though, to the consternation of most, he proposed that they sell the Mansion House and that future lord mayors live in private homes. As ever, the irenic George Roe sought a compromise at £2,000, which was accepted. It was, he said, an 'an unfortunate question because an angry feeling had been excited by it.' [1/2 July 1851; 14/15 July 1851]

A bipartisan spirit, however, was in evidence over the question of the lord lieutenancy and over moves to remove government support for Dublin hospitals and the Royal Hospital, Kilmainham, a home for retired soldiers. [20/21 Jan. 1851; 31 Mar./1 Apr. 1851] At the same time many on the Corporation were keen to disallow discussion of party political matters. George Roe recalled that when he had been lord mayor 'the country was torn and distracted by party politics, and felt all the evils arising from such a cause. But look at the state of the country and of the city in that respect now. Was there ever a period when they were more at peace with each other in this regard than at present? All angry party feelings had been put an end to, and, in consequence, the performance of the duties of chief magistrate would be less onerous and painful than formerly (hear).' [1/2 Aug. 1851] Clearly though what were considered party political matters by some were thought of as reform matters by others. This new tone worked in favour of those who supported the status quo, notably the Tories. Thus when Dublin Corporation received a letter from Cork Corporation saying that they wanted to mount a campaign to abolish ministers' money Hudson and Codd quickly shut the discussion down: 'This was a political question and he (Alderman Hudson) would move that the other business be proceeded with.' [24/25 Feb. 1851] As has previously been noted, ministers' money was a tax in certain Irish towns and cities for the support of the established church clergy. It was thus the urban equivalent of the tithes that had been the cause of a sometimes violent campaign of agitation in rural areas in the 1830s before they were mitigated.

In September there was some sectarian violence in the city when fighting broke out at a meeting of Protestants organized by Tresham Dames Gregg. At the Corporation Codd, who said he believed that it should only deal with 'purely fiscal duties', warned that the incident was a matter for the police and that 'what had just taken place showed the danger of introducing subjects into that council with which it had nothing to do (hear, hear).' [24/25 June 1851; 2/3 Sept. 1851] This was certainly pushing the notion of an apolitical

Corporation to an extreme. He seemed to deny that public order was a proper subject for its attention, when the Corporation had itself historically been deeply connected with the system of law and order.

The supporters of a non-political Corporation had not reckoned, however, with the continued presence of John Reynolds who was nothing if not politically partisan and who returned to his role of scrutineer of finances. The new Corporation began with financial difficulties. The cost of the work of paving for the year was estimated at £72,071, though this marked a huge increase on what it had been. Wide streets had assets of £30,000 and a tax income of £3,500. Pipewater's income was £12,693 as opposed to its expenditure of £11,891. City debt amounted to £232,323, with £8,991 in interest per annum. Under the reform act the Corporation was able to levy a rate of 2*s.* in the pound. The rated property amounted to £634,848. With various adjustments this gave the Corporation an income of £60,311, known as the improvement fund. Charges on the fund (including lighting, cleansing and paving at £72,000) would come to £86,071, leaving a defecit of £25,760. However, as revision of property valuation was likely to reduce the value of property by £100,000 this would reduce the improvement fund to £50,000, leaving a defecit of £36,000. The only other tax the Corporation could levy was the new grand jury and sewer rate which it would have to levy at 3*s.* 4*d.* in the pound on all properties.[9] [2 Jan. 1851] The Corporation was eventually to refinance its loans by borrowing from the Hibernian bank at an interest rate of 4.5 per cent though this only reduced its principal debt to £215,348 after ten years.[10] At the same time its income was reduced by the flight of middle-class people to the townships.

By late 1851, Reynolds was gearing up his attacks against 'this so-called, or rather misnamed, reformed Corporation' on account of its finances and was to clash increasingly with Francis Codd. [29/30 Sept. 1851] The chamber of commerce became Reynolds's *bête noire*. In November, Reynolds, then a mere town councillor, stood at a by-election for the position of alderman in Merchant's Quay ward that had been vacated by the death of the incumbent. He was opposed by but defeated Patrick Sweetman who was a councillor in the ward. [24/25 Nov. 1851] The following day Sweetman defended his own councillor's seat in the same ward but was again defeated. Reynolds was ecstatic at what he saw as the unravelling of a conspiracy against him by his new enemies. At the local level they were the chamber of commerce and the business elite of the new Corporation. At the national level they were those who opposed the new Irish Party at Westminster, to which he belonged, and

**9** Jones, 'Dublin reformed', 2, p. 290. **10** Jones, 'Dublin reformed', 2, p. 289.

its alliance with the Catholic bishops. Thus with the double defeat of Sweetman, '[t]hey had smashed in pieces the whole fabric upon which the clique in the chamber of commerce of this city had erected their rotten dynasty.' That group had set Sweetman against him, another Catholic, 'and thinking that if they succeeded in defeating him it would be a slap in the teeth of the Irish Brigade and the bishops who rallied round them in establishing the Catholic Defence Association.' Sweetman had been beaten 'like a hack the day before' and now again today. 'Last year parties conspired to contest the representation of the municipality from the bona fide ratepayers; and they succeeded in electing a Corporation that did not sympathize with the people.' Reynolds mocked their view of themselves. 'We are an aristocratic Corporation – we are men of station and the ornaments of the city – we are the porcelain of society and who dare say "hoo" to us. They had done nothing since they came into office but double the lord mayor's salary and they were now thinking of putting on a borough rate to maintain their dignity.' He claimed that the lord lieutenant had told them not to allow political discussion but Reynolds said he would campaign against ministers' money. When someone shouted out Francis Codd's name Reynolds said that '[h]e would as soon have a dose of cod-liver oil administered to him as to hear that fellow's name mentioned.' He clearly believed that there was a sectarian animus in the opposition to him and rejoiced that the electors of Mountjoy ward had rejected a candidate associated with the Priests' Protection Society, an evangelical Protestant organization set up in 1844 to proselytize Catholic priests. [25/26 Nov. 1851]

The year 1851 ended with the election of a Catholic Liberal as lord mayor with the support of the Conservatives. Unusually, Reynolds was on the defensive. He was rebuffed when he called for a reduction in the newly raised lord mayor's salary to help with the Corporation's financial difficulties: 'This came with a very bad grace from Alderman Reynolds for when he was lord mayor himself he was anxious to have his salary increased to £2,000 a year (hear, hear).' Reynolds was forced to admit the truth of this, though he claimed that it was because of the legal costs he had been incurring due to the challenges to his position and he went on to try to change the topic by claiming that as lord mayor he had been assaulted in the chair. [1/2 Dec. 1851]

Over the next few years Reynolds was to push two issues, the abolition of ministers' money and, later on, the abolition of the Dublin freeman franchise in parliamentary elections. On 29 December 1851 he announced he was going to promote a petition 'for the abolition of the vexatious impost of ministers' money'. [29/30 Dec. 1851] A general election was looming – it took place in July 1852 – and the *Dublin Evening Mail* believed that Reynolds had 'taken advantage of his elevation to disturb the quiet of this city by an attempt to revive the spirit of sectarian animosity in the town council.' As his purpose, it believed, was 'to be made a champion and a deliverer, he must go forward with a grievance of some sort in his hand.'[11]

Yet when the Corporation came to debate Reynolds's proposal, his opponents, led by two prominent Liberals, were waiting for him. Sir Edward McDonnell, drawing on the apparent new doctrine of the non-political, proposed an amendment: 'That this house, disapproving of the introduction of any subject likely to involve political or sectarian discussion, declines to entertain the motion of Alderman Reynolds.' [5/6 Jan. 1852] He was backed up by Roe who

> had to express his deep regret at the introduction of this question into that assembly (hear). There was no good likely to result from it, but a great deal of evil (hear) ... He saw on the last day a great disposition to revive the old and angry feelings which he hoped and believed had been buried forever (hear) ... But when they reviewed the proceedings of the council for the last year and considered the peace and harmony that prevailed among them, they ought to be very cautious how they would do anything to disturb that peace and that harmony.

Francis Codd was even more direct, clearly aiming his remarks on the substantive motion at Reynolds:

> It was manifestly introduced for the purpose of courting popularity. But there were two kinds of popularity. First, there was that popularity which resulted from a long career of usefulness and honour – a popularity which was indicated by the approbation of the wise, by the confidence of the good, and by the esteem of the virtuous (hear) ... But there was another kind of garlic popularity which resulted from the exercise of the hacknied tactics of an old experienced politician, and was ever indicated by the shouts of an excited and unreflecting mob (hear, hear). That was the popularity which the hon. gentleman was courting by his motion.

In reply Reynolds zoomed back to the recent election. He referred to Patrick Sweetman, who had been twice defeated as 'honest, independent and Catholic Sweetman' but who was, nonetheless, associated with the chamber of commerce, whose connotations were for the most part Protestant and

11 *Dublin Evening Mail*, 9 January 1852.

Conservative. Equally, another candidate, 'in whose favour the whole power of the Codd clique was brought to bear', had also been defeated. For good measure he derided Sir Edward McDonnell as 'a respectable "Cawtholic"'. Reynolds's petition was defeated by thirty-four votes to thirteen.[12] [8/9 Jan. 1852] In the longer term, however, ministers' money came to be seen more as a tax than a political issue and support for opposing it grew in the Corporation. It was eventually abolished in 1857. [19/20 Oct. 1855; 25/26 Feb. 1856; 2/3 Mar. 1857; 6/7 Apr. 1857; 6/7 July 1857]

The Whig government fell in February 1852 and Dublin Corporation at once descended into disagreement as to whether it should present an address to the outgoing and controversial lord lieutenant, Lord Clarendon, for helping with Corporation reform. Opposition to this came from some Liberals such as John Martin and also from Conservatives such as Edward Hudson.[13] Roe denied that Clarendon had been responsible for the Famine. 'Councillor Martin had charged the lord lieutenant with participating in the reduction of the population of this country; but surely he could not be serious in bringing such a charge as that against an individual. They (the council) must be thoroughly impressed with the course from whence that visitation came and for which no human being could be charged.' Codd tried to advance an address that was as neutral as possible but was rebuffed by Hudson. 'And I beg to say that the time has not arrived when I will act at Mr Codd's dictation.' An address, however, was agreed. [1/2 Mar. 1852]

Various issues began to intrude to unsettle the notion of a non-political Corporation. In the spirit of bipartisanship in July the Tory Robert Henry Kinahan was proposed as lord mayor by Roe, a non-partisan Liberal, and by Codd who some time later defined his position as being 'impartial as between all parties in the council'. [22/23 Nov. 1858] Cornelius Dennehy, however, wanted to have Kinahan declare that he would not admit any freemen without legal advice when a member of the Corporation objected. This was because Kinahan's son had been refused freeman status, on the grounds that his grandfather was a freeman, after Reynolds had taken a case to stop Guinness as lord mayor admitting people in this category. Some members objected to undertakings being demanded of someone who would after all be acting in a quasi-judicial capacity in such a matter and the issue was not pressed. [1/2 July 1852] In October there was disagreement over whether the City Assembly Rooms might be used for a conference of the Tenant Right League, that had done well in the recent election, and had gained support that crossed religious

**12** Jones, 'Dublin reformed', 2, p. 275. **13** For many years during the middle of the century there would be two members of the Corporation, one Conservative (representing Fitzwilliam Ward) and the other Liberal (representing Trinity ward), with the name John Martin.

differences. There was an attempt to divert the suggestion by saying the use of the room was at the discretion of the lord mayor. Codd objected to the use of the room for public purposes. The Tory George Woods Maunsell (1815–87) agreed: 'They should make a positive resistance at once to bodies having political aims applying to them for rooms (hear, hear). And he was prepared to say that the tenant right conference was a political body of the strongest character in this country.' The irenic Roe thought they should let 'respectable gentlemen' use the room. Eventually, the lord mayor allowed its use. [6/7 Oct. 1852]

In November there was controversy over attendance at the funeral of the Duke of Wellington in London. Twenty-five places were available to Dublin Corporation but a minority vociferously objected as Wellington had not been popular with Repealers, as he had supported Peel in his opposition to O'Connell. Reynolds said of Wellington that 'amongst those who gloried in fighting he was pre-eminently entitled to every mark of respect; but he would have said that taking him as an Irishman he was a bad Irishman.' John Martin went further. 'Every bloodstained despot in Europe, from Nicholas in the north to Bomba in the south, had gone into mourning for him; he was the very index of aristocratical and monarchical institutions – the people had nothing in common with him (hear, hear).'[14] [1/2 Nov. 1852] Party politics had not gone away and in November 1852 the Dublin Conservatives attempted to strengthen their position by focusing on four wards, where there were outgoing Liberals. They 'sharply contested' the burgess roll at the revision court but when it came to the election they did not make any progress. [2/3 Nov. 1852; 25/26 Nov. 1852]

One of the results of the general election that had taken place in July 1852 was that Reynolds had lost his parliamentary seat for the city of Dublin, gaining only a quarter of the votes and resulting in the return of two Conservatives. He became convinced that he had lost the seat because of the anachronistic presence of 4,000 freemen voters on the parliamentary franchise, most of whom he claimed did not reside in the constituency, and determined to do something about it. He believed that 'the existence of this class of voters is calculated to swamp the rights of the property qualification voters of the city, by depriving them of the power of electing their representatives.' [1/2 Nov. 1852] Reynolds brought forward a motion for the Corporation to petition parliament on the matter but when it was due to be debated there was not a quorum and Reynolds believed that this had been deliberately contrived. 'He complained that there was one member of the council who was always present

14 Emperor Nicholas I of Russia (1796–1855), King Ferdinand II of the Two Sicilies (1810–59), known as 'Re Bomba' or 'King Bomb' because of his brutality to his subjects.

on other occasions – Mr Francis Codd – and who, although he had been sent for by the lord mayor, had not responded to that call ... The moment a house was formed those gentlemen would swarm in to swamp the motion.' After complaining of the costs and fines he had incurred from previous legal cases Reynolds accused the last lord mayor, B.L. Guinness, of having held 'a meeting in one of the rooms in the Mansion House and admitting freemen by wholesale, there being nobody present but the town clerk and his deputy.' The Conservative Maunsell, alluding to another recent controversy, claimed that Wellington had been the one who had ensured the survival of the freemen in the parliamentary franchise. Eventually, at Guinness's initiative, the debate was ended. Reynolds was furious. 'I give Alderman Guinness notice that he may be kept in hot water while he attempts to gag the people of Dublin (cheers).' [8/9 Nov. 1852]

When the debate resumed a week later Reynolds wisely nominated John Martin to speak on his behalf, though Martin was soon interrupted by angry exchanges between Reynolds and Guinness. Once again those who were against what they claimed was political discussion tried to shut the debate down. Hudson said that the 'effect of political and party discussion in that house would be to drive away from it in disgust every man of station and character.' Reynolds's position was defeated in a vote by thirty-five to eighteen, as he descended into accusing the Guinnesses of having been enemies of O'Connell. When the lord mayor, alluding to the forthcoming funeral, mildly praised Wellington's role in Catholic emancipation, Reynolds snapped that the remark was 'a foul libel on the character and services of Daniel O'Connell.' [15/16 Nov. 1852] Reynolds and Martin continued the invective at the formal election of Kinahan in December, with Reynolds inveighing against the understanding that Catholic and Protestant would alternate as lord mayor. 'He had no guarantee that they would not select a Catholic to whom he could have a greater objection than to a Protestant (laughter). They might select a Catholic who was a mere fetch-and-carry for the Conservatives; and he thought there was no more despicable animal on earth than a Conservative Catholic.' [1/2 Dec. 1852]

The matter was raised again by Dennehy in March of the following year, with detailed arguments about the number of rated occupiers registered to vote, the actual as opposed to the notional number of freemen voters, and an allegation that 7,398 voters had effectively been disenfranchised because of the slowness of the process to revise the electoral rolls. For Reynolds, of course, it was personal. Most of the freeman voters had voted for the Conservative candidates at the recent election, not for him. Hudson believed Reynolds's purpose was one 'of crushing or of stultifying a particular class of voters which proved inconvenient to him at the last election.' This was of course true but it did not mean that those voters – the freemen – were not an anachronism that needed to be removed. [14/15 Mar. 1853; 16 Mar. 1853; 10/11 May 1853]

The Corporation commissioned a report into the issue that it then debated in due course. It was now the Conservative strategy to focus the debate on Reynolds. At the time Reynolds's erstwhile parliamentary colleagues, in the Independent Irish Party, were coming in for criticism for taking positions in the new government. Both John Sadlier (1813–56) and William Keogh (1817–78) took office in Lord Aberdeen's ministry. The latter became solicitor-general for Ireland and as a result part of the government of Ireland, based in Dublin Castle.

Thus, Reynolds, according to Maunsell, 'was travelling the road that so many had travelled before him, his goal like theirs being the flesh pots and meal tubs of Dublin Castle (laughter).' Dr Gray, who had returned to the Corporation after nearly five years off it, tried to refocus the debate on the two essential issues, the inefficiency of the revision process that disenfranchised many property voters, and the fact that the freeman franchise, because of its origins in the unreformed Corporation, was essentially a sectarian franchise. He was thus in favour of 'abolishing this sectarian franchise.' Sir Timothy O'Brien, MP, – he had been created a baronet during Queen Victoria's 1849 visit – had milder ambitions. 'The promoters of the report did not want to disfranchise the freemen, or any class of voters; they merely asked for equality and that the freemen should give the numbers of their residence, as was done by the rated occupiers.' [30/31 May 1853] As for Reynolds he was now describing himself as 'an independent member of this council' and turned his attention to resuming hostilities against his old enemy, the town clerk, whose office accounts he described as poetry. [4/5 Apr. 1853]

The year 1853 saw Dublin as the setting for the industrial exhibition, organized by William Dargan (1799–1867) and conceived in the wake of the great success of the Crystal Palace exhibition in London. The Corporation, with all its infighting, was something of a spectator to an effort to encourage Irish industry, an issue about which it had not much thought. The Corporation did little more than congratulate Dargan on his 'munificent exertions to serve the city.' [4/5 Apr. 1853] The Queen, however, decide to thank Dargan in person by making her second visit to Dublin in order to visit the exhibition. The Corporation took umbrage at the low-key visit of whose announcement it had not been given advance warning. One member felt that the citizens of Dublin ought not to go to too much trouble to welcome the Queen on this occasion over 'a visit, the compliment of which was not actually intended for them.' Even Gray joined in: 'Was it treating the Corporation with the respect which was due to it as the chief municipality of Ireland?' [6/7 July 1853] The occasion marked Gray's emergence as the spokesman for the residual nationalism of the times as he led opposition to the address to the Queen that the Corporation agreed and that told the Queen that the people of Ireland had '"at length" come to a knowledge of what the true interests of the country were.' He believed that if it had not been for O'Connell there could have been no thoughts of the need for industry. He further objected to the address telling the Queen that Ireland was becoming more prosperous. For him the address 'does express certain political opinions though in a covert way.' [7/8 July 1853] The November elections that year saw contests in only a third of the wards and minimal change to the Corporation as a result. Three years into its existence the second new Corporation seemed to be running out of steam.

CHAPTER 6

# Markets and superintendence, 1842–65

THOUGH THE PURPOSE OF THIS work is to offer a continuous, developmental narrative and analysis of the politics of the Corporation it will prove necessary at two points to break from the narrative to look at a number of issues that are best understood by being considered over a longer period and in focused detail. A later chapter will look at gas and electricity at the end of the century. This chapter focuses on two of the most controversial issues of the mid-century, markets and jails.

The early decades of the reformed Corporations were noted for controversy concerning these two issues, the Dublin markets and the governing or superintendence of those jails that came under the remit of the city. Both were political issues though in different senses. The board of superintendence that oversaw the jails became a microcosm of the sectarian politics of the Corporation. The good running of the markets, however, was a matter of vital economic importance to the city. Dublin may have been a city but in many ways, and in part because of its port, it was a national hub for agricultural activity and the markets, located at Smithfield on the north side of the river, where animals and provisions were sold, were at the centre of that hub. Cattle, sheep, pigs, hay, straw, coal, butter, corn and potatoes were all sold. The lord mayor had existing powers to oversee the markets and certain Corporation officials had responsibilities there but there were often disputes and regulations were often ignored. The second Corporation reform act, however, further defined the lord mayor's powers.[1]

As early as 1842 the first new Corporation felt its authority was not being respected in Smithfield. By the following year this had focused on a dispute over the probity of the weightmaster at Smithfield, responsible for estimating the weight and thus the commercial value of produce. The lord mayor duly dispatched officials to prevent carts being weighed on the machines that were in place there, only to be told by the police that this would constitute a breach of the peace on their part. A Corporation committee recommended that it establish its own weight house to give it control over the potato market and this was completed by December 1843. In spite of this the Corporation's agent

1 Prunty, *Dublin slums*, p. 96.

at the markets reported that he was being continually defied. Two potato factors complained at the seizure of their weights and scales by the Corporation. The lord mayor hit back, asserting that they were 'fraudulently constructed, and he felt it his duty to seize them in consequence, for he did not see what use there was in having a Corporation or chief magistrate at all if the public were not to be protected from such fraudulent practices (hear, hear).' [31 Jan./1 Feb. 1842; 7/8 Feb. 1843; 7/8 Mar. 1843; 20/21 June 1843; 1/2 Dec. 1843; 12/13 Dec. 1843; 13/14 Feb. 1844; 10/11 Dec. 1844]

In 1846, a markets bill was brought before parliament. It was opposed by Hudson in the Corporation on the grounds that it would effectively impose a new tax and increase the powers of patronage of the Corporation, which would appoint its own weightmasters. These would have to be funded from fees on coal, hay, straw, corn and butter. This objection proved prescient. By 1851, the second reformed Corporation was facing calls for the dismantling of its own system of weightmasters, who were in effect private contractors working on behalf of the Corporation as well as on their own account. This caused attendant disputes as to what the weightmasters should be paid if they were retained and how much compensation they should receive if they were dispensed with. [2/3 Apr. 1846; 2/3 May 1851; 12/13 May 1851]

By the end of 1854 there was a feeling that the weighing of hay had finally been put on a proper basis, by the Liberal lord mayor Sir Edward McDonnell. But this turned out to be a premature judgment. The following year there was pressure on the Corporation over rising prices from consumers of hay, 1,500 of whom had Reynolds present a petition to the Corporation on their behalf. The weightmasters themselves were discontented. One resigned, claiming that with a yearly salary from the Corporation of £120 he was losing money. Another sued McDonnell for £2,000 for loss of business. Some members of the Corporation felt that as McDonnell had dealt with the matter as lord mayor the Corporation should not underwrite his costs. Reynolds believed there was now an urgent need to amend the 1849 improvement act as it was the case that 'the lord mayor was paralyzed in the discharge of his duties as clerk of the market – that he had not the legal right to do the acts which were essentially necessary for the protection of the buyer in the public markets.' Attempts to get the Corporation to take action on this failed, however. [18/19 Dec. 1854; 2/3 Apr. 1855; 7/8 May 1855; 9/10 May 1855; 10/11 Dec. 1855; 21/22 Dec. 1855]

More generally there were calls for a wholescale improvement of the markets and the Corporation found itself having to fend off private legislation brought to parliament to do so and that included proposals to establish a cattle market near the port. [1/2 May 1851; 27/28 Mar. 1861; 22/24 Feb. 1862]

A royal commission investigated the Smithfield cattle market, the most important of the markets, in 1852.[2] By the early 1860s there were growing calls for it to be moved away from Smithfield, to cope with the fact that over half a million cattle, sheep and pigs were being brought to Dublin each year, causing considerable disruption in the city's thoroughfares. [8/9 Dec. 1861; 22/24 Feb. 1862; 14/16 June 1862] By the middle of 1862 the Corporation was itself considering various alternative locations for the cattle market, all of them to the north-west of Smithfield, in the general area of the North Circular Road. Eventually, land owned by the Jameson family at the junction of Aughrim Street and the North Circular Road was chosen. When plans became more specific, however, there were objections to the fact that carrying it through would cost a lot of money. Nonetheless, the Corporation was spurred into action by the prospect of a rival at the port and the new market was in operation by November 1863 [4/5 Aug. 1862; 2/3 Mar. 1863] Over the following decades new markets were opened in other parts of the city for vegetables and other produce. Smithfield itself gradually declined.

The board of superintendence was set for controversy under the second new Corporation. It supervised the jails in Dublin that came under the Corporation and was thus thought to have considerable powers of patronage, particularly through the appointment of officials, though the amount of money at its command was disputed. It was made up of twelve members of the Corporation (though membership of the Corporation may not have been mandatory), six of whom had to be magistrates. There was ambiguity – and thus scope for political tension – concerning how its members were appointed and whether, if at all, they were answerable to the Corporation for the exercise of their functions. [10/11 Jan. 1851; 29/30 Dec. 1852] The power of appointment of officials rested with the board itself, subject to ratification from the Corporation. A move in late 1852 to give the right of appointment directly to the Corporation was defeated by the Liberals. [29/30 Dec. 1852] The Tories continued to press for this because it was believed that the board was under the control of and favourable to Catholics. Reynolds located an anti-Catholic sectarian element in the campaign. 'There was more of the raw material of anger in the discussion than when he brought forward the question of ministers' money.' Early in 1853 Codd managed to get the Corporation to agree to investigate the matter. [3/4 Jan. 1853] Nonetheless, the existing procedure was for the candidates to emerge from a process in the Corporation at the beginning of each year and the following week the twelve members of the board were duly selected by the Corporation by lot. [10/11 Jan. 1853]

2 Liam Clare, 'The Dublin Cattle Market', *Dublin Historical Review*, 55:2 (2002), pp 166–80: p. 166.

Several months later controversy arose over the deputy governor of Richmond penitentiary. As the governor was a Catholic the Tory Joseph Boyce argued that the new deputy should be a Protestant. One speaker objected that this would involve asking candidates their religion. Codd tried to make it less like a sectarian pact by saying that if the governor was a Catholic one would need a Protestant deputy to attend the religious services for Protestant prisoners. [30 Sept./1 Oct. 1853] Reynolds argued that such a rule would run counter to Catholic emancipation [24/25 Oct. 1853]

The next year Hudson pressed for a change in the system of election to the board by lot. There were currently only three Conservative members on it and members of the board had 'compromised themselves and the Corporation by the manner in which they had dispensed the patronage vested in them during the past year.' Of seventeen officers appointed, sixteen had been Catholics. He wanted the members of the board to be elected by open ballot. [6/7 Jan. 1854] But the old system of election by lot continued. Matters remained quiet until the latter part of 1858 when the Tory John Martin (of Fitzwilliam ward) proposed a complex new system under which the six magistrates would be elected by lot and the six others by non-magistrate members of the Corporation who would have three votes each. Yet at the time this system would have favoured the Tories as the new Tory lord lieutenant had just created new magistrates and most magistrates on the Corporation were now Conservatives. The Liberal John Martin (of Trinity ward) accused his namesake of trying to get the power of the board into the hands of his own party. Sir Timothy O'Brien believed that with the creation of many new Tory magistrates 'the Corporation was the only ground left to the Liberals, and why should they allow the ground to be cut out from under their feet in it (hear, hear)? The board of superintendence was the most important board in connection with the council.' The meeting ended with the inevitable row between Reynolds and Codd. [2/3 Aug. 1858]

Following committee discussion the Corporation considered a proposal that each member submit a list of six magistrates and six non-magistrates. Codd thought that the plan would polarize voting and exclude a non-aligned member such as he claimed he was himself. He further believed that it would actually favour the Conservatives who would vote in a disciplined manner, as opposed to the ill-disciplined Liberals. In the end the existing system was retained. [22/23 Nov. 1858] In December John Martin of Trinity ward proposed that the party with a majority in the Corporation should have a majority on the board, a suggestion that provoked much opposition. Codd thought it was giving 'the Liberal party [a means] of seeking an unfair preponderance on the board.' He believed that the board should be 'fairly balanced and that there should be no means whatever of carrying either politicial or secatarian "jobs" (hear, hear).'[3] Another member thought that the 'purpose of Mr Martin's resolution was to crush out every Protestant from the board.' [20/21 Dec. 1858]

Eventually, the self-indulgent infighting of the Corporation was overtaken by more serious events outside. In the late 1850s, a secret organization dedicated to revolution – the Irish Republican Brotherhood – had been founded with Irish-American help. Support for it grew in the early 1860s, particularly among disgruntled young men of the lower-middle class. In 1865, the government took action against the movement with arrests and the suppression of its influential newspaper, the *Irish People*, that had been founded in 1863. Though the Fenians, as they were known, were weakened an attempted rising took place in 1867 in Ireland and there were also incidents in Britain. In the aftermath there was public sympathy for those who had been arrested and convicted, leading to an amnesty movement for their release. An attempt to rescue a Fenian prisoner that resulted in the killing of a policeman led to the execution of the 'Manchester martyrs' in 1867. From the 1870s the Fenians, having formally eschewed violent insurrection, began to exert a more general influence on Irish nationalist politics, though successor American groups pursued bombing campaigns in Britain in the 1880s.[4]

In November 1865, one of the Fenian founders, James Stephens (1825–1901), who had been arrested as part of the government crackdown, escaped from the Richmond bridewell, with the aid of prison guards, as he was awaiting trial. The governor, who had previously both been criticized and defended over charges of laxity, was dismissed. [17/18 Oct. 1853; 24/25 Oct. 1853] The government, which was greatly exercised by what it saw as the Fenian threat to public security, excluded the board of superintendence from the inquiry into what had happened and the power of appointment of lesser officers was reserved to the lord lieutenant. The governor himself had not been appointed by the board. There was offence in the Corporation at these measures. 'The board of superintendence were in no way directly or indirectly responsible for the safe keeping of Fenians prisoners, and everything else connected with them was taken away months ago from the board.' All that was left to the board was to tax the citizens and carry out minor administrative duties. The governor had been appointed by the government and the Corporation was effectively been set up for the blame. 'The government, in order to shield themselves from responsibility, had deprived the board of

3 'Jobs' was a term for corrupt practices. 4 Kanter, 'Post-famine politics', pp 702–4.

superintendence of certain powers which had previously been vested in them and had dismissed two officers who were not originally appointed by the Corporation at all.' [18/19 Dec. 1865] To their complaints the lord lieutenant blandly replied that removing the power to appoint officers 'was not intended to cast any undue share of responsibility upon the board of superintendence for the recent occurrence in Richmond prison.' [22/23 Dec. 1865] At least the episode had united the members of the Corporation and board of superintendence among themselves as they faced humiliation. The episode also showed how remote the Corporation was from some of the realities of the situation in Dublin and throughout the country.

CHAPTER 7

# Taxation and a water triumvirate, 1854–62

BRITAIN WAS THE FIRST COUNTRY in the world to industrialize, leading to the haphazard growth of large cities where conditions were unhealthy and where disease was rampant. The challenges of providing proper housing, a good water supply and public sanitation were ones that concerned both the cities themselves and the government. The latter, consonant with the general Victorian aversion to centralization, sought to play its role in the process by authorizing action on the local level rather than undertaking the work itself. Dublin was not a strongly industrial city but it was relatively large and possessed of an inadequate infrastructure in these areas. Throughout the mid-Victorian period it was the beneficiary of various pieces of legislative intervention in the area of sanitation and public health. There were the Public Health (Ireland) Act (1850), the Nuisance Renewal Act (1853–4) and the Improvement (Ireland) Act (1854), for example. By the 1870s these were joined by the Local Government Act (1871) and the Irish Public Health Act (1878). As early as the 1840s the Bath and Wash Houses Act had led to the erection over time of sanitary facilities. An outbreak of cholera in the early 1850s incurred fewer deaths than in an outbreak in the late 1840s due to the efforts of the Dublin Sanitary Association, a group of concerned private citizens, and the Corporation's sanitation committee. The former was a rare example in Ireland of the sort of associational support that was to enhance the effectiveness of local government in Britain. Dublin's death rate decreased from thirty to twenty-five per thousand during the same period, though thereafter matters deteriorated until by the beginning of the twentieth century it was the worst in the United Kingdom.[1]

Matters were more contentious when it came to Dublin's pipewater supply which had traditionally come from the city's canals. These were owned by private undertakings that were paid for the water. Nonetheless, the supply of water had been the responsibility of the Corporation since 1775.[2] In Belfast it was in private hands, as it was in many British cities. The taking into public ownership of the water supply was one of the features of the advance of local

1 Jones, 'Dublin reformed', 2, chapter 5, 'Dublin Corporation and Dublin health, 1851–60', pp 273–355; Lydia Carroll, *In the fever king's preserves: Sir Charles Cameron and the Dublin slums* (Dublin, 2011), pp 68–75. 2 Cullen, *Belfast and Dublin*, p. 10.

government in Britain in the nineteenth century, and in this respect Dublin was ahead of the times.

The water supplied in Dublin in the early nineteenth century, however, was decidedly unhealthy, in spite of the fact that metal pipes had been introduced to replace original wooden pipes from the 1810s. By the 1850s only sixty per cent of Dublin homes were receiving pipewater. Everyone else had to rely on public fountains, wells and water taken directly from the canals.[3] Two water schemes were proposed in 1847, one each in 1848, 1849 and 1850 and six in 1854.[4]

One of the Corporation's more important committees was thus the pipewater committee. In June 1854 it had to admit that the Corporation 'found it impossible to protect the water at present supplied to the citizens from pollution.' At that point it was estimated that it would cost £200,000 to create a water scheme that would properly supply 258,000 people in the city and 25,000 outside. [2/3 Oct. 1854] Among those interested in the issue were Francis Codd and John Gray, who remarked early the following year of the inhabitants of St Michan's parish that 'the poor occupiers of tenements were constantly afflicted with fever and other diseases, generated by dirt, from the want of a proper supply of pure water.' [15/16 Jan. 1855] Naturally Reynolds was involved and in June of the same year 'launched forth into a violent tirade against Dr Gray' on the question of water bailiffs [11/12 June 1855]

In June 1857, John Martin of Trinity ward, the Liberal member of the Corporation, in proposing a new reservoir in Kimmage, addressed the public perception that the lethargy on the Corporation concerning tackling the water issue was due to the number of canal stock owners who were members. 'He did not believe it would be fair to cast an imputation on any members of the council by supposing that their apathy in the matter was owing to the circumstances of their being proprietors of canal stock, but it was expressed frequently outside the doors of that assembly, that if there were fewer proprietors of canal stock in the council more activity would heretofore have been displayed in getting a good supply of water to the citizens of Dublin.' Gray said that to suggest such a thing was a calumny and Martin agreed that he did not know anyone who had shares in the canal companies. [11/12 Oct. 1858]

There was a certain urgency about finding a new supply as the Corporation's contracts with the canals and other water sources were due to expire in the mid-1860s. [30 Dec. 1859] In October 1859 Gray and Codd presented a report to the Corporation based on work undertaken by two consultants. In light of the subsequent praise Gray was to receive for being the

3 Dickson, *Dublin*, p. 342. 4 Jones, 'Dublin reformed', 2, p. 385.

champion of the Vartry river scheme, which was to be the eventual solution, it is important to note that the Vartry was not part of the debate at the time. Most attention focused on using the River Liffey. The real debate concerned where the waterworks should be located on the Liffey with Kippure and Poulaphuca as candidates. This proposal favoured Sallins. From the start there was opposition. Initially, it came from the Protestant Liberal member John French, though later an ingrained Tory opposition would grow against the possibility of the demonstration of large-scale success for a Corporation led by Liberals, nationalists and Catholics. When the Corporation considered sending a bill to parliament that might implement the report French was irate. Codd and Gray 'had at their back the press, which reported everything they said, while they kept back the statements of other gentlemen (loud cries of no, no). He wanted to have his statements and those of other gentlemen opposed to this bill laid before the public: and he repeated that the lord mayor ought to have directed the town clerk to read the draft of the bill in the first instance.' [28/29 Oct. 1859; 15/16 Dec. 1859]

The year 1860 was to prove a key year for the water supply issue. Tory opposition began to galvanize around the idea that further deep investigation of the issue was required. [20 Jan. 1860] In the Corporation Gray's desire to promote the bill in the Commons was met with queries about the cost of the scheme and with attempts to resile from the approval the Corporation had given in the summer on the grounds that that summer had been a very dry one and people had worried inordinately about the water supply. [20/21 Jan. 1860] There were nasty exchanges about the low water rates that some members were paying under the existing scheme. Gray, Codd and a now amenable Tory, Robert H. Kinahan, were asked to take the parliamentary process forward. It was this triumvirate, rather than Gray alone, as popular memory later encouraged by his son would have it, that bore the brunt of pushing the water scheme through. This also represented that non-partisan approach in the cause of improvement that Tories had said they wanted. Yet the temptation to try to frustrate Corporation success proved too great for many of them. So Codd immediately went on the attack, saying opposition to the scheme came from supporters of the Grand Canal company. An amendment to delay the bill was defeated by thirty-four votes to seventeen. [24/25 Jan. 1860]

Several days of debate followed in the Corporation but private meetings of interest groups lobbying against the measure were also reported in the press. One of these, held in Commercial Buildings, was addressed by Gerald Fitzgibbon, one of the serjeants-at-law, who represented the mill owners whose businesses faced disruption with a change in the flow of the Liffey. He was reported as saying that the water scheme's purpose was so that members of the Corporation could feather their own nests and would produce 'patronage which they would distribute nicely amongst themselves and that alderman John would have this little bit, alderman Tom that, and councillor Tim the other, while the citizens would be shorn of their wool to pay for all.' This was a generalized smear rather than a specific accusation of corruption. Nonetheless, Reynolds for once played a positive role on behalf of the Corporation and sprang to its defence against 'the slanders and calumnies and the abuse so fiercely poured out' against it.' [26/27 Jan. 1860]

But public unease was growing to the extent that half the members of the Corporation signed a requisition to the lord mayor to hold a public meeting to explain what the scheme entailed. Proponents of the bill detected the hand of the Grand Canal company behind opposition. They regarded it with particular suspicion and alleged that it had been especially cynical in negotiating for the use of its water in the past. [3 Feb. 1860] Meanwhile, the triumvirs received approaches from the two canal companies, anxious not to lose their income from selling pipewater, and also from the two railway companies that were rumoured to be seeking to take them over. [14/15 Feb. 1860] This resulted in an offer of ten million gallons of water daily for £4,000 a year. [21/22 Feb. 1860] This new offer seemed so favourable that Gray, Codd and Kinahan supported changing the wording of the bill that was even then before the Commons to substitute the canals for the Liffey as the source of water. However, they were advised by the chairman of the ways and means committee at Westminster that this was not possible and that a new bill would have to be introduced. [2 Mar. 1860; 5/6 Mar. 1860; 31 Mar./1 Apr. 1860] Fresh queries were raised about whether the Corporation had the legal right to promote a water bill at all and a fund to indemnify the members of the Corporation promoting it was established. [31 Mar./1 Apr. 1860]

Many now seemed to be in agreement that this new arrangement with the canals was the answer, or, at least, all previous arguments against the lapsed scheme appeared to have been answered by the new scheme. Yet opposition continued. The recently established *Irish Times*, now joining a number of other papers representing the Tory point of view in Dublin, disagreed. It considered there were still serious objections, particularly concerning the powers the Corporation would have under the proposals. 'It gives the Corporation bailiffs power to enter our houses between the hours of nine and four, and contains other very objectionable clauses.'[5]

The *Freeman's Journal*, in editorial comment, dismissed such views and concluded that the real opposition was to the idea of the Corporation succeeding at a great project such as that of water. 'The opposition has now

5 *Irish Times* [hereafter *IT*], 4 April 1860.

assumed the character of an opposition to the municipality.' [7 Apr. 1860] Such a position certainly reflected the less creditable side of the Tory agenda. John Martin, the Fitzwilliam-ward Tory, seemed to provide evidence for disreputable motivation and took matters to a new low when he admitted that his problem with the scheme now amounted to a belief in 'the inexpediency of bringing water into the rooms of the poor.' Francis Codd was infuriated by this. Martin 'had merely repeated what he had said over and over again – that the council ought to postpone their bill for the present session; and the house had over and over again decided that that was not a course which it would be judicious or becoming to adopt.' [16/17 Apr. 1860] Meanwhile, controversy also continued to follow the Dublin water issue in London. [30 Apr. 1860] The triumvirs shuttled back and forth between the two cities but their efforts collapsed when they discovered that the canal and railway companies were no longer on board with the Corporation's proposals. They concluded that 'they could not hope to receive the cordial aid from the canal and railway companies during the progress of the bill which was essential to its success.' They recommended that if the Corporation still wanted to use canal water it needed to tie the canal companies down to a legally binding agreement before approaching parliament about it. Some darker manipulation was going on, however. The Dublin City MPs were both Tories, Sir Edward Grogan, who had originally been elected in 1841, and John Vance (1808–75), who had taken Reynolds's seat in 1865. They approached the Liberal Irish chief secretary, asking for a government investigation into the Dublin water issue. It looked as though an effort had been made to undermine the Corporation's policy – which the actions of the canals and railways had certainly brought about – so that the Corporation would appear incapable of dealing with the matter. This would have had the effect of playing into the hands of those who wanted the Corporation to fail and, more immediately, of bypassing it on the water issue. The chief secretary, however, refused to agree to the investigation unless the Corporation wanted it. Dr Gray feared that 'an endeavour would be made by some parts to procure a private water company, instead of leaving the water supply in the hands of the representatives of the citizens.' [28/29 May 1860]

The Dublin members then approached the lord mayor, asking that the Corporation support a government investigation in the form of a royal commission. Perhaps surprisingly Gray persuaded the Corporation to agree unanimously to the proposal, as being likely to bring a resolution to the disputes over the water scheme. [14/15 June 1860; 23/22 June 1860] At precisely this moment Francis Codd resigned from the Corporation, saying it was for personal reasons, though whether there was any political reason is unclear. [2/3 July 1860] Codd's party allegiance had always been ambiguous.

Reynolds hoped that the Conservatives would nominate 'a respectable mercantile man' to replace him who might command support across the political and religious communities. [6/7 Aug. 1860]

Meanwhile, the government appointed an investigator into the water issue. [13/14 July 1860] He produced a report in two-and-a-half months. In began by effectively ruling out the canals. In dry weather the canals and river Dodder could only produce eight-and-a-half million gallons of water per day. He considered quite a few alternatives but excluded the use of the Liffey and the Dodder because any scheme would interfere with the river bank and disrupt businesses. In the end he fixed on the use of the river Vartry in Co. Wicklow whose water was pure and needed no filtration, even though at £295,000 it was the most expensive scheme. The proposal was immediately and unanimously agreed by the Corporation, perhaps anxious that there was now no way for any disagreement about it to be resolved in a manner that did not do great damage to the Corporation. [23/24 Oct. 1860] What may have been intended by some to be a ruse to scupper a water scheme, in fact, turned out to galvanize support for one. There were of course objections from the canal companies, which were losing a huge income, and from some of the townships south of the city. Fitzgibbon cited exorbitant figures for future water rates. This caused Gray to investigate the very low rate Fitzgibbon was himself currently paying for his mansion in Merrion Square when compared with higher rates in poorer parts of the city, under the then inequitable system. [18/19 Feb. 1861]

The bill embodying the proposal became law on 21 July 1861.[6] The scheme itself was completed in 1870 and cost £541,000.[7] The Corporation celebrated the passing of the act in early August 1861 with Gray and George Roe presenting the bill to the lord mayor. 'We now, accordingly, present to your lordship a copy of the act (cheers) and we present it to you and the citizens of Dublin as the report which we have to make of the result of our labours (loud cheers).' With the recent death of Kinahan Gray was now the only one of the triumvirs left on the Corporation. Gray proposed to the mostly Conservative opponents of the scheme that they should now 'let bye-gones be bye-gones' but they were in no mood for this and would dog the implementation of the scheme with criticism over the next decade. [1/2 Aug. 1861]

Gray's moment of triumph thus did not last long and he was forced to oversee the implementation of the act against persistent opposition. Disputes soon broke out over water contracts. Gray became so annoyed he attacked the Tories over the negativity of their opposition to the water proposals not only

6 Jones, 'Dublin reformed', 2, pp 411–29. Eventually all the townships, apart from Rathmines, themselves came to use Vartry water, Jones, 'Dublin reformed', 2, p. 430. 7 Dickson, *Dublin*, p. 343.

in Dublin but in London. He was particularly critical of the actions of the Dublin MPs, 'two birds of ill omen,' in getting members of parliament to come over from the Carlton Club, home of the Conservatives, to oppose the water bill and in persuading 'young striplings of the peerage' to come to parliament to do the same. The Corporation representatives had had to compensate the Earl of Meath (1803–87) to the tune of £6,000 who had rights, they had been told, to the Dodder water but Gray had since learned that he had no such rights at all. Gray became uncharacteristically personal and blamed their own law agent Frank Morgan for not telling him this. He believed Morgan had been acting in bad faith, referring to 'Mr Morgan's anti-water works party.' Suddenly Gray's own reputation seemed to be on the line though he was to have an unexpectedly generous ally in Reynolds, who spoke up for him. [7/8 Oct. 1861; 15/16 Oct. 1861] Morgan defended himself, saying he had been sidelined by Gray in London. Peter Paul McSwiney (1810–84), who had been a Liberal member for less than two years, expressed the mood of many. 'Carried away for a moment by the eloquence and ability of Dr Gray he thought Mr Morgan was the veriest imp that ever disgraced humanity.' But having heard Morgan he was now much less convinced. Eventually, though, a motion by Reynolds, supporting the acts of the waterworks committee – and thus of Gray – was passed by twenty-four to twenty votes. [21/22 Oct. 1861] The following week Hudson accused Gray and Roe of having used public money to bribe an official involved in the parliamentary process with £1,000. Hudson said the money came from the indemnity fund and was used to compensate those opposing the water bill for the costs they had incurred. Gray charged Hudson 'with putting that notice upon your paper for the sole purpose of calumniating the character of George Roe and John Gray (hear, hear).' Once again the Corporation voted in support of Gray. [28/29 Oct. 1861] In early November, Gray was accused of having arranged the payment to Lord Meath 'as a peer of parliament, for the purpose of corruptly and improperly securing the passage of the bill through parliament.' [18/19 Nov. 1861] Gray was now clearly a target of Tory attack.

Water was, of course, not the only matter to occupy the Corporation in the decade between the mid-1850s and mid-1860s. One major issue concerned the policing of the city. Dublin had its own force, the Dublin Metropolitan Police [DMP]. In 1854 and 1855 a new Dublin carriage bill caused a debate in the Corporation concerning the financing of the police, as money from hackney cab licenses had gone directly to support them. Reynolds wanted the money to go to the Corporation. [1/2 May 1854; 3/4 May 1854; 15/16 Jan. 1855; 21/22 Apr. 1856] In 1856 there were objections to the provisions of a Dublin police bill before the Commons that allowed the lord lieutenant to deploy the DMP outside the capital. [3/4 June 1856] Reynolds spoke of 'the extravagant nature of the police establishment in the city of Dublin' and wanted the police brought under the control of the Corporation. [1/2 Aug. 1856] John Gray claimed that the taxes that Dubliners had to pay for the police amounted to £22,000 (or £37,000), out of a total annual tax burden of £163,000. Other parts of Ireland no longer had to pay a police tax. [9/10 May 1856]

In part this was connected with a move at the time to reduce taxation in which both Dublin Liberals and Conservatives were in competition to prove themselves the more prudent. A proposal to have the salary of the city marshal increased by £50 a year got caught up in this. There were rumours concerning his financial probity and it did not help him that he was the brother of John Reynolds. [6/7 Oct. 1856; 1/3 Nov. 1856; 14/16 Dec. 1856] The Corporation owned estates at Baldoyle and there was also a good deal of scrutiny of the manner in which they were rented out. [29/30 Sept. 1856]

'Diminished taxation' was the theme of the municipal election of November 1856. Just before the election Reynolds called for a general consolidation of local taxes. [11/12 Nov. 1856] The *Freeman's Journal*, in an editorial, thought the Tories were making a bid to increase their power by campaigning on an issue they had only lately adopted. In the nineteenth century, low spending was generally associated with Liberals not Conservatives. It wondered whether the city could 'rely more upon the recently adopted economics of the Tory Party or on the steady devotion of the Liberal Party to the principles of retrenchment for an effective effort to diminish taxation without undermining the representative system on which our present municipal institutions are based.' [24 Nov. 1856] The latter was a reference to the unwritten convention that had grown up during the decade of allowing the balance between Tories and Liberals on the second new Corporation to remain unchallenged, largely by not contesting some seats. Yet in November 1856 the Liberal Sir Timothy O'Brien lost his seat to a Tory challenge in the South City ward. He was philosophical. He had not wanted to stand and had only done so because his family had persuaded him. Now 'he had got enough of the Corporation. He found it was impossible to keep down taxation, and that was one of the reasons why he was anxious to have done with it.' His son, who was an MP, was less cool. 'He believed the result of the election showed that the principle of equal representation of the Conservative and Liberal parties in the Corporation had been violated (hear, hear). If they lived to see the next election they would find that contests would take place in every ward, and then the Conservatives who had drawn the sword would have to abide the result (hear).' [25/26 Nov. 1856] Things calmed down, however, for in the elections of the following year only four wards were contested. [25/26 Nov. 1857]

In January 1857, the Corporation debated local taxation and the police issue was central to it. On the one hand, some on the Corporation seemed to want control over the Dublin police, while, on the other hand, not wanting to have to pay for it. Others thought wanting to control the police was unrealistic. Local control of the police was common in Britain, though not in London, the capital. Reynolds said he believed they would not be given control but not asking for it would be like 'fixing on the Dublin Corporation the brand of incapacity.' [16/17 Jan. 1857] For others the over taxation of Dublin was a function of the flight to the new townships of the business owners of the city. 'Did they not witness every morning at Westland Row terminus of the Kingstown railway the merchant and other eminent traders of the city, proceeding in from their villas in Kingstown and its locality to their counting houses in town, where they disposed of merchandize at great profit without paying one shilling to the taxation of our city, except for their warehouses?' [1/2 May 1857]

In June 1858, the Tory chief secretary, Lord Naas (later Lord Mayo), introduced a police bill in parliament that incensed many in the Corporation, particularly Codd and Gray. In 1846 the Irish Constabulary (later the Royal Irish Constabulary) had been removed as a local charge throughout the rest of Ireland. This new proposal left the DMP uniquely as a Dublin city charge. [21/22 June 1858] The Corporation debated the bill for several days towards the end of the month. However, the focus of the debate soon turned from financing the Dublin police to the religious composition of its members, because Naas had brought up the matter in the Commons. Large numbers of Catholics belonged to the DMP and Reynolds believed that a sectarian campaign by Dublin Tory newspapers, principally the *Daily Express*, against the DMP, linking them with the Jesuits, had been the cause of Naas's remarks. Martin said that the police 'were under the special tutelage, guidance and protection of the Jesuits.' Gray pointed out that the only connection concerned the timing of a service at the Jesuit church, Gardiner St, to facilitate police schedules. He tried to return the debate to the financial issue. Naas proposed to fund the Dublin police both from the consolidation fund and from Dublin taxes, whereas the national police force was entirely paid for by the consolidation fund. In any event nothing came of the debate as the bill was withdrawn in July. [28/29 June 1858; 29/30 June 1858; 19/20 July 1858] When the Tory government left office the following year Gray objected to the Corporation making an address to the departing lord lieutenant. He had appointed six new Dublin borough magistrates but none of them had been

Catholics or Liberal Protestants. Meanwhile, he claimed that the government had tried to affect the religious balance of the Dublin police by recruiting Orangemen. [20/21 June 1859]

These were also politically acrimonious years on the Corporation. The year 1858 witnessed a recurrence of Reynolds's disruptive behavior. Codd called him 'an incubus on the Liberal Party – that he stood in the way of the Liberal Party (hear, hear, and cries of no, no), and that his custom of abusing every man who differed from him was a source of great injury to the Liberal cause.' However, the nomination of the next lord mayor did not end as badly as it might have. The following year, 1859, was to be a year for a Conservative lord mayor, but the Liberals objected to the Tory candidate who had given offence during the police debates and whose subsequent apology was felt to be equivocal. Alderman James Lambert was elected instead and Reynolds expressed himself pleased by a moderate speech by the Tory leader Edward Hudson on how incoming lord mayors should not interfere with decisions made by predecessors on the franchise. [2/3 Aug. 1858] However, when Lambert refused to attend a dinner at the Mansion House for the cardinal archbishop of Westminster Reynolds exploded. As he told a Merchant's Quay ward meeting, with a disdainful reference to Lambert's profession as a candle maker: 'Lambert, the chandler, who had been nominated lord mayor, but not yet elected (hear), would not defile himself by sitting with this illustrious prince of the oldest monarchy in the world and refused to go (immense groaning).' [3/4 Sept. 1858] He told the Corporation that Lambert's decision was 'an insult to the whole Catholic body' and that he should not become lord mayor. But in the end he did not press a motion on the matter that he had tabled. [13/14 Sept. 1858; 1/2 Nov. 1858] Still, the following year Reynolds refused to attend Lambert's lord mayor's banquet for the lord lieutenant in retaliation for Lambert's boycott of the archbishop. [25 Jan. 1859]

Later in 1858 Reynolds supported the widening of Carlisle Bridge (later called O'Connell Bridge) but came in for some public criticism because of the expense. The criticism occurred at the time of the annual November municipal elections at which the Tories tried to take some Liberal seats, though without much success. In his acceptance speech at Royal Exchange ward Codd presented himself as being above party politics. 'The intellect, independence and integrity of that great commercial ward had said it was not religion or politics that qualified a man to represent them but personal character (loud cheers) and they had recognized in his humble person that qualification (renewed cheering).' He had enjoyed cross-community support in spite of being opposed by a candidate from the 'Protestant club', a group led by R.H. Kinahan. [22/23 Nov. 1858; 25/26 Nov. 1858] None of this prevented Codd from making some very sharp remarks over criticism concerning the dismissal of a Corporation official. He accused one member of having 'stigmatized the conduct of a number of gentlemen, the vast majority of whom were in every respect his superiors, either as men or as gentlemen (oh, oh), as cruel, harsh and unfeeling.' And of another, 'he would ask the council whether they ever heard greater clap trap' than he has spoken? [13/14 Dec. 1858]

Early in 1859, John French accused Codd of having dragged up a joke he had once made about taking bribes as if it were a real admission and Gray of publicizing it in the *Freeman's Journal*. [21/22 Mar. 1859] The following month Reynolds introduced a note of unpleasantness into the election of the city coroner by wrongly claiming that the candidate who was eventually elected – a Liberal – ought to have been elected because the rotation of the position of lord mayor between the political parties also applied to that post. [28/29 Apr. 1859] There was some acrimony during the November elections that year that led to a brief attempt to prevent the person previously agreed from being elected lord mayor, as he had led the Liberal campaign in the election. John Martin, the Liberal of Trinity ward, darkly commented that the Tories should really only have the position every three years, as they were in a minority. [1/2 Dec. 1859]

When it came to nominating a Tory lord mayor in July and August 1860 for 1861 the issue of the freeman franchise for municipal elections was once more resurrected. This was a practice which, as has been seen, was believed by the Liberals to favour the Tories. The matter had arisen in 1858 when Hudson had accused the Liberal lord mayor of admitting anyone who wanted to the freedom franchise. It turned out that the lord mayor had a novel approach to the problem. Rather than supporting the immediate abolition of the freeman franchise he believed its sting could be removed by its wide broadening. He believed that 'the right to freedom was a humbug, that he would like to see every man a freeman of the city and that he hoped the admission would become so extensive that the right would be abolished.' Hudson threatened that 'the arrangement which has hitherto existed in the Corporation that a Protestant and a Catholic shall in turn take that chair can no longer exist.' [28 Feb./1 Mar. 1858]

By 1860 there was pressure for candidates for lord mayor, who had the right to admit new freemen, to pledge that they would not admit to freedom by right of grandfather. Reynolds went through the statistics and claimed that he had lost his parliamentary seat because of the votes against him of the 700 or 800 freemen admitted by grand birth or marriage with the daughter or granddaughter of a freeman. One Tory, seeking to be the next lord mayor, was emollient. He knew 'that the freemen were sore thorns in the sides of the Liberal Party, and it was natural for that party to wish to take these thorns out of their sides.' He admired Reynolds but said he would not take the pledge as he would judge all cases of admission to freeman on their merits. As a result his candidacy for lord mayor was lost by twenty-seven votes to eleven. [6/7 Aug. 1860] He later expressed his view on the matter. 'They had heard a good deal that day of liberality and the Liberal Party, but he said the town council was sinking into absolute tyranny and despotism.' [17/18 Sept. 1860]

In early September the Corporation debated the issue, which in any event was due to be reviewed by the courts. The discussion ended with votes supportive of the pledge, which had initially been agreed by vote on 2 July. Reynolds pushed his view of the lord mayor alternate scheme as meaning Protestant/Catholic rather than Tory/Liberal to propose that they elect a Liberal Protestant as lord mayor and thus avoid the possibility that a Tory would admit grandsons in the following year. [2/3 July 1860; 3/4 Sept. 1860] Roe proposed a compromise, that the pledge would not be enforced on the lord mayor for 1861 as it was due soon to be adjudicated by the courts. [23/24 Oct. 1860] The very future of the Corporation might be at stake. 'There was talk in the city of abolishing the Corporation and he had seen in the public prints letters on the same subject.' Reynolds objected that to adopt Roe's resolution would be seen to be guilty of 'the most unprecedented inconsistency of which a municipal body was ever guilty,' as they had adopted a resolution in favour of the pledge on 2 July. He tried to push Roe to the margins. Roe had voted for Onseley Bonsall, the Tory candidate before Lambert, but Reynolds had voted against him because he had insulted a Catholic priest.[8]

Reynolds claimed his resolution was moderate. It did not require the incoming lord mayor to make the pledge, merely not to reverse the decision of the present lord mayor, pending the decision of the Court of Queen's Bench. The Tories felt that this was a fudge and amounted to the same thing. Hudson said that the Tories would not put forward a candidate if it was under the terms of Reynolds's resolution and, indeed, it might be better to dissolve the compact concerning the rotation of lord mayor. [29/30 Oct. 1860] By November support was draining away from Reynolds's position, in part because the legal advice had changed and it now seemed possible that grandson franchise was, in fact, lawful. In the end the Corporation supported

**8** Bonsall had criticized the Catholic chaplain of the South Dublin Union for alleging mistreatment of women at the workhouse, which allegation had not been proven. He claimed he had been rejected as lord mayor on religious grounds and asserted that Reynolds had said that 'as a Protestant he was too aggressive.' [1/2 Nov. 1860]

Roe's position and voted against Reynolds, with quite a few Liberals staying away from the vote.

The issue then returned to who would be the next lord mayor. The Tory candidate was now Richard Atkinson, who had already been lord mayor in 1857. Reynolds and some others, however, decided to support another Tory, albeit an unpopular one, to cause trouble. [1/2 Nov. 1860] However, Atkinson duly became lord mayor for 1861. He immediately tried to turn down the political heat and to secure the system of rotation from which the Tories greatly benefitted and which Hudson had seemed almost to abandon. He believed that the Corporation should be above politics but that during the past year they had been taken up 'with a question that has given rise to long and angry discussions, occupying time which ought to have been devoted to public usefulness.' He promised that 'no Conservative lord mayor will ever deviate from a consistent, straightforward and impartial course.' He hoped that 'the Liberals will in like manner honourably abide by those understood compacts and never again create an impression on the minds of their fellow citizens outside the house that they are endeavouring, in an unfair or indirect way, to alter the arrangements of alternate Liberal and Conservative lord mayors.' Naturally, this immediately provoked Reynolds into a defence of his actions which, he said, were directed against the grandson franchise. In turn Hudson, instead of complimenting the outgoing lord mayor, as was the custom, alleged 'that during that gentleman's year of office he appeared to think and I believe acted as if he was the lord mayor of a party.' Reynolds again intervened. 'The true translation of Alderman Hudson's attack that day was "the late lord mayor refused to admit the grandsons of freemen."' The outgoing lord mayor in question believed that Hudson was coming 'forward like a snake in the grass to assail my character. I consider that his conduct is beneath my notice.' [1/2 Jan. 1861]

Atkinson admitted 513 freemen under all headings during his time in office. One member of the Corporation lamented the fact that with two Tory MPs Dublin 'was the second city in the British empire, an essentially Catholic city, yet owing to the swarms of freemen on the roll, the citizens were unable to have even one voice in the senate' (the House of Commons). [1/2 Jan. 1862] Lambert objected to a comment that he had been 'running bucks' onto the electoral roll. As ever Reynolds was on hand with statistics. During their two years in office as lord mayor Lambert (1859) and Atkinson (1861) had admitted 814 freemen. Lambert had admitted five freemen for being married to granddaughters of freemen. [10/11 Jan. 1862] One Liberal member threatened to nominate a Liberal for lord mayor in 1863 (a Tory year on the rotation) as the Tories only had one third of the seats on the Corporation.

Other acrimonious matters occupied the Corporation early in 1862, including allegations by the *Irish Times*, whose owner, Captain Laurence Knox, was a member of the Corporation, that the appointment of a surgeon to the city prisons had been anti-Protestant, and objections to Dublin being asked to subscribe to a memorial to the late Prince Albert, husband to Queen Victoria, in London. Reynolds believed that 'they should not send a shilling to London. They should not be treated like a provincial town in the matter but should act in the manner becoming the citizens of the Irish metropolis.' [3/4 Feb. 1862] Later, the placing of a statue of Prince Albert in Dublin would run into nationalist opposition. Ironically, those supporting it were doing so as an assertion of Irish equality in the United Kingdom. April saw the Corporation passing a resolution in favour of the government granting a charter to the Catholic University of Ireland, in spite of Tory objections that it was a sectarian issue. The Catholic University had been founded in 1851 as a counter to the Queen's Colleges but it was not flourishing, in part because it did not have the authority to grant degrees; hence the need for a government-recognized charter. Dr Gray, a Liberal Protestant, gave the principal speech in favour of the charter. This was a 'civic parliament' occasion but there was some embarrassment for the Liberals at the low turnout of their members for the vote. [7/8 Apr. 1862; 8/9 Apr. 1862; 10/11 Apr. 1862]

In July, the Tories nominated John Martin for lord mayor in 1863. Given his connection with the Conservative Registration Society some thought 'it was intended as a gage of battle to the Liberals'. The Conservatives had enjoyed some electoral success in Ireland in the 1850s. The Registration Society focused on registering Conservative voters particularly for parliamentary elections at a time when the issue of the freemen voters was highly controversial. The vote on Martin was tied at eighteen all on a low turnout of Liberal members. [7/8 July 1862] This latter fact showed that there was division in Liberal ranks and turned it into a controversy that damaged them. A meeting of burgesses of Merchant's Quay and Wood Quay wards, supported by Reynolds, called for Liberal members who had not been present for the vote to be called to account. George Roe wrote to the papers referring to a resolution of the meeting that 'it is the duty of the municipal representatives like all other representatives to act in accordance with the wishes of their constituents and when they could not do so consistently, to resign.' Roe announced that he would accordingly resign. [14/15 July 1862; 15/17 July 1862] He had not been soft on some of the key issues. Only a month previously he had successfully had the Corporation adopt a resolution to investigate the freemen voters at parliamentary elections, 'to protect the ratepayers and owners of property in the city of Dublin against being swamped by a body of men, the great majority of whom do not contribute one shilling towards the enormous local taxation of the city of Dublin.' [14/16 June 1862]. He had clearly been pursuing the role of peacemaker between the parties for some time but had obviously now had enough.

The *Irish Times* apportioned blame saying that the meeting had been the work of 'the creatures of Alderman Reynolds'.[9] Meanwhile, Knox accused Reynolds of recuping the expenses for a recent visit to London both from the Corporation and the Carlisle Bridge committee. [18/19 July 1862] Reynolds's callous comment on the departure of Roe was that the Corporation had survived the departure of other prominent members and would survive that of Roe. [28/29 July 1862] The Tory *Dublin Evening Mail* believed that it was remarkable that from both sides 'expressions fell showing the feeling of the council that it is fast falling into contempt and that unless some reform occur very soon it must come to an end'.[10] The increasing bitterness on the Corporation affected the work of the waterworks committee, headed by Gray, that was pushing forward the Vartry scheme. Hudson effectively accused Gray and the committee of corruptly making unnecessary payments to putative landowners on the route of the water pipes. [4/5 Aug. 1862]

The debate on the lord mayor resumed in October. Did the compact concern the alteration of Liberal and Conservative or Catholic and Protestant? Gray was bitter about the fact that there were not more Protestant Liberals on the Corporation. '[T]he reason was, because the gentlemen who controlled the Protestant vote of the city of Dublin had entered into a compact that no Liberal Protestant should get a Protestant vote for a seat in the civic chair (hear).' He said that the agreement in the house 'told every Liberal Protestant in the council that he had no right, no business to be there – that he would not be recognized for civic honours on the one side, and was not in a position to be accepted for them without objection on the other.' O'Connell had alternated between Catholics and Protestants, he claimed.

Martin's supporters pushed his candidacy once more, presenting him in as mild a manner as possible, though Reynolds pointed out that Martin had been involved in the prosecution of Margaret Aylward (1810–89), foundress of the Holy Faith Sisters, who had been imprisoned after a complaint from a Protestant mother about the whereabouts of her daughter who had been in Aylward's charge. [2/3 Oct. 1862] With the Corporation now two-thirds Liberal and one-third Conservative, Reynolds believed of the compact that 'the sooner it was broken the better'. In a vote John Martin was once more defeated. Obviously anticipating this, Martin immediately proposed John

**9** *IT*, 17 July 1862. **10** *Dublin Evening Mail*, 29 July 1862.

Prendergast Vereker instead. Reynolds believed that he would be 'a large manufacturer of rotten freemen.' Vereker said he would judge each case for freeman on its merits. Reynolds called for him to be opposed and yet at a vote Vereker won by twenty-five votes to twenty-three with several Liberals, including Roe, who was still a member, voting for him. [1/3 Nov. 1862]

Thereafter the intensity of animosity between Conservatives and Liberals diminished somewhat. Both sides had sought to gain the upper hand over the previous few years and neither had really won. Even Gray noticed a new more cooperative mood from Tories on the waterworks committee. [8/9 Dec. 1862] The twelve years of the second new Corporation had been an unsatisfactory time. Whatever consensus there had been that the Corporation should work on a non-partisan basis had not worked out. The Tories loudly proclaimed their belief in the system, which after all was to their advantage, but their dogged opposition to the water scheme, even when it went against their own best commercial interests, showed that they too could be very partisan. Tensions focused on conflicts about the parliamentary freeman franchise, admission to which was in the gift of the lord mayor, and on the rotation of the position of lord mayor itself. The origins of the latter were obscure – it was certainly not a direct gift from O'Connell even if he had himself initially promoted some Liberal Protestants to the office and no one knew whether it was on the basis of religion or party. The rotation came under strain in the late 1850s with Tories having to sacrifice their first choices to choices more acceptable to the majority.

Oddly, in an era, the 1850s, when the Conservative party was weak in the United Kingdom, it was strong in Ireland. Dublin's MPs were Tories. Equally, the call, heard most frequently in the early 1850s, for the Corporation to be non-party political and for national questions not to be debated may have added to the internecine bitterness between Liberals and Conservatives on the Corporation that grew in the late 1850s and early 1860s. In part this lack of national partisanship was because Irish Liberals were out of sympathy with British Liberals on such issues as the Ecclesiastical Titles Act (1851), which sought to limit the use of British territorial designations for Catholic dioceses, and Italian unification, which British Liberals supported but whose success was at the expense of the pope's temporal power. As Mary Daly has pointed out, 'Local politics, in the absence of clear-cut national issues tended to concentrate on sectarian questions.' Thus in 1860 John Reynolds was one of the moving forces behind a meeting in Dublin to express support for the pope.[11] In the midst of this, then, it was all the more remarkable that the Corporation

11 Daly, *Deposed capital*, p. 210.

managed to succeed in pushing forward its greatest achievement of the century, the Vartry water scheme. Its success can be gauged when compared with the situation in the modern, industrial city of Belfast. Only with the Belfast Water Act (1840) was responsibility for water supply removed from the spring water commissioners, a private body appointed by the Charitable Society, and vested in the water board, elected by ratepayers. Thirty years later with the Vartry scheme in Dublin in operation twenty-four million gallons of water were being supplied daily in Dublin, compared with only half that amount in Belfast where a large number of water sources were being employed. It was only towards the end of the century and with another water act that Belfast gained a more stable water supply from the Mourne Mountains, though Belfast was ahead of Dublin when it came to the disposal of sewage.[12]

Nationalism now began to reassert itself in the wider community in the 1860s and not only in the form of the Fenians but also in new more robustly nationalist politicians of the constitutional kind. With its limited franchise, those elected to the Corporation soon seemed to be out of touch with the pace of political developments. Liberal-Tory disputes seemed irrelevant. There were, however, a few voices representative of the new trend within the Corporation, not least A.M. Sullivan (1829–84) who was elected to it in 1862. But the energy of the times in Dublin was no longer with the traditional political parties of the Corporation but with the political meetings, the disputes over statues and other political symbols, and the revolutionary musterings that were occurring elsewhere in the city. In face of these activities the Corporation often seemed like a bystander.

**12** Cullen, 'Belfast and Dublin', pp 170–1; Royle, 'Workshop of the empire', p. 217.

CHAPTER 8

# Acrimony, on the sidelines of revolution, 1863–70

THE 1850s AND EARLY 1860s had been years when British governments had not much bothered about Ireland. There had been other things to preoccupy them including international crises such as the Crimean war (1853–6) and the anti-colonial rebellion which the British termed the 'Indian mutiny' (1857–8). The thirty years from the mid-1860s to the mid-1890s, however, would be years when Ireland attracted considerable attention in Britain. This was not only because of developments in Ireland such as the rise of the Fenians in the 1860s, the growth of new forms of parliamentary nationalism in the 1870s, under Isaac Butt (1813–73), and in the 1880s, under Charles Stewart Parnell (1846–91), and the agricultural depression of the late 1870s that lead to the founding of the Land League and to the 'land war' of the 1880s and beyond whereby the demands of tenant farmers for the moderation of rents began a process that would by the early twentieth century lead to tenants becoming the owners of their farms, with the help of government loans. It was also because British political leaders were determined to solve the Irish question, which for them consisted in granting such reforms to Ireland, consistent with the integrity of the United Kingdom and British empire, that might finally gain a settled legitimacy for the British connection in the majority Irish population.

In his first term in office as prime minister (1868–74) W.E. Gladstone (1809–98) pursued an active policy of reform, of which the disestablishment of the Irish church was the element that perhaps most impinged on the political mood in Dublin Corporation. Yet he left office relatively unpopular. In his three subsequent periods in power (1880–5, 1886, 1892–4) he had to be reactive to rapidly changing events in Ireland but brought in radical solutions to the land question and eventually, though unsuccessfully, promoted partial Irish self-government, or home rule, as it was called. Though his first government was supported by large numbers of Liberal Irish MPs he watched with equanimity as the Liberal Party fell into desuetude in Ireland, preferring an alliance with the Irish Parliamentary Party, as a substitute. This had implications for Liberals on Dublin Corporation, as shall be seen.

The Liberals were not the only ones to seek to mollify Irish political alienation. During his second period in office as Conservative prime minister (1874–80) Benjamin Disraeli (1804–81) managed to bring reform in areas of Irish grievance that had eluded the Liberals, not least in education where *inter alia* a system of indirect endowment and external examination eased the position of the Catholic University, an issue that again was a frequent subject of debate in Dublin Corporation. The Conservative governments (1885–6, 1886–92, 1895–1903) under Lord Salisbury (1830–1902), who was personally unsympathetic to Ireland, nonetheless pushed forward the policy of land ownership for tenants, believing that the principle of 'dual ownership' that Gladstone had introduced was an unstable one. Aided by and thus also influenced by the Liberal Unionists who contributed to their majority and who had broken away from Gladstone over home rule, these governments also pursued a policy of mollifying reform under Salisbury's nephews, the brothers Arthur (1848–1930) and Gerald (1853–1945) Balfour who separately held office as Irish chief secretary (1887–91, 1895–1900). They pursued a policy that came to be known as constructive unionism or 'killing home rule with kindness'. Its most important effect for Dublin Corporation lay in the reform of local government at the end of the 1890s that extended both the municipal franchise and the boundaries of the city. It also contributed to a certain softening of attitudes to Dublin Tories on the Corporation.

As for Dublin Corporation during this period, it saw itself transformed. By the end of the period it found itself in the grip first of the united Irish Parliamentary Party in the 1880s and then of its fractious successors, following the fall of Parnell in the early 1890s after a divorce scandal. The 1870s were one of the most irenic, non-political and perhaps productive periods the Corporation was to enjoy. The mid and late 1860s, however, the years covered by this chapter, were a period of continuing acrimony and rancour on the Corporation, at a time when the country was facing the challenge or opportunity, depending on one's viewpoint, posed by the Fenians. Though the presence of a new nationalism and the change in political culture it ushered in were felt in the Corporation, not least in the person of A.M. Sullivan, the Corporation itself seemed to be something of an irrelevant observer on the sidelines of possible revolution. On the other hand, with the coming of Gladstone's reform agenda, the Corporation found itself in serious debate over disestablishment, land reform and university education and to this extent was acting for a time along the lines of a civic parliament.

Innumerable issues causing conflict presented themselves during these years, some with a sectarian hue as disestablishment loomed. They included loyal addresses on royal occasions, the railways (particularly the trunk connecting line over the Liffey), erecting statues in Dublin, the mounting of exhibitions, the ballast board, expenses relating to representations to parliament, publicans (or vintners as they were often termed), the opening of St Stephen's Green to the public, as well as some old perennials such as the appointment of the lord mayor, finances and taxes and the freeman franchise. Some of the conflicts were highly personal with Reynolds against Sullivan, Reynolds against Gray over expenses, Knox against Gray over expenses and the railways, Tory newspapers against Gray over the water supply and even Tory John Martin against fellow Tory Knox. Many of these issues were intertwined in subtle ways. Sometimes the Corporation would zigzag between matters of high national importance and matters of very local concern. In 1869, for example, as it struggled with articulating a view on the issue of the disestablishment of the Protestant episcopal church it was also facing the wrath of Dublin publicans, brewers and distillers over proposed new licensing laws.

Amid the acrimony though, there were occasional moments when the Corporation was reminded that it was an ancient and prestigious body, known beyond the borders of Ireland and even the United Kingdom. The latter part of the nineteenth century was an era of great exhibitions in European and American cities that afforded the hosts the opportunity to display their industrial prowess. Several exhibitions took place in Dublin though they were not on the same scale as those in London, Paris and Chicago. These latter events allowed the opportunity for local municipal participation and in 1867 the Corporation was thrilled to learn that the Emperor Napoleon III had reserved seats for Dublin representatives at his Paris exhibition. 'The emperor of the French had been munificent towards the poor of Dublin and from ancient times to the present day friendly feelings had existed between the two nations,' declared a delighted A.M. Sullivan. [22/24 June 1867] In the event matters were spoiled by the news of the execution of the Emperor Maximilian, whom Louis Napoleon had backed as ruler of Mexico.

The year 1863 began with controversy on the Corporation over one of the perennial partisan points of tension for a leading body enmeshed in the ceremonial structures of the British state, loyal addresses and celebrations on royal occasions, in this case the marriage of the Prince of Wales. [27/28 Feb. 1863] A.M. Sullivan, the new and more pronouncedly nationalist voice on the Corporation who had objected to having to take the oath of loyalty to the crown on his election, was strong in his view that 'this was not the time for a public illumination and that such a display would ill accord with the condition of the country and of the people.' [3/4 Mar. 1863] Later in the year he objected to addresses of welcome for the visiting channel fleet of the royal navy. [20/21 Sept. 1863] Eventually, a private committee put on an entertainment for the fleet, though this was derided as a 'shabby entertainment' by Reynolds and as 'a miserable failure' by Sullivan.[1] [1/2 Dec. 1863]

It was the Conservative Party that suffered from internecine strife, however, with a dispute between John Martin and Captain Knox, founder of the *Irish Times*, both of them members of the Corporation. Martin had been accused of profiting from his association with the Conservative Registration Society and in turn accused Knox of not being a true Conservative and of conspiring with 'disloyal' members of the Corporation [31 Aug./1 Sept. 1863] Eventually the Conservative Registration Society mediated between the two and got them both to withdraw their charges.[2] Martin also got into a dispute with Reynolds over the promotion of the metropolitan railway scheme for Dublin. [2/3 Nov. 1863]

Finances continued to prove difficult during these years. Taken together all the city taxes in 1863 came to 7*s.* 8*d.* in the pound on the poor law valuation, amounting to £216,744 which was £10,000 less than the then current expenditure. According to Reynolds the Corporation owed £610,000. [6/7 Nov. 1863] In 1865 the Corporation considered asking to have the city revaluated as means of improving matters. [22/23 Jan. 1865] One source of increased debts was the need for the Corporation to resist acts of parliament deleterious to its interests. At the start of 1866, for example, it had been agreed to oppose the Bray township bill and the Enniskerry railway bill while it was facing various bills from the ballast board to take over the Grand Canal docks. There were also impending bills from the gas company and concerning the Dublin trunk connecting railway. Reynolds estimated that all this would cost the Corporation £20,000 over two years. [11/12 Jan. 1866]

Attempts in 1864 to get the Corporation to agree on the terms of an improvement bill to be presented to parliament got mired in bickering over expenses for London trips with Knox once more being cast in the role of villain. Sir John Gray (as he had recently become) accused Knox of writing in his paper 'that members of this council contrived to get themselves put on committees and deputations to London for the purpose of living and feasting and fattening at hotels at the public expense (hear, hear).' [13/14 Jan. 1864]

In the city more generally there was considerable controversy concerning the erection of statues of figures, iconic of different political views and sponsored by politicians anxious to bolster their own standing by association. Statues were planned for O'Connell, supported by Sir John Gray, and for the late Prince Albert. Supporters of the latter initially wanted it erected at

1 That year also saw the election of the former Young Ireland leader John Blake Dillon (1814–66) to the Corporation, though he was to die three years later. 2 *IT*, 31 August 1863.

St Stephen's Green. When this was not approved they fixed on College Green, provoking Sullivan's opposition to a site which he felt should have been reserved for a statue of Henry Gratten, who was associated with late-eighteenth-century Irish parliamentary independence, for the realization of which he then began working. Yet the site was in the gift of the Corporation and it voted in favour of the Albert statue to Sullivan's rage. 'The names of those who had voted for the resolution would be branded with infamy to all posterity. The statue of the foreign prince would be hateful in the eyes of the Irish people and would provoke the hissing and execration of every true-hearted Irishman who went by it (applause in the gallery).' Sullivan was not only cheered but those who opposed him were groaned. All of this shocked Reynolds who claimed he had been threatened when coming into the meeting. After making a rather lugubrious joke about Grattan having once been pelted with mud by people called Sullivan, Reynolds proceeded to attack the upstart Sullivan. 'He had given thirty years of his life gratuitously to his fellow citizens. He was unplaced and unpensioned. And then from this politically polluted source, which he should refer to by-and-by, this mushroom sprung up amongst them (groans from the gallery).' But perhaps most shocking of all for him must have been the realization that he was out of touch with a new, more radical public mood. It was a realization that he seemed to acknowledge, even as he denied it. 'Mr Sullivan had the audacity to say the people of Dublin would regard the statue of Prince Albert with hostility. He knew the people of Dublin better than Mr Sullivan and he denied that statement. If the people were led by such men they would be led into hopeless contests in which human blood would be shed.' [15/16 Feb. 1864]

Sullivan held a public meeting in protest against the decision on 22 February which had to be rescheduled for a later date when it was broken up by Fenians, who regarded Sullivan as a dangerous rival for the nationalist support they were seeking to attract. Sullivan had succeeded in turning public opinion and in the spring the Corporation voted once more, this time to deny College Green to the Albert statue, in spite of Queen Victoria having recently given her approval for it.[3] Tensions did not end there, however. In November 1865, a fight broke out at the end of a meeting of the O'Connell statue committee, which was held in the Corporation council chamber and the police had to be called. [1/2 Nov. 1865]

All of this was the prelude to a move made by John Reynolds just over a year later. At that stage he had just two years to live and, feeling perhaps that

3 Murphy, *Abject loyalty*, pp 135–45. The Albert statue was eventually located on Leinster Lawn and a Grattan statue on College Green.

the end was coming, he now set about assuring his legacy. In January 1867, he proposed, in his own bid for surrogate recognition through statuary, that Hogan's marble statue of O'Connell be moved from the rotunda of City Hall (the former Royal Exchange) to outside the building. This was done but the statue began to deteriorate in the open air and was soon moved back in again. Reynolds's proposal that the inscription on the new pediment for the statue include a reference to him as O'Connell's 'staunch ally and sincere friend', however, did not meet with approval. Indeed, the proposal was greeted with laughter in the chamber in view of Reynolds's complex relationship with O'Connell. [1/2 Jan. 1867; 7/8 Jan. 1867; 4/5 Mar. 1867; 10/11 May 1869]

Back in 1864 Reynolds had voted for the Conservative candidate, Sir John Barrington, for lord mayor in opposition to Sullivan. Barrington, whose nickname was 'soapy' on account of the fact that he was a manufacturer of soap, was duly elected and Reynolds was severely criticized his vote. Sullivan called Barrington 'the nominee of a party convicted of gross intolerance.'[4] [4/5 July 1864] Sullivan tried to put a brave face on his defeat and when he was reelected to the Corporation – though actually on a tied vote – in November, he declared to his constituents that '[t]hey knew that his voice had been raised in the city assembly on the side of toleration and justice and he now felt that he was not returned to perform sectarian or factious duties but, as an Irishman, to serve his country (hear).' [25/26 Nov. 1864]

Reynolds was by now back in his old form and that same month raised the question of the trunk connecting railway bill, for a rail link across the Liffey. He was a supporter and his friends had spent £28,000 promoting various schemes. He was enraged that a petition against the bill had been sent to parliament on behalf of a sub-committee of the house on the matter that had not received the approval of the whole Corporation. He claimed that the Queen's Counsel Charles Robert Barry (1823–97) had been retained by the Corporation at the Commons for twenty-one days at the cost of ten guineas per day. He even produced a law agent called John Smyth whom he proceeded to cross examine about the matter before the Corporation, though the exchange did not go well:

> Alderman Reynolds – Did you, sir, employ Mr Barry to oppose the railway bills?
>
> Mr Smyth – No (laughter). I did not give Mr Barry a single line of instructions (roars of laughter). I did not employ him in any shape

4 Michael J.F. McCarthy, *The Irish revolution, 1. The murdering time, from the Land League to the first home rule bill* (Edinburgh, 1912), p. 456.

or form in the matter (renewed laughter). I merely asked him as a personal favour to myself to see that a few clauses were right which were introduced into the bill; he did so, and for that he did not get, nor will he get, a single sixpence (hear, hear and applause).

Alderman Reynolds – When those clauses were accepted – (cries of question).

Sir John Gray – I think, my lord mayor, the house is now satisfied –

Alderman Reynolds – I won't allow Sir John Gray to interrupt me when I want to get at facts (oh, oh). He must deal with the facts –

Sir John Gray – Before I come to the facts, I must sweep away falsehoods – falsehoods which were put forward and which you perverted in repeating for the purpose of concealing the facts (cheers). No attempt on your part will prevent me from exposing the fictions you have dealt in (cheers). [8/9 July 1864]

This of course was part of the wider dispute between Martin and Knox concerning railways and expenses and for good measure Gray accused Reynolds of being in alliance with Knox. Over the next few days a humbled Reynolds admitted he had been wrong about Barry and Knox resigned from the Corporation. [9/11 July 1864; 11/12 July 1864] Knox's newspaper the *Irish Times* was ferocious in its castigation of the Corporation:

> And now, the citizens of Dublin will remark that no man of any party or position, possessed of the courage and strength necessary for resistance to any proceeding however mischievous, remains in the town council ... We admit that we can, under existing circumstances, no longer argue against the abolition of the Corporation. The members of the council ... showed on Saturday that they are utterly incapable of resisting a single man if only he will roar loud enough and shake his fist in their faces.[5]

The man supposedly shaking his fists was Gray and, in retaliation against him, the Tory newspapers, the *Dublin Evening Mail*, the *Daily Express,* the *Warder* and Knox's own *Irish Times*, began to harry him over the work of the water committee. [22/24 Oct. 1864] Gray became very sensitive over such attacks. In 1867, he threatened to sue a councillor over allegations that he had misappropriated money. [4/5 Feb. 1867; 11/12 Feb. 1867] The same year John French, now described as a Conservative councillor, whose interest was wider

5 *IT*, 12 July 1864.

than simply Gray, was described as 'a constant maligner of the Corporation and its committees', intent on finding 'materials upon which to found calumnies against the Corporation.' 'Except while sleeping and taking his meals Mr French spent his days in the waterworks committee examining books and papers and the fullest facilities were afforded to him (hear, hear).' [24/25 Apr. 1867]

In the early months of 1865 the city faced the question of opening St Stephen's Green as a public park which would involve the Corporation having to pay considerable compensation to the residents of the area whose private park it currently was. Opposition to the measure carried the day in the Corporation at least, in spite of an impassioned speech from Peter Paul McSweeney about the public good involved in opening the green. 'If the Corporation persisted in opposing this bill they would degrade themselves in the eyes of civilized Europe, leaving themselves open to the imputation that they were obstructive to anything tending to the social wellbeing of the humbler classes (hear, hear).' [4/6 Mar. 1865; 6/7 Mar. 1865; 23/24 June 1865]

But this was only a prelude to the controversies, some of them religious, that would mark the following few years on the Corporation. The early months of 1866 saw the Corporation, at some financial cost, persist in its opposition – described as 'futile and vexatious' in the House of Lords – to the Dublin trunk connecting railway bill. This would have seen the construction of two large new railway stations in central Dublin, one north of the river at Sackville St and one south of the river near Dame St. [14/15 Mar. 1866; 23/24 Mar. 1866] Eventually, the proposal petered out. [25/26 May 1866] Nonetheless, parliamentary expenses continued to be high. Sullivan reckoned they had amounted to £28,000 and proposed that commissioners sit in Dublin to consider Irish bills as a way of mitigating the expense. [4/5 June 1866]

In May a further effort was made to ask parliament to abolish the freeman franchise. It received Corporation support by eighteen votes to fourteen, in spite of initial Conservative reluctance to be present and ensure a quorum. Tellingly, though, this meant that only just over half the members of the Corporation were in attendance. Meanwhile, the Corporation entered the fray over the question of Irish church disestablishment and disendowment with the Liberal lord mayor, James William Mackey, sent to London with a petition concerning church temporalities, as its property and revenues were known. [8/9 Apr. 1866]

The previous year had begun with a foreboding of the sectarian sourness that the coming, successful Liberal campaign to disestablish the church would bring. One member refused to join in the thanks to the outgoing lord mayor, Peter Paul McSwiney, because he had attended a meeting in favour of disestablishment. In response a Liberal member referred to the Conservatives on the Corporation as 'those who looked upon those who thought with him as an inferior race.' [2/3 Jan. 1865]

The rising interest in disestablishment, which would lead to Gladstone's Irish church act of 1869, renewed pressure in the Corporation on the selection of lord mayor. Depending on how one viewed the nebulous alternating pack it was either the turn of a Conservative or of a Protestant to be lord mayor in 1867. However, Reynolds objected to the Conservative nominee on the grounds that he was not a supporter of religious liberty, meaning disestablishment; others called the nominee a bigot. Acting apparently on his own initiative and in perhaps his last political triumph on the Corporation, Reynolds contrived to have the Protestant Liberal, William Lane-Joynt (1824–95), elected as lord mayor by the considerable margin of thirty-six votes to fourteen, over the objections of the Conservatives. [2/3 July 1866] The argument that Conservatives could not be supported for office because of their political views would be one later used by Irish nationalists on the Corporation in the 1880s and 1890s, though on different grounds.

There was considerable confusion in July 1867 over the nomination of the following year's lord mayor. The Conservatives favoured James Vokes Mackey but Sullivan pronounced that he was unacceptable as he did not favour franchise reform and did favour the retention of the ascendancy, at a time when the Conservative government under Lord Derby seemed to be leaning towards reform.[6] Matters were not clear on the Liberal side, however. Some wanted Lane-Joynt to stay on for another year, as no suitable Liberal Catholic candidate had come forward. Lane-Joynt himself was not very keen on this. He had not enjoyed his tenure because of criticism from his own side for not granting them favours or 'jobs' to use the expression of the time.[7] Nonetheless, a motion to give him another year was only lost by one vote, twenty-four to twenty-five. Dr William Carroll then emerged as the Liberal candidate. Some Liberals announced that they had been previously pledged to J.V. Mackey and this led to rumours of an alliance of Tories and a group of Catholics to keep the Liberals out of office. Nonetheless, Carroll was elected by thirty votes to twenty-three, the latter figure consisting of the votes of nineteen Tories and four Liberals. [9/10 July 1867; 15/16 July 1867] The fact that Mackey had been labelled as a supporter of ascendancy echoed the increased use of that term as debate over disestablishment intensified. The term had been given

6 James Vokes Mackey ought not to be confused with James William Mackey, a Catholic and Liberal, who had been lord mayor in 1866. 7 When he left office there were unpleasant scenes when a vote of thanks was proposed for him. [1/2 Jan. 1868]

currency in the 1790s in the old Dublin Corporation. Sullivan felt it was time to set the record straight: 'it would emphatically be the duty of the Corporation to atone for such a pitiful past and if the voices of their predecessors were heard crying out for ascendancy, the shout of the present Corporation should be heard demanding full, civil and religious liberty (hear, hear).' [11/12 Nov. 1867]

These events coincided with a debate initiated by the Liberal Protestant, Sir John Gray, in favour of the granting by the government of a charter to the Catholic University. The issue of religious endowment and university education was a complex one, as has been seen. The Catholic University had been founded by the Irish Catholic bishops but was languishing both financially and because its qualifications had no state recognition. This was an occasion for the Corporation to act as civic parliament as in the days of O'Connell, debating larger, national issues. However, the Conservatives had decided that these occasions only gave publicity to causes favoured by nationalists and Liberals. So they stayed away. Gray made a long speech which was met with support from the twenty-seven members present. It gave Reynolds one of his last opportunities to inveigh against opponents as he asked what had happened to the nineteen Tories and their clique of Liberal adherents. [13/15 July 1867]

The year ended with an attack by a councillor called Cornelius Dennehy on the new leader of the Liberal Party at Westminster, W.E. Gladstone, who had spent many years as chancellor of the exchequer, introducing income tax to Ireland in 1853, and whose recipe for reform in Ireland focused on disestablishment and a certain degree of tenant rights. Dismissing these reforms, Dennehy pinned what he called the 'deplorable state' of Ireland on Gladstone's increase in taxation. [23/24 Dec. 1867]

Over the decades the Corporation found itself at odds with other local bodies which at various times were centres of power or influence when it came to the running of the city. These included the chamber of commerce and the gas company, the latter, particularly, late in the century. The end of the 1860s saw the Corporation at odds with the ballast board, which had charge of the port of Dublin. In many ways the ballast board was a hangover from the days of the old Corporation and the bodies that surrounded it, such as the wide streets commission. As John Reynolds put it: 'In no great port of the three kingdoms was the harbour board constituted as it was in Dublin; in Liverpool, Glasgow, Bristol, and other ports the boards were elected.' Most United Kingdom harbor boards were made up of a balance of members elected from the local city council and of representatives of merchants and ship owners. Dublin's ballast board was largely self-perpetuating and was thought to be under the influence of commercial vested interests such as the Bank of Ireland and chamber of commerce. [11/12 Jan. 1866; 16/17 Jan. 1866; 5/6 Feb. 1866] The Corporation did have a limited representation on the body, though that had effectively been reduced when the first reformed Corporation was formed. Under the old Corporation the court of aldermen had appointed three aldermen to the ballast board and the councillors had sent the two high sheriffs. Under the reform the sheriffs were now appointed by the lord lieutenant and the ballast board refused to accept alternative nominees from the new Corporation. In the mid-1860s the ballast board set about increasing its tax levying powers on goods entering the port of Dublin, though it said it was prepared, in theory at least, to allow more representation by ratepayers and ship owners. [8/9 Dec. 1841; 15/16 Dec. 1841]

In 1867, the ballast board proposed a new bill whereby the Corporation would have four representatives, eight would be elected but there would be twelve nominated by the existing oligarchy. The Corporation wanted more representation but the chamber of commerce clearly did not agree. This gave John Reynolds an opportunity to attack his old nemesis Francis Codd, no longer a member of the Corporation, whom he dubbed 'the autocrat of the chamber of commerce'. It was to be the last such occasion as Codd was to die within a short period. Codd, Reynolds said, had been very troublesome to the Corporation and had an 'abhorrence' for it. He proposed that all sixteen members of the ballast board be elected, not by the council of the chamber of commerce but by its entire membership 'which constituted the mercantile body of Dublin'. This radical proposal, however, was not representative of the consensus on the Corporation, which was intent on continued and enhanced representation for itself. The stage then moved to London where witnesses were produced at Westminster concerning the degree of Corporation representation. Things did not go so well for the supporters of the ballast board's proposals, however, when one of their witnesses supported Corporation representation. By April though it looked as if parliament was not warming to the Corporation's position and A.M. Sullivan suggested they did not waste any more money on parliamentary representation. 'He called the self-constituted, irresponsible, closed doors ballast board a relic of old times, an antique unsuited to modern times. Knowing the Lords liked antiques, and the least likely to extend the representative principle, they [the ballast board] went first before the Lords.' The resulting act created the Dublin port and docks board which was a defeat for the Corporation as its membership included a mixture of life members, members elected from a limited group of merchants and a small Corporation representation. [7/8 Jan. 1867; 4/5 Feb. 1867; 27/28 Mar. 1867; 3/4 Apr. 1867; 29/30 Apr. 1867]

One of the most remarkable features of Dublin Corporation during the late 1860s was how little it seemed affected by the often dramatic presence of revolutionary Fenianism in the city at the time. On 17 March 1858, James Stephens launched the Irish Republican Brotherhood in Dublin. The year 1861 saw an enormous public demonstration at the funeral of Terence Bellew MacManus (1823–61), who had been transported to Van Diemen's Land after participating in the Young Ireland rebellion of 1848. By 1865, there were fifteen Fenian circles in Dublin. That year the government suppressed the Fenian newspaper the *Irish People* and arrested Fenian leaders. The following year *habeas corpus* was suspended and over 200 men were arrested in Dublin. In March 1867, a brief and unsuccessful attempted rising took place in Tallaght outside Dublin. There were 5,000 British soldiers in Dublin at the time. Almost two-thirds of Dublin Fenians were artisans such as tailors, carpenters, shoemakers and bricklayers. One in ten was a shop assistant and a further one in ten was unskilled.[8] These were not men from whom the limited electorate of the Corporation was drawn. Throughout these years the Corporation found itself in the position of a bemused observer on the sidelines of events rather than as an active or central participant.

The issue on which the Corporation was most closely involved during those years was one on account of which its members felt they had been humiliated and had a grievance. It involved, as we have previously seen, the Corporation control over certain jails through the board of superintendence. In 1865 after Stephens' escape from Richmond bridewell the lord lieutenant had taken away its powers to appoint junior officers to the jail, after dismissing a man who had not even been appointed by the board of superintendence. 'It had been most unjustly charged against the board that they were parties to the escape.' There was thus great indignation on the Corporation over what was seen as an attempt by the government to blame it for the escape when the responsibility for the care of Fenian prisoners rested with the inspector general of prisons. There was also indignation concerning conditions of close confinement under which the prisoners were held and which were not popular with the public.

This sense of grievance came up again in a debate the following year concerning an address to the departing lord lieutenant, Lord Kimberley (1826–1902). He was said to have replaced the dismissed man with 'a man who had been convicted in the courts of a criminal act.' Members of the Corporation were also peeved at accusations of disloyalty concerning Irish people from official sources, such as in a departing speech from Kimberley.

8 Shin-ichi Takagami, 'The Dublin Fenians, 1858–79' (PhD, TCD, 1990), pp 18, 28, 30, 33, 82.

One member 'did not believe the Irish people deserved the heavy accusations made against them in that speech. They had passed through eighteen months or two years of unexampled temptations to disloyalty, having regard to the extraordinary efforts made to corrupt them, and their loyalty had been, notwithstanding all that, as undoubted as the loyalty of the people of Canada.' The latter was soon to be granted partial independence. In the course of a debate about an address to the new lord lieutenant, Sir John Gray objected to the reference to 'a wide-spread conspiracy' in Ireland in the new Tory government's Queen's speech, a statement of the government's priorities, and feared that the incoming lord lieutenant would rule accordingly. One member believed there was no point in denying there was discontent in Ireland and used the occasion to push the Gladstonian agenda of land and church reform. 'As a loyal subject of her majesty, he thought the very best thing they could do was to openly declare the fact of the existence of discontent, as Lord Kimberley had done, and try and point out the cause of that lamentable state of things with a view of getting rid of them as quickly as possible (hear, hear).' Here was a moment when the Corporation seemed to be acting as the civic parliament. Sensing this the Tories, in accordance with their policy on such occasions, withdrew from the chamber so that there was no longer a quorum for a vote. However, the next day a Conservative member took up the challenge with a speech attacking recent Liberal policy in Ireland. [18/19 Dec. 1865; 16/17 July 1866; 13/14 Aug. 1866; 14/15 Aug. 1866]

The Corporation was shaken by the Fenian rising of 1867 and nervously scrambled to disassociate itself from revolution and to assert its loyalty, while also hinting at the need for reform. Closest to home had been the incident at Tallaght, to the west of Dublin, on the night of 5 March where the mustering of Fenians there was dispersed after an attack by the Irish Constabulary. The lord mayor told the Corporation that 'they ought not lose a moment in expressing an opinion, as the first great Corporation in Ireland, and give a tone to all other public bodies in the country (hear, hear). They should declare their unswerving loyalty and attachment to the throne and constitution – their desire to maintain peace and order – and their confidence in the government maintaining the supremacy of the law and the rights of property and then adopting measures that would conduce to the amelioration of the condition of the country (hear).'

A variety of interpretations of what had happened were then articulated. Peter Paul McSwiney, merchant, former lord mayor and ally of the newly elevated Cardinal Cullen, archbishop of Dublin, was keen to imply the opposition of the Catholic Church to the rising. 'For the first time in our chequered history the peasant youth of Ireland had been seduced from their allegiance to religion and led to despise the teaching of those who are divinely commissioned to teach them – their prelates and their pastors.' Another councillor wanted to blame it on Americans, whose civil war had recently ended. Disaffection 'had been introduced into the country by foreign gentlemen, who for some years glutted themselves with rapine and murder during an internecine war, and now came over to create disturbances for their own purposes.' A.M. Sullivan disagreed with the whole tenor of the meeting and tried to turn responsibility for events against the government. 'He was not one of those who believed that it necessarily lay upon them to rush in a moment of terror before the representative of Government and fall upon their faces declaring their loyalty and offering their services ... They had a right to remember that while authority must be upheld for the sake of society, the abuse of authority was the most revolutionary of all influences.' He then linked the rising with a nationalist narrative of 'seven centuries of crucifixion' under English rule. Reynolds condemned Sullivan's intervention as a 'mischievous speech' and dismissed the Dublin rebels, by citing their class origins, as 'butchers' boys, bakers' boys, boys with caps and boys without caps'. His was quite a subtle view and one that perhaps unwittingly referenced the class view that insulated the Corporation from a threat that in the longer term was more formidable than it realized. There was, he claimed, no need for the Corporation to declare loyalty because '[t]here was no rebellion of the people at all. The respectable tradesman did not go to Tallaght, nor did the decent agriculturalist.' Eventually, a balanced resolution, proposed by Gray, was passed. [8/9 Mar. 1867] As for Sullivan he was to become something of a hero on the Corporation as early in 1868 he was imprisoned for seditious libel on account of his support for the 'Manchester martyrs', those Fenians executed for killing a policeman in the course of a rescue attempt of a fellow Fenian. [2/3 Mar. 1868] Even for those who had not supported the Fenian rising, the punishment of captured Fenians evoked a traditional Irish nationalist sympathy. This applied, too, as in the case of Sullivan, to those who had been punished for supporting executed Fenians.

The trend towards debating national politics continued two months later when a resolution was introduced welcoming Gladstone's stated view that Ireland should be ruled according to 'the desire of the country itself.' The Conservatives withdrew, however, so that it could not progress. Three days later the Liberals returned with a majority and passed the resolution but with no Conservatives present it was a damp squib. The Conservatives sent a letter deprecating the development. They believed 'that the introduction of political questions into the town council is highly inexpedient, inasmuch as the discussion of such topics interferes with the transaction of the legitimate duties of the council, tends to arouse discord and party feeling, and to prevent that harmonious action which forms the best guarantee for the effective and satisfactory discharge of the business of the city by the Corporation.' [13/14 May 1867; 17/18 May 1867]

Supporters of the Vartry water scheme must have found this ironic, given Tory efforts to undermine their work. And political questions continued to be raised in the Corporation over the next couple of years, not least that of disestablishment of the Irish church. The latter question in particular inflected the party politics of the Corporation with sectarian animosity.

The spring of 1868 saw a visit by the Prince of Wales to Dublin.[9] There was anxiety in the Corporation that too ostentatious a display of loyalty would backfire with a public mood sympathetic to the militarily defeated Fenians. Equally, there was a fear that a lack of display would be interpreted in other quarters as disloyalty to the crown. When the idea of public illuminations was voted down Sir John Gray warned that 'if that bald resolution went out without any observation or explanation it would be subject to grave imputation and the character of the Corporation would be seriously damaged.' [6/7 Apr. 1868] In the end though all went well with the visit.

From jail, A.M. Sullivan announced his resignation from the Corporation, which naturally was not accepted. Members of the Corporation signed a memorial to the lord lieutenant in favour of him and a fellow jailed journalist, together labelled 'the press prisoners'. The memorial was said to have been suggested by Conservative members, many of whom signed it. However, after a long delay it was rebuffed: 'the fifty-three members of the council who signed the memorial had been treated with the greatest possible discourtesy … Six weeks were allowed to elapse, all the while it being kept dangling before the eyes of these gentlemen that when the Prince of Wales came over the prison doors would be opened.' In June Sullivan was released and received an ovation on his return to the chamber though he discouraged offers of the lord mayoralty. [2/3 Mar. 1868; 6/7 Apr. 1868; 4/5 May 1868; 8/9 June 1869]

The mayoralty itself became controversial when the Conservative James Vokes Mackey was once more proposed for the office in July. Things initially went his way but he was opposed on grounds that he supported church establishment, though he said that he would be neutral on the matter as lord mayor. McSwiney was clear on the matter: 'no Liberal can consistently elect him to fill the office of chief magistrate.' Electing Mackey would be 'construed into an acquiescence by the citizens of Dublin in the continuance of an alien church establishment'. The only way Mackey could be elected would be if he

9 Murphy, *Abject loyalty*, pp 162–7.

were to positively pledge in favour of disestablishment and 'to support during his year in office, the movement in favour of religious equality against Orange ascendancy.' It was obvious that Mackey had prepared for his candidacy by negotiating with Liberals who had opposed him on the previous occasion. However, some of his new supporters, who now included Sullivan, began to get cold feet. Sullivan said Mackey's words about neutrality implied a religious indifference that disturbed him. [6/7 July 1868; 13/14 July 1868] Stories began to circulate that in retaliation the Conservative Registration Association would make every effort to displace Liberals at the forthcoming municipal election. Alarmed by this the Liberals, who were notoriously unstructured in terms of organization, formed a central municipal committee to fight back [26/27 Aug. 1868]

On 7 September the Corporation debated disestablishment, with Gray leading the Liberal case in favour. This time the Tories stayed because of what was to follow the inevitable victory of the motion. Gray proposed that in view of the resolution no one could become lord mayor who did not support disestablishment. This was supported by twenty-nine votes to nineteen. Mackey drew attention to the irony of the fact that the disestablishment debate has centred on religious liberty. 'If they were to take a prudent and honourable course they had no right to restrict the office of chief magistrate to one side or the other. They all knew it was a non-politicial office.' John Prendergast Vereker warned Gray and Sullivan that 'in the hour of victory they should not play the tyrant.' [7/8 Sept. 1868]

There were consequences on all sides at the annual November elections. A Conservative was defeated by a Liberal in Arran Quay ward, claiming he had been opposed for supporting Mackey for lord mayor. Reelected in Rotundo in spite of being opposed, a Liberal claimed his election was 'the fittest reply to Mr James Vokes Mackey's attempts to vilify the Catholic religion and people.' When a Conservative took a Liberal seat in North City ward his election was met with a form of applause known as 'Kentish fire', associated with sectarian Protestantism. Perhaps alarmed by this he told his supporters that he was a cabinetmaker and employed fifty-nine Catholics. [25/26 Nov. 1868; 30 Nov. 1868] When it came to the formal election of the lord mayor in December, Mackey withdrew. Gray, who was not present, was elected, though there was doubt as to whether he would accept. In the event he did not and the then current lord mayor, Sir William Carroll, as he had become in June of 1868, was reelected for a second year. Dennehy blamed the whole controversy of the election of a lord mayor on the Conservatives. When Mackey had been nominated in the summer the Dublin Tories had celebrated this as a victory over disestablishment. It had therefore been necessary to displace Mackey. [1/2 Dec. 1868; 11/12 Dec. 1868]

Early in 1869 the Corporation, without any objection from Conservatives, agreed to cooperate with other Irish Corporations to petition for amnesty for Fenian prisoners. Meanwhile, drawing on its privileged position alongside London and Edinburgh, Dublin Corporation presented a petition on disestablishment to the Queen in person in Windsor Castle. Sir John Barrington humorously refused an invitation to join the delegation. A.M. Sullivan commented: 'I am very sorry to see such a lack of loyalty on the part of the gentlemen on the Conservative side of the house as that no one will come forward to honour himself with an interview with her majesty.' Replying to this for the Conservatives John Byrne was not amused. 'This side of the house is loyal to the throne and what this petition asks to have abolished is one of the principal supports of the throne. If it were possible for a member of that deputation to state to her majesty the truth on the subject and the sentiments that actuated the large majority of this house, it could be shown that they asked by this document to strike from under the throne one of the principal supports – a matter that is looked upon with dismay by her majesty's co-religionists. The truth of the matter was that nobody would venture to go upon this sham deputation (oh, oh).' In August the Corporation agreed motions congratulating Gladstone and Gray on the passing of the disestablishment bill. [18/19 Jan. 1869; 9/10 Mar. 1869; 23/24 Mar. 1869; 23/24 Aug. 1869] Gladstone had got the measure passed, in spite of the evident danger of a constitutional clash between the House of Commons, which supported it, and the House of Lords, which did not, through the private interventions of Queen Victoria.[10] Gray had also been Liberal MP for Kilkenny City since 1865 and had campaigned at Westminster and through the *Freeman's Journal* for disestablishment.

Meanwhile, the Corporation turned its attention briefly to a matter of some concern to the commercial classes that were important in Dublin civic politics. A measure was being debated in parliament relating to the licensing of premises selling alcohol. Commonly called the permissive bill it made provision for local votes on licensing. Sullivan supported it but was facing considerable opposition from Dublin publicans, brewers and distillers whom he described as 'a powerful, extensive, wealthy and well-organized body of gentlemen, merchants, manufactures and traders.' Dennehy opposed him on the interesting grounds that the text of the bill libelled the leading citizens of

**10** Murphy, *Abject loyalty*, pp 169–76.

Dublin and claimed that alcohol 'was the fruitful source of crime, pauperism, disease, insanity and premature death. He contended that if they adopted such a proposition they would brand some of the best men of this city – its Guinnesses, Roes, D'Arcys and others – with a responsibility for those evils.' Perhaps surprisingly McSwiney said he had been won over by Sullivan's arguments. 'Councillor Sullivan had shown them that private interests should not interfere with the public good.' Once more Gray cautioned about the bad publicity, which the inevitable voting down of Sullivan's motion would cause the Corporation, branding it as an opponent of temperance. This was a clever move as it induced Sullivan to withdraw his motion and allowed the Corporation to pass a bland resolution about discouraging intemperance.[11] [12/13 Apr. 1869]

With this issue out of the way the Corporation turned its petitioning attention to that of land reform, which was also on Gladstone's reforming list. In September 1869, Sullivan proposed a motion in support of fair rent and fixity of tenure, which passed unanimously. McSwiney expressed pleasure at Conservative support but cautioned that they should not ask for too much and needed to set aside 'all wild and visionary schemes.' Some time later Gladstone's disappointing reply about Fenian amnesty was received by the Corporation in response to its memorial on the matter. It lead to darker ruminations about land reform. [16/17 Sept. 1869; 27/28 Oct. 1869]

The following March Sir William Carroll proposed that the Corporation recommend a particular general as the new Irish commander-in-chief. This bizarre suggestion, which seemed so far beyond the general remit of matters dealt with by the Corporation, led to some heated exchanges between Sullivan and others about the role of the military in Ireland. [7/8 Mar. 1870] But it was Gladstone's land bill whose terms came as a disappointment to Irish Liberals and nationalists, when they were published, that attracted much of the Corporation's attention. Sullivan introduced a motion, which was agreed, condemning the proposals as likely to increase rather than decrease tensions between landlords and tenants. 'It was a compromise bill – another monument to English incapacity in legislating for Ireland (hear, hear).' There was a dispute, however, over the use of the term 'irreconcilables' by McSwiney, for those who were demanding too much, in his view. [14/15 Mar. 1870] Larger matters intruded towards the end of the year with great support on the Corporation for the French in the Franco-Prussian war, which saw the French defeated. [24/25 Oct. 1870]

11 The matter came up for debate again in June 1870 [6/7 June 1870; 13/14 June 1870; 20/21 June 1870].

Fenian amnesty became a live issue again in November 1870. There was widespread praise for the moderate terms of the resolution, supported by the Conservatives, that Gray drew up on the matter, as it was felt that this would be more effective than a demand. Sullivan believed that amnesty would only work at pacifying the country if it were offered without government conditions. 'Let the government of England do for once an act of generosity in reference to its Irish policy and it will be the first time it will have discovered a new method to pacify Ireland (loud applause).' This, however, was to be the end of A.M. Sullivan's career on the Corporation, though not of his national political career. He was sensationally defeated at the municipal election two days later, by 'one very influential body of electors' who, he claimed, had intimidated poorer electors and who certainly shouted him down when he tried to speak after the result. [23/24 Nov. 1870; 25/26 Nov. 1870]

The year was to end with further sensation when Cornelius Dennehy publicly rebuffed a social invitation from the lord mayor. 'Councillor Dennehy considers the time inopportune for municipal festivities, when by the grossest mismanagement, in every way, the Corporation has been sunk to the lowest possible point in public estimation.' This insulting behaviour led to an outpouring of sarcasm and vituperation against Dennehy who had made a reputation for himself as a difficult and accusatory colleague:

> He, indeed, is the regenerator of this city of Dublin – he, indeed, is the only independent and honest man amongst men who are as independent and as honest, perhaps honester than he is, and yet are to be called by him to account for their public acts in the discharge of their duties to the citizens! There is scarcely a gentleman of the committee on which this man is that is not threatened to be brought into the Queen's Bench – in fact, this man has reached a condition that he will have to be labelled 'dangerous' (laughter and applause). My lord, get a man with a craze – especially a legal craze – and if you don't worship the vanity, if you don't bow down before the egotism, if you don't believe in the craze, that man becomes your enemy for life (hear, hear).

Dennehy had recently made charges concerning the alleged misappropriation of £40,000. The attacks on him were not universal, however, and he did have an ally in John French who, as has been seen, was also considered a difficult member. By the time the Corporation resumed its consideration of the matter nine days later, however, Dennehy had backtracked. Now facing libel action, he apologized to the lord mayor and Corporation for his previous accusations.

'I never for an instant intended, by speaking or writing of the mismanagement of the council businesss, to impute in the most remote degree to any honourable member of this council any act of corruption. I know their characters are without spot or stain.' French, too, apologized for accusing members of 'misapplication' of public funds. As ever the irenic Gray attempted and succeeded turning these words into an apology acceptable to the Corporation. [19/20 Dec. 1870; 28/29 Dec. 1870]

This was the dramatic end of a four-year period when the Corporation had found itself engaged in something approaching the style of a civic parliament with national political matters beyond the concerns of urban Dublin. Indeed, what could have been less urban than land reform. The reason for this lay in the rise of Gladstone with his defined agenda for reform in Ireland. It had been preceded by several years when the Corporation found itself on the fringe of political and security developments concerning revolutionary Fenianism. The new decade, the 1870s, would be different again. Nationalist politics began to reassert itself at the parliamentary level under Isaac Butt as a prelude to Parnell's Irish Parliamentary Party of the 1880s. However, these movements showed little interest in local politics until well into the Parnell era. Dublin in the 1870s continued to be the domain of Conservatives and Liberals, though there was little of the heat of party politics of previous decades. Disestablishment had taken the heart out of the Conservative battle for Dublin. The decade would thus be one of the Corporation's most non-political and peaceful ones but, perhaps for that reason, one of its most productive.

CHAPTER 9

# From drains to boundaries, 1871–80

HAVING DEALT WITH SOME SUCCESS with providing fresh water, the Corporation still had to face the problem of waste water, with its attendant health hazards. It would be a long haul and Dublin's sewage system was not opened until 1906. One problem lay in the fact that the Dublin port and docks board, successor to the ballast board, owned the quays and bed of the Liffey and thus it needed to give its permission for a main drainage scheme. At the end of the 1860s the issue initially presented itself as a plan to purify the river Liffey by diverting sewage from the river into the sea. Plans for a sewer system were drawn up by Parke Neville (1812–86), the Dublin city engineer since 1851, and Sir Joseph Bazelgette (1819–91), who had successfully introduced a sewage system to London in 1865. Neville had previously proposed intercepting sewers on either side of the Liffey as far back as 1853. In 1865, he suggested that the sewage collected by the intercepting sewers be discharged to a storage tank on the East Wall and used as fertilizer. A year earlier another plan had proposed that the sewage be processed on the North Bull island though the residents of nearby Clontarf objected. Neville's ideas were the basis of the plan that was eventually adopted, and his and Bazelgette's proposals became the Dublin Main Drainage and Purification of the Liffey Act (1871). Little real progress was made in implementation though for many years.[1]

From the beginning one key question concerned whether the surrounding townships would join in with any scheme. [11/12 June 1869; 24/25 June 1869; 8/9 Aug. 1870] To the annoyance of people like French, the committee to oversee the project was not strictly a Corporation committee but was a body made up of twelve Corporation members and six members from the other local authorities. [17/18 Oct. 1870; 1/2 June 1871; 5/6 Jan. 1874, 10/12 Jan. 1874] This, of course, led to the usual dispute on the Corporation over whether the members it would send should be elected or chosen by lot. 'Mr French said there were very respectable men on the committee, but there were some old women on it (Oh). What was the use of having persons on the committee who knew nothing about the works? (Oh).' However, the lack of progress the committee was making soon became an issue of concern and one

1 Cullen, 'Belfast and Dublin', pp 10, 14, 144, 147–52.

that reflected on the competence of the Corporation, as one Conservative member emphasized. 'For a long series of years they had been moved by all the organs of public business to proceed with this business and adopt a proper system for the drainage and purification of the river Liffey. He deprecated the manner in which the main drainage committee had been spoken of and maligned – held up to the public as incapable of transacting public business – and hoped there would be an end of these calumnious and slanderous charges.' [10/12 Jan. 1874; 18/19 Nov. 1874; 21/22 Dec. 1874] A related issue concerned the large amount of money it would all cost and whether the government would be willing to make a loan to the Corporation. [18/19 May 1875; 25/26 May 1875; 12/13 July 1875; 12/13 Oct. 1875; 27/28 Oct. 1875] Eventually, the government refused to provide the £500,000 for which the Corporation was looking. It was unconvinced that the Corporation could carry through the scheme efficiently and unimpressed by the securities the Corporation had proferred for the loan. Some members of the Corporation were relieved.

Things now began to descend into confusion with no clear way ahead. A new bill in parliament did not make progress. Dennehy believed that the Liffey could be purified by 'compelling the suburban townships to provide for or dispose of their sewage otherwise than by polluting the Liffey.' He proposed two intercepting sewers on either side of the Liffey beneath the quays and claimed that they could be built for £30,000. [6/8 Nov. 1875] The issue of a royal commission was also raised, perhaps as a way of preventing Dennehy's proposal from gaining momentum. A royal commission had, after all, previously found a solution to the water supply question. Meanwhile, Dennehy believed that the reasons for the failure to date of the main drainage scheme were not only because the cost had turned out to be much higher than expected but also because, unlike in the case of the waterworks scheme, all viewpoints were not listened to. 'The fact that they had shut the door upon the citizens who were opposed to the measure – opposed to this enormous expenditure – they had shut the door to their appearing before the committee and showing that instead of being a service it would [be] an injury.' Questions were also raised about the legality of some of the costs incurred by the committee. When John Byrne suggested an inquiry by the local government board, a new body whose role is considered below, he was accused of trying to undermine the Corporation at the behest of the (Conservative) Constitution Club or the citizens' committee, which were among the groups which had been opposing the old scheme.

The only active proposal was Dennehy's but this came in for severe criticism. 'Was Mr Dennehy serious in asking the city to contribute £100,000 to a drainage system which left the whole North Dock wall and the South Dock wall undrained and brought the intercepting sewers on the south side to Sir John Rogerson's Quay? Did he think the commissioners of Clontarf [the local authority in that township] would allow the sewer to terminate on the North Bull [wall]? It was all moonshine; it was merely a cloak to prevent the drainage or improvement of the city, in any shape or form, being carried out.' No one seemed to want to make a decision so that when a vote on a way forward was called in 1876 some members left the chamber so that there was no quorum. [27/29 Nov. 1875; 28/29 Jan. 1876]

Eventually, even Dennehy seemed to come round to the idea of a royal commission, claiming it would vindicate his view. 'There was a bad smell from the river during about two months in the year. That was a matter quite distinct from the main drainage of the city, but the two questions had been mixed up together. He believed the result of the royal commission would show that the nuisance would be effectually abated at one-tenth of the cost originally contemplated.' Yet when it came to a vote on a royal commission in late 1876 it was lost and even Dennehy voted against it. The next year the Corporation had to oppose a bill from Rathmines and Pembroke that would have discharged their sewage in such a way as to cause it to wash back up into the Liffey. Edmund Dwyer Gray, son of Sir John Gray, who had died in 1875, pointed out that the dangers of competing and mutually disadvantageous bills from the Corporation and the townships could have been obviated had a royal commission looked at the views of all sides. Failing a royal commission bilateral negotiations took place between the Corporation and Rathmines and Pembroke over the possibility of a joint scheme. In the end though Rathmines and Pembroke got their own scheme through parliament and a royal commission was appointed to look into the Dublin city situation.[2] [13/14 Mar. 1876; 6/7 Nov. 1876; 5/6 Mar. 1877; 27/28 Mar. 1877; 9/10 Apr. 1877; 23/24 July 1877; 5/6 Jan. 1880] The report of the royal commission was a turning point and a scheme eventually evolved that involved two parallel sewers on either side of the Liffey with a treatment centre at the Pigeon House. Yet action continued to be slow. The Corporation took six years to respond formally to the royal commission and it was not until 1896 that real work began and not until 1906 that the scheme was finally completed.[3] The Corporation had also to set about securing government funding and in the end high estimates of its costs were proved accurate. [7/8 Dec. 1891; 13/14

2 Prunty, *Dublin slums*, p. 87; Séamas Ó Maitiú, *Dublin: suburban towns, 1834–1930: governing Clontarf, Drumcondra, Dalkey, Killiney, Kilmainham, Pembroke, Kingstown, Blackrock, Rathmines and Rathgar* (Dublin, 2003), pp 86–7, 99–101. 3 Dickson, *Dublin*, p. 416; Michael Corcoran, *Our good health: a history of Dublin's water and drainage* (Dublin, 2005), pp 91–8.

June 1892; 6/7 Feb. 1893] The Corporation eventually received a £350,000 loan from the local government board. The plan implemented followed that of those proposed earlier though with the outfall at the Pigeon House Fort.[4]

The main drainage issue was part of a larger matter to do with disease and public health. Various acts between 1849 and 1866 had established 'inspectors of nuisances', later renamed 'sanitary sub-officers', and a public health committee connected to the Corporation. In 1874, the Public Health (Ireland) Act provided for fifteen medical officers of health in Dublin. Dr (later Sir) Charles Cameron (1830–1921) was appointed chief medical officer and held the post with distinction for many years. The 1874 act was followed by another and very significant health act in 1878, which improved the physical environment of the city, and by 1885 there was a sanitary staff of thirty-six in Dublin.[5] There were various pieces of legislation later in the century that promoted slum clearance and artisans dwellings, notably the 1875 Cross act, and many also had a public health dimension to them.[6] These were accompanied by sundry government investigations. A royal commission into the Dublin death rate in 1879 concluded that the problem lay with poor housing. 'It is not in defective sweeping, defective paving, defective street scavenging or any polluted state of the river Liffey, so much as in these horrible room tenements which exist to the direct injury of more than 100,000 of poor inhabitants and at the indirect-charge and direct money loss of the entire community.' [1/2 Oct. 1880]

Overall the response to poor housing in Dublin was a desultory one. By contrast Cork Corporation began to tackle its poor housing with some determination after 1880, seeing it as a public health issue. In the ten years after 1882, when the population of the city was around 75,000, some 3,000 labourers' cottages were built on the outskirts of the city and not in areas of tenements.[7]

The rise in the demand for home government, or home rule, in the 1870s left the Corporation largely untouched. In July 1871 three members of the new Home Government Association, which in its early stages included Irish Conservatives hostile to Gladstonian Liberalism, asked to make a presentation to the Corporation. Sir John Gray was in favour on the old O'Connellite grounds that the Corporation was a model of the advantages of self-rule. [3/4 July 1871] However, the Liberal and Conservative politics of Dublin

4 Cullen, 'Belfast and Dublin', p. 152. 5 Denis J. Carroll, 'Waste disposal and waste management in Dublin, 1850–1922' (PhD, Maynooth University, 2005). 6 Prunty, *Dublin slums*, pp 76–8; Jacinta Prunty, 'Improving the urban environment: public health and housing in nineteenth-century Dublin' in Joseph Brady and Anngret Simms (eds), *Dublin through space and time* (Dublin, 2001), pp 166–220: pp 191, 195; Carroll, *Cameron*, pp 103–19. 7 Stack, 'Victorian

Corporation continued without seeming interruption during a new era that was to witness the revival of nationalism. At a meeting to announce one of the results of the November 1871 annual Corporation elections a somewhat isolated voice from the crowd cried 'What about home rule?' Indeed, Tories gained some notable victories during this contest with John Jameson, of whiskey fame, elected alderman for Arran Quay. He sent an employee to deliver his acceptance speech. His victory, it should be noted, was in an open ballot and his employees might have felt constrained to vote for him, as his distillery was close by. The secret ballot was not introduced until the following year. [25/27 Nov. 1871; 27/28 Nov. 1871] When Maurice Brooks, a Protestant Liberal, was nominated in July 1873 as lord mayor for 1874, Byrne expressed annoyance that he was not a Conservative. This led to a perhaps over hopeful retort from another member: 'He deprecated the use of the words Catholic and Protestant, Liberal and Conservative. If they could conduct their business and keep these in the background it would be in accordance with the spirit of the country.' Yet, that year at the November elections only three seats were contested and those contests led to no changes. It was certainly part of a wider trend towards Dublin electoral amity during this time. [7/8 July 1873; 25/26 Nov. 1873]

When there were wider political flare ups the Corporation liked to keep its distance. In August 1871 there was a major riot in the Phoenix Park at an amnesty meeting following a royal visit. One member of the Corporation tackled the lord mayor on his inaction: 'Did you, as father of the city, go to the hospitals and examine the people in the wards?' When he received a peremptory negative to his question, he retorted: 'Then what is the use of having a chief magistrate? (cries of oh).' The general feeling was that the Corporation should stay out of such matters.[8] Eventually, a mild enough memorial on the incident was forwarded to parliament. [8/9 Sept. 1871; 14/15 Aug. 1871; 22/23 Aug. 1871]

More energy was generated by the Galway election petition case in 1872 and by the apparently anti-Catholic remarks of the judge in the case, William Keogh.[9] As has been noted Keogh had been a controversial politician in the early 1850s, widely criticized for accepting a job in the government when he had pledged not to do so. He severely criticized the Catholic clergy of Galway during a case in which he overturned the results of a parliamentary election. P.P. McSwiney successfully steered a resolution about the incident through the Corporation, though one member, adverting to his consistently pro-Catholic

Cork', pp 181–4. **8** Murphy, *Abject loyalty*, 181–6. **9** James H. Murphy, *Ireland's czar: Gladstonian government and the lord lieutenancies of the red Earl Spencer, 1868–86* (Dublin, 2014), pp 90–2.

stances, suggested he had 'tied himself to the chariot wheels of an unconstitutional hierarchy,' by which he meant the Catholic bishops. Yet when he served as lord mayor in 1875 (eleven years after his first term in that office) he proved himself a doughty defender of the Corporation's reputation. 'I would respectfully invite the attention of those who are constantly abusing the Corporation to inform themselves of the amount of business accomplished by this body and, instead of finding fault with the elected representatives of the people, to prepare themselves to take a share of the work (hear, hear).' It had, inter alia, constructed 2,796 sewers and house drains. Its income was now £194,000. It and its committees met on an impressive number of occasions annually and one of its councillors had attended 235 meetings in the past year. Moreover, Essex Bridge, hitherto named after a lord lieutenant, had been renamed Grattan Bridge, after the father of eighteenth-century Irish parliamentary autonomy. [8/9 July 1872; 1/2 Jan. 1875] Three years later, however, a select committee criticized the Corporation for neglect of its duties and the poor attendance of its members.[10]

If there was conflict in Dublin it was often with other centres of power, such as the port and docks board.[11] This board was an independent body with twenty-five members, seven representing traders and manufacturers, seven representing ship owners, seven representing the commissioners of Irish Lights (the coastal safety authority that maintained lighthouses) and three representatives of the Corporation together with the lord mayor himself. Corporation influence was thus that of a small minority on the board. In December 1878, the board issued a blank denial that the Corporation had any right of oversight into its finances. The following year there was a row in the Corporation when William Lane-Joynt, by then no longer a member, was appointed as one of the Corporation's representatives on the port and docks board. His supporters successfully argued that the board would benefit from his expertise. A particular point of conflict with the board was Carlisle Bridge, the main crossing point of the Liffey in the city, which needed either to be modified or replaced at a large cost. The Corporation feared it would have to foot the bill and the issue caused considerable friction during its meetings. There were concerns that the port and docks board was attempting to increase its powers in general at the expense of the Corporation. In the end a new bridge was built by the port and docks board, though it chaffed rather when the Corporation decided to name it O'Connell Bridge. [11/12 May 1875; 17/18 Sept. 1875; 22/23 Sept. 1875; 13/14 Dec. 1875; 16/17 Dec. 1875; 24/25 Apr. 1876; 2/3 Dec. 1878; 24/25 Mar. 1879; 26/27 May 1880; 30/31 Dec.

**10** Crossman, *Local government*, p. 81. **11** Cullen, 'Belfast and Dublin', pp 7–8.

1880] There was even some controversy over the finally achieved opening of St Stephen's Green to the public, thanks in part to the munificence of the Guinness family, which some alleged was a form of political bribery. [23/24 Oct. 1876; 8/9 Dec. 1876]

Later in 1872, a disgruntled Liberal member made a speech at the Corporation reflecting the general disillusion with Gladstone's government, albeit a speech that, because of its novelty, elicted a bemused response. He 'said that members of the council who admitted what they knew to be the fact, that Ireland was going to the bad, were the very persons to cheer the lord lieutenant at the agricultural banquet, when he asserted the prosperity and advancement of the country … Mr Gladstone and other members of the cabinet were quite aware of the true state of things and the only way to hit the premier was to return two home rulers for Dublin (laughter and applause).' [1/2 Nov. 1872] In 1874 the Corporation had agreed to allow Irish MPs of the Home Rule League to meet in its council chamber. [24/25 Feb. 1874] By 1876 the Corporation was becoming even more supportive of the new nationalist movement led by Isaac Butt. That year it petitioned parliament in favour of his land bill. [10/11 Apr. 1876]

This new mood apparently gained symbolic expression in a brief return to the statues wars of the 1860s with controversy over the placing of a statue of Lord Gough, a general in the British army who had been born in Co. Dublin. The promoters of the statue wanted it placed in Westmoreland St and threatened to take it to England if they were refused. An eventual compromise saw it placed in the Phoenix Park. Whatever the public mood on the issue was, the tone of the debate in the Corporation was a moderate one. [28/29 July 1879; 11/12 Aug. 1879]

Sewage does not recognize the boundaries of local government. The issue of drainage had brought the Corporation into conflict with the circle of townships, largely Tory-dominated, that now surrounded it, particularly the prosperous townships of Pembroke (modern Ballsbridge) and Rathmines immediately to the south of it. Greater Dublin was clearly one entity and the formal city of Dublin with its Corporation, constrained as it was within the boundaries of the two canals, resented that it had to bear much of the cost of greater Dublin's infrastructure while being deprived of its more prosperous ratepayers. The absorption of the townships into the city of Dublin was clearly an ambition of many on the Corporation. The sewage issue stoked the expansion ambition. It was eventually largely accomplished – though remoter Blackrock and Kingstown (later known as Dunleary and then as Dun Laoghaire, at least in print) were never conquered – but it took a long time.

Kingstown was the first township to be founded, in 1834. Rathmines was founded in 1847 and proved the most successful, eventually taking in Rathgar, Harold's Cross and Milltown. Pembroke was founded in 1863. In 1873, the structure surrounding local government in Ireland was given an extra dimension with the creation of the local government board for Ireland. This was a sign of a move away from the policy of having a minimal structure at the national level to deal with matters of local government. The process of founding townships was enabled legally by new legislation in 1847 and 1854, and economically by the advent of railways that allowed for suburban living. The percentage of the metropolitan population living in the suburbs rose from one in eight in 1831 to thirty per cent in 1891. In 1871, thirty-seven per cent of the population of the townships was Protestant compared with only eighteen per cent of the city. One of the results of this was that the number of wealthier Protestant businessmen on the Corporation diminished and the number of grocers and publicans increased.[12]

Agitation for increased authority for the Corporation began as early as 1874. This initially focused not so much on boundary extension as increased powers of patronage, such as the restoration of the right to appoint a high sheriff – albeit by the lord lieutenant from a list of three candidates nominated by the Corporation – which, indeed, was granted in 1876, as was the power to create honorary freemen of the city.[13] That year, however, saw considerable opposition to a bill introduced in parliament by Sir Arthur Guinness that E.D. Gray claimed would have had the effect of reducing rather than increasing municipal democracy by giving more voting power to owners of property. He linked the move with that perceived generalized criticism of the Corporation from naysayers. 'These gentlemen to whom he had alluded were ever ready to find fault with them, but they were equally ready to shunt the responsibility from themselves (hear, hear). If eminent gentlemen – merchants or others of high position in Dublin – whether Conservatives or Liberals, who desired to do duty and not to give vexatious annoyance in the council, put themselves forward, they would be fairly and fearlessly elected by the Catholic and Liberal electors of the city (hear, hear); but they seemed to find it a far easier task to come forward to make a row and urge complaints (hear, hear).' Byrne, for the Conservatives, disagreed, saying it was 'a myth and moonshine' to think that Conservatives would be elected in Liberal wards. Others drew attention to the relatively small number of municipal electors in Dublin, 5,584 for a population of 267,717. Belfast had almost exactly the same number of electors for a

**12** Dickson, *Dublin*, pp 325, 329; Ó Maitiú, *Suburban towns*, pp 23–40, 50, 67. Daly, *Deposed capital*, p. 152. **13** Crossman, *Local government*, p. 79.

population that was two-thirds of that of Dublin. Meanwhile, in the city of Bradford in England there were 29,412 voters for a population of 145,830.

Dublin Corporation decided strenuously to resist the legislation proposed by Guinness by giving evidence to a committee in the House of Commons and things seemed to go well for it. One member of the Corporation gloated over the fact that 'the attacks made on the Corporation had utterly broken down. Gentlemen who had been loud in their denunciations previously when submitted to the cool atmosphere of a committee-room of the House of Commons, if they had the facts that they boasted of, certainly did not produce them there.' There was even an element of cross-party cooperation which resulted in McSwiney congratulating a Conservative member 'for the honourable, straightforward and able evidence he gave before the committee of the House of Commons'. Dennehy hoped that a wider franchise might increase the quality of individuals offering themselves as councillors. [13/14 July 1874; 23/24 Feb. 1876; 29/30 May 1876; 3/4 July 1876]

Atttention then turned to the real issue, the extension of boundaries. Initially, the Corporation tried to promote its own bill but this fell away because of government initiatives for more thoroughgoing reform. A parliamentary select committee on taxation of July 1876 had expressed the view that there would need to be an investigation into municipal boundaries before increased taxation could be contemplated. In July 1878, there was a recommendation that the boundaries of Dublin, Belfast, Waterford, Limerick and Drogheda be extended.

As a result a commission into Irish municipal boundaries of three members – a barrister, a local government inspector and a civil engineer – was established and began work in 1879.[14] There were actually mixed feelings about the possibility of an expanded city on Dublin Corporation. Would it stabilize the city's finances or lead to the return of Conservative rule? E.D. Gray welcomed it without qualification. 'Their city was over-taxed in order that those living outside the boundary might have all the advantages of the city without contributing anything towards the expenditure (hear, hear).' On the other hand Dennehy believed that it 'would emasculate the Liberal Party in the council – it would put in an overwhelming majority of Conservatives' even though they would be coming from the former townships which opposed amalgamation. [14/15 Jan. 1878; 11/12 Nov. 1878] The commission took evidence in Dublin throughout April and May 1879 and returned in the autumn to take further evidence in Rathmines. When the commission published its report the following March it seemed to presage a stunning

14 Ó Maitiú, *Suburban towns*, p. 110.

victory for the Corporation. It proposed that the city of Dublin absorb the townships of Rathmines, Pembroke, Kilmainham, Drumcondra and Clontarf and part of county Dublin; it further proposed a Corporation of sixty-four members of whom forty-five would come from the existing wards with the rest coming from the townships. The Corporation sent a delegation, that included three members who were also MPs, to the chief secretary to urge the immediate implementation of the recommendations. In his statement Gray tried to calm things down, claiming that 'the difference of taxation in the townships as compared with the city was more nominal than real', perhaps to temper fears concerning the prospects of higher taxation for the denizens of townships if absorption went ahead. When nothing happened as a result of this delegation the Corporation sent another delegation, this time to the lord lieutenant. The latter eventually replied that a more efficient means of rate collection would have to be implemented before there could be any thought of boundary revision. [28 Mar. 1881; 28/29 Sept. 1881; 13/14 Dec. 1883; 21/22 Jan. 1884] The townships vociferously objected and their case, as bastions of loyalty, was strengthened by the fact that, as will be seen, the Corporation itself was in the process of being taken over by Parnellite nationalism. At the same time the government did nothing to meet Corporation requests for a revaluation that might have increased its capacity to borrow and thus make absorption more attractive for the townships.[15] It was clear that the report was a dead letter.

There was some apparently good news though for the Liberals/nationalists on the Corporation concerning the municipal franchise. This appeared to have been greatly widened thanks to the efforts in parliament of the suave Charles Dawson (1842–1917), who had been twice lord mayor of Dublin in the early 1880s and who managed to get the residence qualification period for burgesses reduced. Yet the *Freeman's Journal* was premature when it claimed that the municipal electorate had been increased to 20,000 voters. Dawson admitted a few years later that his reform had been stymied by the law officers who had argued that it applied only to the parliamentary franchise, which was now increased to 40,000, and not to the municipal franchise, which ended up stuck at 8,000 voters. The municipal franchise was hardly a priority with the Irish Parliamentary Party. The following year Dawson appeared on a platform for municipal reform organized by working-class organizations, including the United Trades Council and the Labour League. He candidly told them, however, 'that it was not wise or patriotic to divert the attention of the people from the great question of national government to subordinate reforms and, no matter what hobbies he had, he always had been and always would be ready

15 Daly, *Deposed capital*, p. 233.

to surrender himself to the guidance of Mr Parnell and the Irish Party (applause).' [18 Apr. 1885; 2 Nov. 1885; 5/6 Sept. 1887; 21/22 Oct. 1888] Social advancement was to be subordinated to national advancement. In fact, several Irish Parliamentary Party MPs associated with Dublin – T.D. Sullivan, E.D. Gray, Tim Harrington and W.M. Murphy (1845–1919) – had sponsored a private members bill in parliament in 1885 to allow Dublin to absorb the five inner townships but it had failed.[16]

If sewage – symbolic of issues that crossed municipal boundaries – was one factor that seemed to press for the absorption of the townships, then finance was the other, with Dublin responsible for services and an infrastructure that its ratepayers could not afford to maintain. Worry concerning finances pervaded the workings of the Corporation in the 1870s. As early as October 1873 there was a debate on deploying the ultimate solution, the burdensome extra tax known as the borough rate. It had been levied in the course of two years in the 1840s, during O'Connell's dominance of the Corporation, but not since then. Of growing concern was a distinct fund called the borough fund, which consisted of monies due to the Corporation as rents, shippage and anchorage dues and city marshal's fees and from which city debentures and the growing expenses of the public health department had to be met. In 1875, it was reported that receipts for the fund in 1874 had been £22,518 and the expenditure £23,009 meaning that it was in deficit. It was predicted that the deficit would quadruple. The blame was laid at the door of the public health committee. [18/20 Oct. 1873; 4/5 Oct. 1875]

Another significant draw on Corporation finances was the cost of promoting or resisting bills in parliament at a time when matters of infrastructure were still not dealt with under the provisions of general legislation overseen by a government department but by means of private bills promoted by local government authorities or commercial interests, though this would begin to change with the introduction of the local government board. During the period between 11 June 1872 and 24 March 1873 the Corporation had been forced to spend £18,099 on promoting or opposing bills. This was an unusually expensive year, however. In 1875, the figure was a mere £4,240. But the list of bills opposed was still a long one and is worth reproducing: the midland railway bill, the Dublin port and city railway bill, the central railway bill, the Dublin bridge and quay walls bill, the great southern and western railway bill, the Dublin tramway bill, the Kingstown bill, the Kingstown extension bill, the alliance gas company bill, the north Dublin street trams bill, the south Dublin street trams bill, the Dublin, Wicklow and Wexford railway

**16** Ó Maitiú, *Suburban towns*, p. 125.

bill, the citizens' committee main drainage bill, the Dublin south city markets bill, the Dublin port and docks board bridges bill, the Rathmines and Pembroke township drainage bill, the great northern railway bill, the Dublin central tramways bill, the midland great western railway bill and the Greystones and Hollywood provisional order bill. [9 May 1878] Most of these bills involved issues to do with transport or the townships. Then there were new demands for further loans, particularly for the artisans dwellings that recent legislation had encouraged. Thus in June 1879 the Corporation agreed to ask the commissioners for public works for a loan of £20,000 for such work. At the time it produced some adverse comment in the Conservative press. Dawson sprang to the defence of Liberal endeavours to improve the condition of the city. 'The newspapers representing the other side were continually saying that Liberal members like himself were ready for everything sensational but that they were not ready for practical business. He smarted under that injustice very much, and it was unfair for the great public works were inaugurated by members on that side of the house.' Loans were also sought during these years for the main drainage scheme, for paving and for a much needed public abbatoir near the cattle market. [3/4 June 1878; 17/18 June 1878; 24/25 June 1878; 1/2 Mar. 1880; 8/9 Mar. 1880; 25/26 Apr. 1880]

All this had already led the Corporation to take action on the financial front. In November 1877, it had voted to levy a borough rate of 3*d.* in the pound. However, in July of the following year John McEvoy took action in the Court of Queen's Bench to prevent it from levying this tax and the court supported him. The Corporation received legal advice that if the borough rate could not be levied it would have to cut back on the work of the sanitation committee. Meanwhile the collector general ceased collecting the borough rate. He advised that had it been fully collected it would have brought in £7,830. Responses to the crisis on the Corporation varied. Gray reported that the work of the sanitation committee was at a standstill and urged the Corporation to appeal to the local government board, which he believed had the power to increase rates on their behalf. Others thought it was an opportune moment for financial retrenchment and for curbing the £2,000 annually being paid on salaries for sanitation officers. The local government board eventually agreed that sanitation costs could now be charged to the improvement fund rather than the borough fund. In fact, that year the Corporation's finances were not in too perilous a condition overall. Total receipts came to £256,997 and total payments £259,738, leaving a small enough deficit. Total indebtedness was £1,150,000. There was general pleasure at the outcome to the borough rate crisis though French objected that the improvement fund could not bear the costs. He also said that McEvoy was a good man when mention of the latter's name was greeted with laugher. French himself was the object of laughter some time later when he sought a place on the paving, cleansing and lighting committee, a move unwelcome to many councillors who disliked French's persistent hostility to his colleagues. One member commented that the work on that committee was onerous and that of the work on his previous committee, '[h]e had heard Mr French several times confess that he was troubled with a rheumatic affection in the hand which prevented him from being able to sign the cheques (laughter).' French died ten months later. [28/29 Nov. 1877; 6/8 July 1878; 1/2 Aug. 1878; 12/13 Aug. 1878; 19/20 Aug. 1878; 30/31 Oct. 1878; 18 Nov. 1878; 23/24 Feb. 1880; 15/16 Nov. 1880]

As for John McEvoy himself he was one of the last of the independent, buccaneer figures that would adorn the Corporation before its absorption into nationalist politics. In some ways he was like John Reynolds with an eye for financial detail, though he did not share Reynolds's nationalism. In 1875, he had taken legal action to try to stop the Corporation's main drainage amendment bill in parliament with a submission that many thought libelled some members of the Corporation. In 1878, he had published a pamphlet on municipal reform and often used *ad hoc* committees, called ratepayers or citizens committees, as platforms for his campaigning. He would eventually be elected to the Corporation though in the aftermath of the borough fund crisis he failed in a contest with Sir William Carroll. The crowd jeered him as being in the pocket of the (Conservative) Constitution Club, though he was to tell the Corporation that he was not a member of either party. [18/19 Nov. 1875; 27/29 Nov. 1875; 25 May 1878; 25/26 Nov. 1878; 5/6 July 1880]

Modern cities take water and sewers for granted. Victorian cities such as Dublin had to invent the processes that put them in place. Modern countries have also mostly found acceptable and efficient ways of delineating civic boundaries. In nineteenth-century Dublin boundaries were a matter of conflict and rivalry as well as ones of putative good government. Yet the conflict concerning sewers on the Corporation from the 1870s onwards did not have quite the same intensity as had the conflicts concerning the provision of a new water supply several decades earlier. Conservatives had abandoned the fight for control of the city by trying to undermine the possibility of successful projects. Equally, the conflict between the city and the townships became more intense. The latter, though their own internal politics could be complex, were the new Conservative redoubts against control by the Corporation.

CHAPTER 10

# Gas and electricity, 1872–98

IF THE CORPORATION HAD FACED rival centres of power at various points in the form of the chamber of commerce and the ballast board, and its successor the port and docks board, the major vested interest it was forced to contend with in the last few decades of the nineteenth century was the Alliance and Dublin Gas Consumers company [hereafter the 'gas company'], which had been formed in 1866 from an amalgamation of two previous companies. Not only did it control the supply of gas for public lighting and domestic use, but it sought to become the leader in a new field, electricity and electric lighting. Along with artificial road surfaces, water supply and sewers, electricity and gas, together with the telephone, would be indispensable features of the twentieth-century city. Yet nineteenth-century cities had to undertake the initial task of putting the infrastructure that supported them in place. Dublin Corporation's duel with the gas company over three decades now requires particular attention. That that duel was more a matter of commerce than ideology is evidenced by the fact that, unlike some previous rivals of the Corporation, the gas company was thought to be nationalist in outlook, inasmuch as politics mattered to its commercial decisions. Perhaps though this was the reason why the Corporation, itself an overwhelmingly nationalist body, was chary about taking radical action against the gas company, such as taking it into public ownership.

As early as 1872–3 the Corporation, which relied on the gas company for street lighting, made moves to take it over through the introduction of a bill into parliament. After seeking legal advice, however, the bill was withdrawn. Nonetheless, the Corporation established a gas committee to monitor what was now an important issue. [14/16 Dec. 1872; 16/17 Dec. 1872; 12/13 Mar. 1873; 1/3 Nov. 1873] Part of the problem was that the price of gas was thought to be exorbitant. Dennehy raised the issue in 1876 only to be criticized for having prevented the takeover of the gas company. 'Mr Byrne said if the citizens were paying £54,000 a year more than they ought for gas, they might thank Mr Dennehy for being one of those who imposed that burden upon the city, because he would not allow the Corporation to become possessed of the gas works.' After months of pressure, including public pressure from a citizen's gas committee, the gas company did come to terms with the Corporation over the question of prices. [10/11 Apr. 1876; 10/11 Nov. 1876; 24/25 Nov. 1876]

The gas company was ambitious and in 1879 the Corporation found itself having to oppose a bill in parliament from the company that would have given it a monopoly on the production of electricity. [27/28 June 1879] The issue erupted again in 1883 when the gas company sought to promote another bill to strengthen its position in a number of ways. The Corporation was effectively forced to concede ground to the gas company on the issue, because it candidly admitted that when it came to support in parliament it was in the weaker position.[1] [30/31 July 1883] Battle was resumed the following year over allegations that the company was overcharging the Corporation for gas for public lights, and had been doing so since 1873. The matter was rendered more difficult because of the complex ways in which a tally of the amount of gas actually used was made, as only a small number of lamps were metered. For the gas company William Francis Cotton (1841?–1917) wrote to the papers defending the price, when compared with that charged in English cities, getting himself into a wrangle with McEvoy over the matter. Meanwhile in the Corporation Dennehy proposed that the Corporation itself go into the business of producing gas. Some suggested that, were the Corporation to consider this, members who were shareholders in the gas company ought to recuse themselves from the deliberations. The question 'was whether the Corporation on behalf of the citizens should not practically go into business in opposition to the gas company.'

Perhaps alarmed by this suggestion the gas company set about devising new and more efficient ways of estimating the consumption of its gas in public lamps by the Corporation. A consultant recommended payment per lamp not via meters. By 1888, the Corporation was considering appointing an inspector of public lighting to keep an eye on the gas company and accusations of fraud against the company and its pricing system were circulating.[2] [14/15 July 1884; 17 July 1884; 18 July 1884; 28/29 July 1884; 1/2 Sept. 1884; 14/15 Dec. 1885; 9/10 Apr. 1888; 16/17 Apr. 1888]

The same year saw a new strategy for getting round the gas company with a proposal to turn the Corporation lamps into electric lights. Some claimed it

1 Ó Maitiú, *Suburban towns*, pp 163, 165. 2 In 1888, Thomas J. Cotton was appointed as Corporation gas inspector. [7/8 May 1888] He was a brother of William F. Cotton who had himself worked for the Corporation as lighting and gas examiner (1861–73). In 1866, W.F. Cotton encouraged the Corporation to buy the gas company. Although agreement was reached it was blocked by a parliamentary committee in 1871. See Pauric J. Dempsey, 'Cotton, William Francis' in James McGuire and James Quinn (eds), *Cambridge dictionary of Irish biography*, https://dib-cambridge-org.proxy.bc.edu/home.do, accessed 10 November 2019.

could be done in two-and-a-half years, thought the board of trade advised that the gas company would have to be compensated. There had previously been an electricity company but it had failed. The Corporation therefore decided that it would itself become the electricity supplier. The gas company immediately made plans itself to supply electricity, as did two other companies. Meanwhile some on the Corporation thought it a reckless plan. Dennehy said he would take legal proceedings to ensure that any losses were personally borne by the individuals who voted for it. [20/21 July 1888; 22/23 Oct. 1888; 29/30 Oct. 1888; 1/2 July 1889.]

By the beginning of 1889, matters were turning decidedly ugly to the extent that some proposed that the dispute between the Corporation and the gas company be referred to arbitrators. The situation had been made worse by what the Corporation's gas inspector, who was being harassed by officials of the gas company on his inspections of their premises, had reported:

> Since the appointment of Mr Thomas Cotton, as inspector, the committee had had numerous reports from him as to the defective condition of the testing station. They are informed by their officer that an examination of the maps referred to by the secretary of the gas company completely confirmed his reports that only a very small portion of the gas supplied to the city was being tested, or had been tested for years past at the company's station, Burgh Quay. The idea of the appointment of this gas station was not that it was to be a gas company station but a Corporation station under the sole control of the officers of the Corporation and not under the control of officials of the gas company. They had the report of their inspector that when he went to test the gas not only was there an officer of the gas company there but he was followed about from room to room by an official of the gas company with notebook who took down every word said, everything done and every motion by the Corporation official. [7/8 Jan. 1889]

The Corporation's gas committee concluded that things could not go on as they were. They came down in favour of continuing with gas meters. However, some of the equipment at Burgh Quay was now half a century old and 'no proper test of gas could be made there.' With the gas company on the defensive the Corporation pressed home its own solution. It would buy up all the public lights and provide its own meters (one for every twenty lamps) to determine the use of gas. [7/8 Oct. 1889] Meanwhile, the Corporation also went forward with plans for its own electric plant at Fleet St. [12/13 May 1890; 19/20 Jan. 1891; 9/10 Feb. 1891]

Yet relations between the Corporation and the gas company were now so poor that the gas company sued one councillor who was also a member of the Corporation gas committee, Thomas Mayne, for slander. The action failed, albeit on grounds of privilege rather than of veracity. However, James Shanks, a Protestant home ruler, then holding the post of high sheriff, was not best pleased. He had been accused at the trial 'that he utilized his position as a member of the Corporation corruptly in the interests of the gas company. He regarded that as an abominable accusation and if it were true the council ought to expel him.' [20/21 July 1891] Suspicions over the probity of the gas company and its charges continued. When Henry J. Gill (1836–1903), publisher and member of the Corporation, criticized its inspector Thomas Cotton, saying, 'I do not believe these tests of your inspector,' he was reminded that he was himself a director of the gas company 'and therefore prejudiced no doubt.' [5/6 Feb. 1894]

The century ended with the Corporation seeking various legislative means of coming to terms with the gas company. It proposed a bill in 1894 that dealt principally with other matters such as the townships but also attempted to find a way forward for resolving disputes between the Corporation and the company. When it was withdrawn, shares in the company rose considerably. [12/13 Nov. 1894; 8 Mar. 1895; 8/9 Apr. 1895] In 1896 the Corporation promoted another bill and attempted a more conciliatory approach, offering to hold a meeting with the gas company. However, the company turned down the offer on the grounds that the Corporation had treated it badly over the years and the bill could only damage it. The bad relationship had not been good for either side. Litigation with the gas company had cost over £4,000. As for the bill, it did not fare well in parliament and by October the gas clauses had effectively been removed. [13/14 Jan. 1896; 5/6 Feb. 1896; 24/25 Feb. 1896; 20/21 Apr. 1896; 7/8 Oct. 1896] In 1897, W.F. Cotton, secretary of the gas company and an active nationalist, was nominated at an election for a seat on the Corporation but withdrew before it took place. [17 Nov. 1897] Two years later he was elected as an alderman.

As the second reformed Corporation neared the end of its existence it seemed to have reached an impasse with one of the most important suppliers of a public service in the city. Perhaps the oddest thing about the conflict was how tentative Dublin Corporation was about it, given what was happening elsewhere and given the fact that municipal purchase of Dublin's gas company had once been proposed by W.F. Cotton himself, when he was working for the Corporation as a younger man, and had almost came to pass in the early 1870s. Elsewhere 'municipal socialism', as it came to be called, was commonplace. In 1869, the city of Leeds in England had bought over its two gas companies. The first great achievement of Joseph Chamberlain's time as mayor of Birmingham in the early 1870s was the municipalization of gas. Closer to home Belfast had municipalized its gasworks in 1873, with an increased output of 400 per cent by 1905. Increasingly, though, Dublin Corporation was returning to a preoccupation with national politics rather than with local improvement.[3]

3 Barber, 'Municipal government', pp 319–24; Ward, *Birmingham*, pp 73–7; Royle, 'Workshop of the empire', p. 228.

CHAPTER 11

# Parnellite takeover, 1881–9

IN 1880, GLADSTONE RETURNED TO power as prime minister of a Liberal government for the second time. Now, however, he was having to be reactive to events in Ireland, relating to land agitation and the nationalism of the Irish Parliamentary Party. He introduced a land act in 1881 to moderate and regulate rents on farms but, faced with rural disturbances, found himself relying on special criminal legislation, generally referred to as coercion. Leaders such as Parnell were imprisoned for a time. An agreement with them in May 1882 was overtaken by the assassination of the chief secretary and under-secretary. Eventually, Gladstone was converted to the idea of home rule and formed an alliance with the Irish Parliamentary Party but failed to get the measure passed by parliament in 1886 and again in 1893, during his brief third and fourth terms as prime minister. For most of the last decade-and-a-half of the nineteenth century, a Conservative government was in office, implementing strong security policies in Ireland and yet trying to ameliorate Irish grievances with reforms.

The early 1880s would mark a fundamental shift not only in the politics of Dublin Corporation but in the way that politics was conducted. With the Liberal government highly unpopular, Dublin Liberalism would be swept away on the Corporation and replaced by a nationalism that was beholden to the outside control of the national leadership of the Irish Parliamentary Party. Initially, though, in the late 1870s and very early 1880s the Corporation, as a political entity, was not greatly affected by what was happening nationally, except in rather subtle ways.

In the late 1870s there was an agricultural downturn and many feared the return of famine. Traditionally, the lord mayor of Dublin had been a locus for fund-raising in times of distress. In December 1879 the lord mayor received a telegram from the mayor of Adelaide in South Australia: 'Does distress exist in Ireland to warrant a public appeal here?' To this he replied: 'Great distress anticipated in the south and west of Ireland: public aid most desirable.' [22/23 Dec. 1879] That autumn the duchess of Marlborough, wife of the lord lieutenant, had already set up a relief committee. In January 1880 a Mansion House committee was also established in Dublin to fund relief. On 20 January, E.D. Gray, who was then lord mayor, presided at a meeting of Irish nationalist

MPs which was critical of relief efforts, though some regarded him as a rather partial and ambivalent nationalist. In retaliation, Marlborough refused to attend the traditional banquet given in the early part of the year by the lord mayor for the lord lieutenant. It was a mistake on the part of Marlborough as the banquet was a useful occasion for the lord lieutenant to interact with Dublin politicians. Though the traditional banquet was held in 1881 under the last Tory lord mayor under the rotation system, George Moyers, it was the end of the tradition, as the Corporation gained a more nationalist hew.[1] Gray dramatically announced the cancellation of the banquet and donated the £500 saved from the banquet to the Mansion House fund. 'Now I think that the banquet, being given solely for the purpose of entertaining his grace, and in reality for the purpose of eliciting the views of the representative of the government on the state of the country and apparently his grace not being ready to inform the people of Ireland as to the views of the government upon the state of the country (hear, hear), or as to the steps the government may be about to take to avert destruction from the people – I think the reason for holding the banquet is ended, and I see no good reason for holding that banquet.' [26/27 Jan. 1880]

When Moyers took office at the beginning of the following year Gray raised the old possibility that the Corporation might become what O'Connell had perhaps hoped it might, Ireland's civic parliament, albeit by claiming that national issues, such as land, were also Dublin issues:

> The question had frequently arisen as to whether it was the right and privilege of that council – and if it were, whether they should exercise that right – of considering the great political questions affecting the well-being of the city … O'Connell held it to be one of the highest privileges and one of the most paramount duties of municipal Corporations to concern themselves with political questions and when they came to such a question as that respecting the land, which affected not merely the tenant-farmers and the landlords, but every man in the community and in which all the professional classes were vitally if not directly interested, he held that they would be neglecting one of the most important duties that they had to perform as representatives of the people did they not take into their serious consideration a question so vitally affecting the well-being of the city. … He only said this – that whether they were Conservatives or Liberals, whether they were Land Leaguers or opposed to the present agitation, they were all affected by it. [1/3 Jan. 1881]

1 Murphy, *Abject loyalty*, pp 305–7.

He announced his intention of proposing a resolution to be presented to the Commons on the land issue, claiming by way of encouraging interest in the topic in the Corporation that 'it had been invariably found that the members of the council who took the most active part in bringing political questions before it were also the most active as regard its ordinary duties.' [1/3 Jan. 1881] Later in the year Gray proposed that where possible the Corporation should buy Irish, an idea that gained cross party support. The Tory J.P. Vereker, however, could not resist alluding to what he saw as the anti-industry effects of some forms of Irish agitation:

> It would be a cruel thing to recapitulate the vast series of cases where valuable mills were established and capital invested which were extinguished by outrages and threats and driven to a more pleasant, more secure and happier land. Let them all join heartily and hope that these things were at an end. Those who wished to promote Irish manufactures should teach the people that the only way is to promote obedience to the law and security, without obedience to the law and security capitalists would fly to the remotest corners of the globe until they found security and peace. [5/6 Sept. 1881]

By the autumn concern had turned to clashes involving the police on the streets of Dublin and what was thought to be an excessive show of force. Complaints were led by Charles Dawson, the rising star on the Liberal–nationalist side. But the Tory lord mayor Moyers would not allow discussion and McEvoy warned the house that 'You are going to make yourselves partisans in a controversy (cries of "No, no"). I say you are – in a controversy between what we have come latterly to call the "two governments" – the government of the Queen and the government of the Land League.' [17/18 Oct. 1881]

All of this, however, was merely a prelude to a greater intrusion into the Corporation of the nationalist politics of the time. This change was effectively to reduce the Corporation from being an independent political body to being an adjunct to a wider politics, with the Corporation taking its orders from outside. It was sparked off by what might have been supposed to have been the most felicitous of civic duties, the awarding of the honorary freedom of the city, a right that recent legislation had conferred. In October 1881, it was proposed to grant the freedom of the city to Charles Stewart Parnell and John Dillon (1851–1927), son of the Young Irelander John Blake Dillon. Together with some others they had been arrested on 13 October and were being held without trial under special legislation. Moyers refused to hold a special meeting of the Corporation to consider the matter, which twenty members had asked for in a special requisition, and framed his reasons in overtly personal political terms:

> I have refused it because the requisition is, in my opinion, one in which I cannot personally concur ... I consider the resolution which was proposed for the consideration of the council tomorrow is one which is calculated, in my mind at all events, to materially affect, depreciate, and lessen the dignity and honour of this house (hear, hear, and no, no) ... I think the first duty of a constitutional government is the protection of the lives, liberties and properties of the subjects (hear, hear). The responsible government of this country, in view of this responsibility, has deemed it necessary to arrest two very estimable gentlemen. [24/25 Oct. 1881]

In spite of Moyers's resistance the Corporation met the next day to consider the matter. Gray began his long speech with an ironic reference to the Corporation's loyalty to the crown: 'possibly it has been rather more free in those expressions [of loyalty] than was necessitated by the amount of consideration extended by the crown to the inhabitants of this country (hear, hear).' In urging the granting of the freedoms Gray linked Parnell and Dillon with the early days of the first reformed Corporation, with differences between O'Connell and Young Ireland now elided: 'I say that this is an opportune time and the most opportune time that could be selected for doing to these gentlemen all the honour that is in our power – when all England is vilifying them as it vilified O'Connell, as it vilified Dillon's father, as it vilified Smith O'Brien, as it vilified Gavan Duffy when he was a living power in Ireland.' Tellingly, his strongest words were for the Liberals on the Corporation. They were being pressurized not to vote for the proposal. If the Corporation did not approve the measure then its name would be 'a reproach to Irishmen all the world over.' Not to vote for the freedoms would be a vote 'against Ireland and in favour of coercion'. Dublin Liberalism had always been a broad notion that had included various forms of nationalism within it. At times of very pronounced nationalism Dublin Liberalism found itself superseded by nationalism. This had been the case with O'Connellism in the 1840s and Gray was signalling that this was to be the case now. The difference this time was that Parnellism would spell the end of Dublin – as, indeed, it would of Irish – Liberalism.

In reply to Gray, John McEvoy noted that the motion about freedoms had been proposed and withdrawn and then proposed again only after the issuing of the 'no rent manifesto', which called for the withholding of rent as a strategy in the land war, and was thus intended to endorse Parnell's call on tenants not to pay rent. Parnell had after all been incarcerated by Gladstone's Liberal government. Charles Dawson noted that none of the Dublin Conservatives had spoken, thus hoping to benefit by leaving the Dublin Liberals exposed to nationalist pressure. When it came to the vote there were twenty-three in favour and twenty-three against. Moyers used his casting vote against the motion which was lost. [25/26 Oct. 1881] From that moment the nebulous but, nonetheless, real rotation agreement of lord mayors, whether it was between Protestant and Catholic or Conservative and Liberal, that had operated for thirty years, was doomed.[2]

The repercussions from the vote were swift and devastating for Dublin Liberals. A quarter of the members of the Corporation had not taken part in the vote. Some of these felt compelled to write to the newspapers explaining why they had not been there. The annual municipal elections were approaching and one newspaper correspondent said it would afford the Dublin burgesses the opportunity to show their 'detestation of mendacious Whiggery and spiritless and mere lip nationality.' Another promised to stand for election against one member 'who has betrayed the trust reposed in him as well as to do my utmost to drive from office in the other wards those who treacherously voted in favour of the Tories, over whose action Mr Gladstone can now joyfully exult.' Of course the animus against Dublin Liberals was fed by the more general unpopularity of the Liberal government itself. [28 Oct. 1881; 29 Oct. 1881]

Ward meetings enthusiastically proposed more nationalist candidates. These included James Carey (1845–83) who would later play a prominent role in the trials that followed the Phoenix Park murders of May 1882, though he would be prevented from standing at the immediate election by a legal ruling from the lord mayor. Wood Quay ward was particularly pointed in its condemnation of their representative who left the meeting before the vote 'and it was thus by his cowardly conduct that the motion was lost.' He later resigned. Indeed, the next meeting of the Corporation learned of the resignation of several councillors, presumably to forestall electoral rejection. [2/3 Nov. 1881; 31 Oct./1 Nov. 1881; 17/18 Nov. 1881]

T.D. Sullivan (1827–1914, brother of A.M. Sullivan) was nominated to stand in Wood Quay. He made it clear that times were changing for the old alleged consensus on the Corporation:

2 Dickson, *Dublin*, p. 348.

> They were told the Corporation was no place for politics, but the men who talked that way made the Corporation a hotbed of politics as long as they could have it all their own way, the relics of the old ascendancy class who squandered away the city property and made the rates of Dublin so heavy today. The leaven of slavery was not yet out of the hearts of the Catholic citizens of Dublin, or at least out of a good many of them who found their way into the Dublin Corporation; it was a want of courage, spirit and patriotism that lost that vote a few days ago and he felt there was a little bit of corruption in it too. [7/8 Nov. 1881]

Meanwhile, E.D. Gray, perhaps to show how truly nationalist he was, dramatically announced his own intended resignation from the Corporation, on the grounds that it had effectively betrayed the nation, though he was not actually to leave. He had joined

> because I was sincerely proud to be a member of a body which I considered truly representative of Irish national feeling. I was therefore glad to assist as an individual member in demonstrating that the representatives of Dublin city were as well able to discharge their public functions as those of any other municipality … I earnestly trust and firmly believe that the Corporation of Dublin will yet remove the stigma which in my opinion now justly attaches to it of having at a critical period of Irish affairs ranged itself against the true interests of the country and against the great principles of constitutional and personal liberty to which it had always been faithful. [12 Nov. 1881]

A changed and more nationalist Corporation met in December 1881. Charles Dawson was elected lord mayor for the next year without any controversy. However, the Conservatives objected that, contrary to custom, no Conservative was included on the list of nominees for high sheriff. The intention of the nationalists was that Gray become high sheriff and they feared that if a Conservative be included on the list the lord lieutenant might prefer him to Gray. If a name of 'any other smelling less sourly in the nostrils of those who ruled the country than Mr Gray's were sent forward, the opportunity might be taken of snubbing the council by appointing the gentleman last on the list.' Gray became high sheriff but it indirectly led to him spending time in prison the following year for publishing in the *Freeman's Journal* a report concerning misbehaviour of a jury at a trial instead of first reporting the matter to the proper legal authorities as his office required him to do.[3] A gold medal

3 Murphy, *Ireland's czar*, pp 248–9.

presented to him on his release was later added to the chain of the high sheriff. [1/2 Dec. 1881; 8/9 Jan. 1883; 5/6 Feb. 1883]

All this must have in the larger view been a source of satisfaction to Gray, who lived in dread of the Irish Party setting up a daily paper as a rival to his *Freeman's Journal* if he, or it, did not prove nationalist enough. The political commentator, M.J.F. McCarthy (1864–1928), however, was clear that Dawson's time as lord mayor marked a change of tone, though this was due as much to the changed composition of the Corporation as to Dawson personally. 'It was in Dawson's years in office, 1882 and 1883, that the Mansion House came under genuine popular control. In Gray's year, the nationalists had not established their power in Dublin.' McCarthy believed that Dawson 'fulfilled all the requirements of the new Irish democrat'. He was a successful baker, 'a typically clever young Catholic combining implicity belief in Catholic dogma with a certain assertion of political free thoughts. Like most of the new leaders, he took up special branches of political philanthropy, notably the improvement of artisans.' Dawson turned the Mansion House, the lord mayor's official residence, into a centre for social activity to rival Dublin Castle, using an enhancement in the lord mayor's salary to do so, according to McCarthy. He ended the practice of inviting the lord lieutenant to dine at the Mansion House and his reelection for a second year in office ended the practice of alternating lord mayors on religious and political lines.[4] Indeed, his first year in office had got off to a sour start when he refused to vote in favour of a motion of thanks to the outgoing Unionist lord mayor, George Moyers. The motion was defeated by twenty-eight votes to eighteen. [2/3 Jan. 1882]

John McEvoy thought that the new nationalist majority on the Corporation would lead to a realignment and strengthening of the opposition, presumably now that the Dublin Liberals were in the process of being swept away. 'Instead of the puny ridiculous minority which they had at present to deal with, it might come to pass in a few years that the party now in the ascendant there would be met by an intelligent, influential minority, which would perhaps afterwards become a majority, composed of independent citizens, who would be Conservatives in a non-sectarian and non-sectional way, desiring to maintain the integrity of their existing institutions, their connection with Great Britain and the settlement of property as it now stood.' H.J. Gill, MP, thought that what McEvoy really wanted was the abolition of the Corporation in favour of a small governing clique.[5] [1/2 Dec. 1881]

4 McCarthy, *Irish revolution*, pp 223–4. Patrick Maume, 'Charles Dawson and the public sphere in late Victorian and Edwardian Dublin', *Éire-Ireland* 50:3 (2015), 113–32, at 123. 5 There was a divided response among Protestants to the rise of nationalism in Dublin in the 1880s, with some trying to forge a non-sectarian Unionist identity, whereas others, such as the members of

The Corporation lost no time in addressing the question of the freedoms of the city for Parnell and Dillon. A meeting was held on 20 December at which fifty-three of the sixty members were present. However, a great row arose over whether it was a properly called meeting between the lord mayor, Moyers, aided by the Tory alderman Alfred Wormser Harris, and the lord mayor elect, Dawson. The meeting ended in disorder with cheers for Parnell and Dillon and cries of 'to h—l with Shylock.' This led to an altercation between Harris, who was Jewish and against whom the anti-Semitic taunt had been aimed, and the nationalist John O'Connor, which nearly came to blows. 'Alderman Harris charged Mr O'Connor and his friends with having degraded the council as the House of Commons was degraded by the Irish members. This observation was made use of while the alderman stood in close proximity to Mr Redmond, MP, but the later gentleman took no notice of it.' The presence of John Redmond (1856–1918), one of Parnell's lieutenants but not a member of the Corporation, was itself significant, and indicative of the interest of the Irish Parliamentary Party in extending its control to Irish local politics. [20/21 Dec. 1881]

The granting of the freedoms of the city to Parnell and Dillon was now speedily passed early in 1882 though the lord lieutenant refused to release them so they could receive the honour or to allow the Corporation to proceed to Kilmainham gaol to confer them there. They were eventually to receive the freedom of the city in August, after their release. [3/4 Jan. 1882; 9/10 Jan. 1882; 6/7 Feb. 1882; 16/17 Aug. 1882]

The public mood took a different turn with murders in the Phoenix Park in Dublin of Lord Frederick Cavendish (1836–82) and T.H. Burke (1829–82) in May, by a small group of radical nationalists known as the Irish National Invincibles. Cavendish was the incoming chief secretary, the political head of the government in Ireland, and Burke, the principal object of the attack, was the long-standing under-secretary, the head of the civil service. The lord mayor and fourteen members of the Corporation, not all of them Conservatives, had taken part in the traditional ceremony of welcome for the new lord lieutenant on the morning of the murders. In their aftermath Dawson had hastened to the lord lieutenant to express Dublin's sympathies and a special meeting of the Corporation was held to condemn what had happened. But the mood soon turned again with the introduction of what would become the crimes act, a coercion measure designed in part as a response to the murders. The

the conservative Workingmen's Club, veering in a more sectarian direction. See Martin Maguire, 'The organization and activism of Dublin's Protestant working class, 1883–1935', *Irish Historical Studies*, 29:113 (1994), 65–87.

Corporation approved a petition against it, with McEvoy, to hisses, claiming it was a vote in favour of the murders. [7/8 May 1882; 16/17 June 1882]

In the autumn the Conservatives proposed the freedom of the city for the Dublin-born general, Sir Garnet Wolseley, but the move was defeated. They were accused of trying to get the motion passed by subterfuge as they brought it forward at a time inconvenient for the five nationalist MPs who were also members of the Corporation. H.J. Gill, MP, blamed this on the remaining non-nationalist Liberals, or Whigs as he called them, distinguishing them from 'our party', meaning nationalist members. He accused these Whigs of being in alliance with the Conservatives. The Whigs were 'the followers of the Tory party in the way that the jackals are the followers of the lions'. Meanwhile, McEvoy, for the other side, made a very telling accusation of his own. He said that there had been a majority for the award but that some nationalists had been deterred because 'the Irish Parliamentary Party interfered from London to dictate what was to be done.' This was an indication of what was to come, with a Corporation that was more nationalist and keen on debating national political issues, but as something of a puppet of the national political leadership outside. [10/11 Nov. 1882]

As if by arrangement a dispute over the freedom of the city had for the second year in a row raised nationalist feeling just in time for the annual municipal election. At the end of the year Dawson was reelected for the next year, now in practice bringing to an end the rotating system. The lines between the two parties in the Corporation, nationalist and Conservative, who now numbered around twelve, were deep. As McEvoy put it, the divide was no longer between Liberals and Conservatives but, as he saw it, 'between the party of disaffection in this country and the party which would maintain the British constitutional connection' [1/2 Dec. 1882; 18/19 Dec. 1882] On the question of disaffection, the November 1882 election saw James Carey finally elected to the Corporation just in time for him to become a figure of popular infamy as the person who gave evidence against the Invincibles responsible for the Phoenix Park murders that resulted in their executions. In June 1883 he wrote to the Corporation that he was going to return following 'my unavoidable absence from my corporate duties.' Instead, he left for southern Africa where he was assassinated. Some had believed that he might have had a successful career on the Corporation. M.J.F. McCarthy records that he was being promoted as a possible lord mayor for the working man.[6] [25/27 Nov. 1882; 18/19 June 1883]

**6** McCarthy, *Irish revolution*, p. 320. Murphy, *Ireland's czar*, pp 180–97.

The fact that there were five nationalist MPs who were members of the Corporation in 1883 was itself a telling indication of the Corporation's new position as a mere part of a wider political system. So, too, were the variety of constituencies for which they served. Maurice Brooks was the most conventional, being MP for Dublin City between 1874 and 1885. He was also considered a rather tepid nationalist. [3/4 June 1884] Charles Dawson, the lord mayor for 1882 and 1883, was MP for Carlow borough between 1880 and 1885. H.J. Gill was MP for Westmeath between 1880 and 1883 and then for Limerick City between 1885 and 1888. T.D. Sullivan, who would be lord mayor between 1886 and 1888, was the other MP for Westmeath between 1880 and 1885 and would be MP for Dublin College Green between 1885 and 1892 before ending as MP for West Donegal, 1892–1900. E.D. Gray was MP for Tipperary between 1877 and 1880, Carlow County between 1880 and 1886 and, finally, Dublin St Stephen's Green between 1885 and 1888. Others were to follow. Thomas Mayne was elected MP for Tipperary County at a by-election in 1883 and held its successor seat until 1890. John O'Connor, who had been involved in the fracas with Harris, became a singularly inept lord mayor in 1885 and would be MP for South Kerry from right at the end of his term in December 1885 until he resigned the seat in September 1887. He was from Co. Kildare, not Dublin. On one occasion he introduced his remarks to the Corporation by identifying himself as a tenant farmer's son. In terms of sectional interests, though, he was accused of being in politics to protect the vintners' trade.[7] [3/4 Jan. 1881]

There was also Thomas Sexton (1848–1932), perhaps the greatest lord mayor of the period, though in 1882 not yet a member of the Corporation, who held office from 1888 to 1889. He was from Co. Waterford but was successively MP for Sligo County between 1880 and 1885, Sligo South between 1885 and 1886, Belfast West between 1886 and 1892 and North Kerry between 1892 and 1896. It was thus the case that, with the exception of the year 1884, all the lord mayors in the eight-year period between 1882 and 1889, when Parnellism was at its height, were also nationalist members of parliament. Even Michael Davitt (1846–1906), erstwhile leader of the Land League, was briefly a member of the Corporation in 1886. [4/5 Jan. 1886; 30/31 July 1886]

Another indication of changed times was the participation of national figures, formally unconnected with the Corporation, in municipal elections. At the November 1883 elections the Irish Party was keen to secure the reelection of William Meagher who was to be lord mayor in 1884. Three MPs spoke in

7 Murphy, *Abject loyalty*, p. 228.

his favour in North Dock ward. Thomas Mayne was a member of the Corporation but Tim Healy (1855–1931) and Tim Harrington (1851/2–1910) were not. [22/23 Nov. 1883] Harrington would eventually become a member but for some years before that would act as a controlling figure over nationalist members of the Corporation without himself being a member. The Corporation was on its way to becoming an instrument of the Irish Party. Speaking in a different ward at the same election Thomas Sexton, MP, not yet a member of the Corporation, warned against what he said was an alliance of Liberals and Conservatives against nationalists and set out the new position. 'He graphically described the influence of corporate bodies in formulating national objects and pointed out that the positions hitherto held by Whigs and Tories should be, if possible, now in the hands of nationalists.' He disagreed with the view 'that municipal bodies had no other duties to perform than looking after the lighting, paving and cleansing of their towns, and that forsooth the introduction of political matters into their debates was discreditable in the highest degree.' [25/26 Nov. 1883]

The municipal election of 1883 was another political turning point for the Corporation. There had been six alderman vacancies, all on the north side. Before the election they had been filled by two nationalists, two Liberals and two Conservatives. After there were five nationalists and one Liberal. Fifteen councillors were up for election. Before the election there had been seven nationalists, four Liberals and four Conservatives. After there were twelve nationalists, one Liberal and two Conservatives. Interestingly, the nationalist expansion was at the expense not just of Liberals but of Conservatives too. [26/27 Nov. 1883]

The changing political composition of the Corporation was mapped onto a changing social composition, too, though in complex ways. This change may have been behind debates in the early 1880s concerning raising the lord mayor's salary from £2,000, where it had been since 1851, to £3,000. During the debates there were references to the position currently only being accessible to wealthy men, who could afford the costs of entertainment involved. Specifically, it was alleged that the raise was proposed by Liberals/nationalist so that Charles Dawson, 'a man not of that gigantic richness', might become lord mayor, though Dawson, in fact, owned a successful bakery business. The increase was approved and Dawson duly became lord mayor. However, several months into his term the waspish McEvoy proposed that the raise be rescinded, in view of 'the lord mayor, in the exercise of wise economy, having dispensed with the customary inaugural banquet, given in the month of February.' This was tongue-in-cheek praise for the nationalist ending of the annual dinner for the lord lieutenant. [25/26 July 1881; 8/9 Aug. 1881; 15/16 Aug. 1881; 13/14 Feb. 1882]

All this may have been an indication of a perception that members of the Corporation were not now the wealthy men, the big businessmen, they once might have been as in the days of the distiller, George Roe. There were other perceptions about the social composition of the Corporation, too, specifically that it was coming under the influence of smaller merchants, such as publicans, with their own economic agendas. These changes reflected economic and social developments in the city, with the flight of persons of wealth and rank to the townships. In the city itself retail was certainly becoming a more socially acceptable occupation.[8]

Whether this social change favoured nationalism was a moot point, though overall it probably did. During the controversy over the Parnell freedom it was rumoured that the secretary of the Vintners' Association had been working against the granting of the freedom. [28 Oct. 1881] In the run up to the annual municipal elections in 1883, T.W. Russell, a temperance candidate for the Royal Exchange ward, promised 'to make an end of that publican domination that cursed and overshadowed this city (applause)' [14/15 Nov. 1883] To emphasize the point he took his audience through the occupations of the sixty members of the Corporation. There were four doctors and three newspaper proprietors. There were two representatives of the following occupations: mineral water manufacturers, bakers, printers, china merchants, soap and candle merchants, coach builders and furniture dealers. The following were the occupations of one member each: financial agent, seedsman, builder, market gardener, stationer, accountant, druggist, tailor, solicitor, dressing case manufacturer, undertaker, book manufacturer, miller, barrister, chemist, fowl merchant, hatter, auctioneer, bookseller, pawnbroker, ironmonger, tobacconist, salesmaster and leather mearchant. The remaining fifteen members were 'drink sellers.' For Russell the Corporation's neglect of the infrastructure of the city and focus on nationalist politics all favoured the agenda of the publicans:

> There were miles of streets where the poor were huddled together, where decency, not to say comfort, was an impossibility, and it was precisely in these streets that this traffic that dominated the city was fattening and luxuriating. It was only in Dublin that men were chattering about politics when the very foundations of the state were being undermined and sapped. He knew much had been done of late

8 L.M. Cullen, *Princes and pirates: the Dublin chamber of commerce, 1783–1983* (Dublin, 1983), pp 74, 76; Dickson, *Dublin*, pp 342, 344.

> in sanitary matters, thanks to the exertions of men like Mr Gray (hear, hear) … and whom these very publicans were striving to drive out of the Corporation. [14/15 Nov. 1883]

This was a serious charge: that the focus on national politics in the Corporation was distracting it from addressing Dublin's social problems and advantaging publicans whose businesses provided an escape for the victims of those social problems. Russell stood as a Liberal in Royal Exchange but was beaten by the nationalist candidate who was a vintner. The terms nationalist and Liberal were used in a confused state at the time, sometimes in opposition to each other and sometimes as being in continuity. Nonetheless, Russell was brave to set himself up against nationalism. In Mountjoy ward a resolution had been passed to the effect: '[t]hat we, the Liberal burgesses of the Mountjoy ward, take this opportunity of expressing our unbounded confidence in Mr Parnell and the national party and we pledge ourselves not to adopt any candidate at the forthcoming municipal elections whose principles are not thoroughly in accord with the popular party.' [26/27 Nov. 1883; 9/10 Nov. 1883]

In her analysis of the occupations of members of the Corporation Mary Daly gives the figure for publicans/grocers as nine in 1880, with twenty-one merchants and thirteen manufacturers. Undoubtedly, Russell was giving his figure dramatic effect by distinguishing various forms of manufacturer from each other. The number of publicans on the Corporation was on the rise though, with nineteen by the end of the century. Equally, the number in big business was falling, from twenty-three in 1850 to eleven in 1880 and only three by 1900. So there was no doubt that there was a trend towards retailers, especially publicans or vintners, and away from wealthier businessmen. The latter trend was due to the move of wealthy Protestant businessmen to the townships.[9] That the publicans' lobby on the Corporation was a strong one and one that nationalism had to take account of was illustrated by an incident before the 1884 municipal elections and in which T.W. Russell once more featured. At a meeting in Trinity ward a man who worked as a pawnbroker was nominated to run in the election against another man who was a coach builder. The former went on to just about defeat the latter but there was one problem with his candidacy: some years before he had 'refused to sign a memorial against Sunday closing and supported Mr Russell.' At the meeting he was profuse in his apology and said he had changed his ways. [7/8 Nov. 1884] Candidates had to bow before the interests of publicans/vintners.

9 Daly, *Deposed capital*, pp 204–5.

Nationalists had to negotiate around their interests and this could become a problem at times, as it did during the visit of the Prince of Wales in 1885.

From 1884, the tone on the Corporation became more overtly nationalist and certainly less deferential to institutions such as the monarchy. When one of Queen Victoria's sons died the usual vote of condolences was passed but only after the strenuous opposition of the maverick nationalist John Clancy (1844–1915). 'I won't stay here in my position as town councillor and have a vote of condolence passed to any foreign prince, who I am not aware ever did anything for the interest of Ireland. It may be very well for some parties who are brought up in the sycophancy of the castle, or who are always full of adulation for royalty whenever the question crops up. But I, as a representative of Inns Quay ward, am present here to do civic duty, and not to acquiesce in, propose, or second, or take part in anything like a vote of condolence to any foreign prince whatever.' He credited Queen Victoria with being a good mother but 'there are other mothers just as good as she is who have lost sons who were ornaments to their country, who were either expatriated for their love of their country, or suffered on the gallows, or in some other way, and I never yet knew the Corporation to take the initiative in passing a vote of condolence to any such of our people.' Abraham Shackleton, nationalist, Quaker and miller, tried to calm things down. 'He believed those who knew his private opinions were aware that he was one of the last persons in this country who would attempt any toadyism. His opinions abstractly were in favour of republicanism, but as long as the present state of things existed he believed it was right and proper that the council should testify its respect for the lady who was placed by the will of the people at the head of the state.' [7/8 Apr. 1884] As for Clancy his reputation had already been used by the Corporation in what was becoming its annual attempt to manipulate the lord lieutenant into choosing its preferred candidate for high sheriff by nominating two other unacceptable candidates with him. Wishing a particular alderman to have the post it also nominated Clancy and Tim Harrington. McEvoy professed himself amused. He recalled that the preferred candidate had been absent from 'the memorable Parnell discussion – asthma, or some other disorder, obliged him to stay at home. He had since been interviewed and was, he (Mr McEvoy) believed, thoroughly straight on the Parnell question.' Clancy was an ex-Fenian and Harrington was controversial. 'If the nationalist party were going to act strictly according to their aspiration, why did they not send forward to his excellency three gentlemen of the same class as Mr Clancy and Mr Harrington? Why did they not boldly challenge the government by the naming of politicians of the Fenian or Land-League type, and sending them forward, and thus embarrass the government at once?' He believed there was collusion between the nationalists and the government to avoid this.[10] [1/3 Dec. 1883]

Yet Clancy's stance was really the official one of the Irish Parliament Party concerning the political culture of Dublin. A few months later William O'Brien, MP (1852–1928), spoke at a meeting in Trinity ward, chaired by the lord mayor, and at which Charles Dawson, MP, and Tim Harrington, MP, were in attendance. He commended the change in the Corporation but thought that there was a need to purge the city of its sitting MPs, the old home ruler Maurice Brooks and a Liberal. The next parliamentary election would be fought on a wider franchise. Concerning the capital his ambition was

> to make Dublin the capital of Irish nationality (cheers) and not as it has been – the mere capital of English rule in Ireland. Up to a few years ago Dublin was really an English city. In fact he should rather say that it combined the worst – it combined all the snobbery and all the anti-Irish prejudices of an English city, with the poverty and misery of an Irish city cursed, as this is, and blighted by English rule … If they took its members of parliament, or its Corporation, or its poor-law boards, or other local boards – whether they were travelling from Bray or sitting in the stall of the theatre, they had the same feeling of breathing in Dublin an atmosphere of hostility and antipathy to the Irish cause and the Irish people. If they wanted to find any traces of Irish nationality in Dublin they had to hunt where what was purest and best was found – they had to hunt in the back streets and among the poor and lowly. [3/4 June 1884]

Another new feature was how overtly Catholic the politics of the Corporation was becoming. At the 1884 municipal elections it was noticeable how many of those standing for election had themselves nominated by priests. In the traditionally Tory Fitzwilliam ward which since the reform 'had never been represented by a man of the popular creed', one candidate proclaimed himself as a nationalist and a Catholic and was only narrowly defeated by his Conservative opponent. [13/14 Nov. 1884] At the election the nationalists were clearly targeting the Tories. The old notion of some kind of balance between the two communities was now over. The nine nationalist seats up for

**10** The account in the *Freeman's Journal* says the candidate was J.J. Clancy but this appears to have been a mistake. John Clancy (1844–1915) was a former Fenian who was a member of Dublin Corporation, who served as sub-sheriff for fourteen years from 1885. J.J. [John Joseph] Clancy (1847–1928), on the other hand, was a more moderate nationalist who would become an MP in 1886.

consideration were uncontested. All six non-nationalist seats were contested and the nationalists gained two of them. After twenty years representing South Dock, Sir John Barrington, a Conservative and merchant, lost his seat. He said, 'he was sorry the national party should have shown such a strong feeling against him.' However, the Conservative Sir George Owens and John McEvoy, now identified as a Conservative in a polarized political world, retained their seats. So, too, did Sir William Carroll, a non-nationalist Liberal, though someone shouted, 'You rotten Whig', at him during his acceptance speech. [25/26 Nov. 1884]

The new, more nationalist, Corporation faced a major test with the visit of the Prince and Princess of Wales to Dublin as part of a wider Irish tour in the spring of 1885. The visit was announced at the end of February and various protests against it were held in Dublin at which Irish Party parliamentarians spoke. Things were not helped by the vacillations of the lord mayor, John O'Connor, who was caught between nationalism and the commercial interests of publicans, whose creature he undoubtedly was. Like his immediate predecessor he owned public houses, six in all. He had been a leading campaigner against the Sunday Closing Act of 1878. M.J.F. McCarthy, then employed by the Grocers' and Vintners' Association, recalled being at one dinner at the Mansion House, during O'Connor's time, which was packed with publicans. They were delighted by the presence of the Catholic archbishop of Dublin, which they took as a sign of support for them.[11]

O'Connor announced he would not fly the lord mayor's standard over the Mansion House during the royal visit but soon changed his mind, at the behest, it was said, of the secretary of the Vintners' Association who had said that disrespect towards the prince might lose them the support of British breweries in their ongoing battle against Sunday closing. Parnell, however, sent a letter to the nationalist members of the Corporation asking them to be neutral during the visit. As a result the Corporation decided not to make a loyal address to the prince. O'Connor himself fell into line with the more hostile approach and at one point had an undignified exchange from the balcony of City Hall with a crowd supportive of the visit and hostile to him. He taunted them with being Orangemen, landlords and, surprisingly, freemasons, as many in the British drinks trade were certainly also freemasons, and threatened to make things difficult for the royal couple when they travelled to the south of the country.[12]

Aside from the concerns of the vintners, the importance of the visit was that it was a moment in which it was made clear to nationalist members of the

**11** McCarthy, *Irish revolution*, pp 372, 413. **12** Murphy, *Abject loyalty*, pp 231–40; Murphy, *Ireland's czar*, pp 342–5.

Corporation that they had to adhere to the policy of the national party and had to be disciplined about doing so. They had to obey voting instructions and could not absent themselves from the Corporation for votes they did not support. Perhaps most significantly was the fact that it was announced that the Irish Parliamentary Party had designated T.D. Sullivan as its spokesman in the Corporation on the issue of the royal visit. The unhappiness of some nationalist members became clear during the debate in the Corporation. Shackleton said he would not vote under coercion. 'But he wished to take the opportunity of protesting against the principle which he had already referred to and which he believed would be a disastrous one for nationality for the tightening of the harness of the political party would drive men of moderate views out of it.' He was a Quaker and disliked authority. 'He thought that the Irish Parliamentary Party had interfered a little too much with the privileges of the Corporation.' [13/14 Mar. 1885; 16/17 Mar. 1885; 12/13 Jan. 1891]

Shackleton subsequently resigned. It lead to an attack on the Corporation from the Conservative *Daily Express* that so stung T.D. Sullivan that he quoted it mockingly to the Corporation. 'Where are now the legitimate successors of the ... eminent citizens who entered the Corporation when it was reformed and reconstituted through the efforts of the chamber of commerce, who desired to see business attended to, and not politics, in the City Hall?' Harris, however, echoed the sentiments of the newspaper and attempted to focus them on recent changes to the personnel of the Corporation. He recalled the 1870s as a positive time of reform on the Corporation. But all this had changed after 1881. Shackleton and others 'had been driven out of the council and their successors in point of ability were not to be found there today. The subject of discord had been thrown into the council and from that moment that body had been sinking in the estimation of the citizens of Dublin.' Another member disagreed with the criticism but saw it not so much in terms of the rise of the influence of the Irish Party in the Corporation as that of the publicans, in a reflection of the complex interaction between the two phenomena. 'It would serve the members of the trade very much more to stay at home and mind their own business than to attend in the council and be abused for it. The working classes had now taken up their parrot cry; yet they had got more employment from the trade to which he belonged than from any other trade in the city.' Nonetheless, when in early 1888 a bill in parliament in favour of Sunday closing was considered by the Corporation the lord mayor vetoed an attempt to require the publican members of the Corporation to abstain from the vote on account of their interest in the matter. [23/24 Apr. 1885; 12/13 Feb. 1888]

In July, the Conservatives, of whom there were apparently still twelve, walked out of a meeting of the Corporation when the lord mayor refused to pass on correspondence he had received concerning the state entry of the new Tory lord lieutenant. One of the departing Tories remarked that the Corporation was forfeiting its position under its charter, to which Dennehy replied that their power came from the people. In the November elections that year, however, the Conservatives lost four seats, increasing the Irish Parliamentary Party hegemony on the Corporation. [6/7 Nov. 1885; 16/17 Nov. 1885; 25/26 Nov. 1885]

In 1886, T.D. Sullivan became lord mayor. He began his term by refusing to toast the Queen and refusing a ceremonial military escort, preferring to use the Irish trade band instead, during his inauguration.[13] Parting thanks to O'Connor rather rewrote his record of vacillation. Concerning the royal visit he had come through 'scathless' when 'one of the greatest political dodges of modern times was tried out not only on the citizens of Dublin but upon Ireland at large. The blow was aimed first at the chief liberties of the city and the Corporation and afterwards at the country at large, the object being to bring them back to what they have given up and what is commonly known as West Britonism.' When Sullivan was nominated for a second term, Sir George Owens complained about the new hegemony. 'It was most unfair that no Conservative or Liberal differing from the gentlemen opposite was now-a-days appointed to any positon of honour or emolument in the Corporation. No member of the Loyal and Patriotic Union [founded in 1885 to unite Irish Liberals and Conservatives against home rule] received such appointment. It was a bad example as to what they might expect if home rule were carried.' [1/2 Jan. 1886; 5/6 July 1886]

The new nationalist dominance created its own uncertainties. One nationalist member of the main drainage committee feared taking decisions because of newspaper criticism and because 'the business of this council was not being conducted in this council at all.' Sir George Owens believed that the Corporation would attempt to influence the poor law union elections. There were now only seven Conservative members. When they proposed an address to the incoming Conservative lord lieutenant in late 1886, Dennehy was once more on hand to claim that power did not come from the sovereign, whose representative the lord lieutenant was, but from the people. He proposed an amendment, which was passed, and which asserted '[t]hat we decline to take any part in welcoming to Ireland the representative of a government which is opposed to the only measure that can ever give peace, contentment, and

13 McCarthy, *Irish revolution*, p. 442.

prosperity to our country – the restoration of our native parliament.' [8/9 Feb. 1886; 16/17 Sept. 1886]

The position of the Conservatives, and remaining Liberals, was weakened even further at the November 1886 municipal elections. The election for aldermen was in the wards south of the Liffey, where Conservatives were strongest. Of the outgoing aldermen, there had been three Conservatives, three Liberals and three nationalists. Of the incoming aldermen two were Conservatives and seven were nationalists. Before the election there had been two Conservatives, one Liberal and twelve nationalists in possession of the councillor seats in contention. After the election there were thirteen nationalists and two Conservatives, the Conservatives having lost one seat but having gained the Liberal seat. Of the twenty-four seats contested four were won by Conservatives and twenty by nationalists. The nationalists gained five seats at the expense mostly of the Liberals who lost four seats. The Conservatives were only down one seat. This, however, was to be the last of the major realignment municipal elections as by this time most of the Corporation seats had been up for reelection since the nationalist takeover of 1883. Among other things it certainly marked the end of Dublin Liberalism. [25/26 Nov. 1886]

There were three noteworthy features of this election. The first was that McEvoy stood for election as alderman in Royal Exchange. This had been held by a Liberal who had decided not to stand and perhaps the Conservatives thought they might gain it. McEvoy did not succeed and afterwards remarked that he had not expected to. The following year when his seat as councillor came up at South City he did not stand for reelection. [5 Nov. 1887]

The second was the case of John Clancy who was convincingly defeated when he stood for reelection in Inns Quay ward by another nationalist. The latter had been nominated by the National Registration Association and they complained to the Corporation, alleging that some of its employees had been campaigning for Clancy during working hours. Some people felt that Clancy had not been sufficiently loyal to Parnell and this defeat was a means of punishing him. Tensions had run so high that the Catholic archbishop of Dublin had had to write a letter asking the different sides to stop warring. The association, which was pointedly pledged to help elect a candidate who would 'consistently support the policy of our trusted leader, Mr Parnell', had a large number of priests among its members. Presumably the archbishop's words carried some weight with them.[14] It was not the end of Clancy, however, and he soon found another seat. [14 Oct. 1886; 19/20 Oct. 1886; 25 Oct. 1886; 22/23 Nov. 1886; 7 Dec. 1886]

14 *IT*, 8 October 1886.

Undoubtedly, the major upset was the election of Thomas Sexton, MP, to represent Fitzwilliam ward. As Sexton remarked afterwards: 'This was the citadel of toryism in this city.' Sexton immediately set about using his new position in the Corporation to make speeches about national issues. [22/23 Nov. 1886; 25/26 Nov. 1886] He was clearly being lined up to be lord mayor. The problem with one large party becoming dominant is that conflict ceases to be between parties and becomes something intramural. Thus it was that Sexton found himself opposed by Gill who also wanted to be lord mayor. The Irish Party's emerging method to dealing with internal dissent was popular pressure, as we have seen in microcosm in the case of Clancy. And thus it was that in July 1887 a demonstration was held in the Phoenix Park in favour of Sexton, with three other MPs present apart from himself. The growing populist element was turned against Gill and against James Winstanley who had also put his name forward at a meeting of nationalist members of the Corporation. 'It was all very well to say that Mr Gill was a large employer; but why was any man a large employer. It was because he made money by it and by all accounts Mr Gill did not pay his employees very well.' As for Sexton: 'Mr Sexton had not devoted himself to a profession. He had devoted his brains solely to the service of Ireland. It was only men who were jealous that had started this opposition. Mr Sexton was prepared to stand or fall by Parnell; he was his chief lieutenant. Those who would vote for Winstanley would be opening the first branch of the Liberal Unionists [the name for those Liberals who had opposed Gladstone on home rule] in the Dublin Corporation.' Once Parnell and his party had expressed their view there could be no more discussion, it was declared. Sexton himself said he had lived in Dublin from boyhood. He had only been to two or three meetings of the Corporation but that was because he was required in parliament in London. He had been persuaded to stand because of his knowledge of national politics. His friends had told him that '"[w]e want a man next year who is acquainted with the basis of the long struggle between this country and Britain."' Sexton was unanimously nominated for lord mayor at the next meeting of the Corporation, being nominated, indeed, by Winstanley who meekly regretted his candidature and claimed he was no opponent of Sexton. [3/4 July 1887; 4/5 July 1887]

Meanwhile, political denunciation was becoming commonplace in the Corporation. Queen Victoria celebrated her golden jubilee in 1887. When Owens proposed a message of congratulations the hostility from the public gallery was so intense that Sullivan and Dawson had to try to explain it away and sought to express opposition to the address in more moderate tones. When it came to addressing recent evictions on the Lansdowne estate a few months later Dawson was at pains to explain why urban Dublin spent its time debating rural Ireland's issues:

> This was a question which came home to the dwellers in towns. They talked about town industries and the working classes did not in this country seem always fully to realize the fact that the bases of all industries were to be found in the rural districts and in an abundant population … The first thing was to create a contented population in the rural districts who would come into the towns and support the industries there established. But foolish and absurd would be the efforts to establish industries at vast expense and then to go looking for the customers to buy them.

Typically, it was the maverick Clancy who challenged this weak point in the dominance of the Irish Party over Dublin politics, namely that its priorities were rural not urban. 'He was inclined to believe that the artisans and working classes had been more or less lost sight of and it was time that some consideration should be given to them by public men.' [14/15 Mar. 1887; 2/3 May 1887]

In fact, the labouring classes were beginning to stir themselves politically. As early as 1880 the working men of Harold's Cross had complained to the Corporation that it was not giving Dublin tenders proper consideration for contracts to their employment disadvantage. In 1886, during his brief tenure on the Corporation Michael Davitt had supported moves to hold meetings of the Corporation in the evening so that members who might be working men might attend. That same year the lord mayor had had to address a group of 500 men who were discontented at not getting more work from Corporation projects. When a Liberal lord lieutenant, popular because of Gladstone's conversion to home rule, took formal leave of the city some months later the lord mayor praised the presence of the 'deputation from the working classes of Dublin' in the procession as a sign of popular participation. Yet there was unease which resulted in a denunciation from Tim Harrington for a potential candidate at the November 1887 municipal elections who 'represented himself as coming forward as the candidate of the workingman.' There was also nationalist nervousness about widening the municipal franchise in a way that might include more workers. In late 1888, Charles Dawson spoke on the subject to a meeting of the United Trades Council and Labour League in Dublin. He certainly supported an increased municipal franchise but cautioned that the first priority ought to be the national question and supporting Parnell. In the end working-class politics failed to establish itself during this period.[15] [2/3 Feb. 1880; 1/2 Feb. 1886; 15/16 Mar. 1886; 30/31 July 1886; 23/24 Nov. 1886; 21/22 Oct. 1888]

It required a certain courage to be one of the handful of remaining Conservatives on the Corporation during this period, though most of them seem to have been knighted by the government for their pains. The late 1880s saw a renewed phase of the land war called the plan of campaign (1886–91). In September 1887, following the Mitchelstown massacre, during which several men were shot dead by the police in the course of a political demonstration related to the campaign, a motion condemning the incident was debated in the Corporation. Only two Conservatives turned up to oppose it. When Sir Henry Cochrane was continually interrupted his colleague, James Dobson, objected. He effectively alleged that the nationalists on the Corporation were in favour of physical force methods: 'it was not until after Carey became an informer that a single voice could dare be raised against him on that council ... The goal of their ambition was self-government but they must first show that they had the capacity of governing themselves. He contended that the time had not yet arrived when Irishmen had shown that they were capable of governing themselves (cries of "oh" and hisses).' He and Cochrane were accused of 'supporting the policy of butchery of the government' though Sullivan, as lord mayor, intervened once more to calm matters down. [16/17 Sept. 1887]

The following month Sullivan deployed the ceremonial dignity of his office – which was considerable and was one of the reasons why the Irish Party wanted its senior members to hold it – when he was required to turn up at the Dublin police court to answer charges under the coercion act. He took the opportunity to make the most of the juxtaposition of the trappings of his office with the indignities of his court appearance to turn the event into a slight against the Corporation and its nationalist voters. The civic regalia, sword and mace, were arrayed before him and he expressed outrage when they were temporarily confiscated by the police. The Corporation should investigate 'whether the police had power to arrest the sword bearer, to wrest the sword from his grasp and to prevent those emblems from being taken into the court in the presence of the lord mayor.' Dawson, with reference to the Corporation's ceremonial links with the monarchy and with obvious tongue in cheek, said that '[t]he great anxiety he felt was as to the insult which had been offered to the crown by what was done in the police court.' When Sullivan was later snubbed by not being placed on the city commission, a judicial body, as was the custom for lord mayors, it was proposed that he proceed once more in state

15 M.J. Kelly, *The Fenian ideal and Irish nationalism, 1882–1916* (Woodbridge, 2006), p. 52.

to Green St court to protest. However, Sullivan faced serious enough charges, namely of having published in his newspaper, the *Nation*, a report of the proceedings of a suppressed branch of the National League (successor to the Land League). On 2 December 1887, while still in office as lord mayor, he was sent to jail for two months. [10/11 Oct. 1887; 1/2 Dec. 1887; 3 Dec. 1887]

Retribution in the Corporation fell on the Dublin Conservatives. Sir George Owens and Robert Sexton (who would inevitably later become Sir Robert Sexton and was no relation of Thomas Sexton) were removed as visiting justices from the Dublin city prisons. As Dawson put it: 'It was not the two individuals that they wished to strike off, but it was Balfour and coercion they struck off, which policy was represented there by Sir George Owens and Mr Sexton, and they should elect them again if they were not supporting a policy of coercion (hear, hear).' [2/3 Jan. 1888] A.J. Balfour (1848–1930) was the Conservative chief secretary for Ireland at the time (1887–91) and was to pursue a strong line on security enforcement with the aid of a new coercion act, passed in 1887.

At the end of the year Robert Sexton sought a place on the list of nominees for high sheriff. Dawson opposed it though on the subtle grounds, which Sexton denied, that if he got it Sexton was bound to favour his own side in his decisions. Thomas Mayne, MP, felt there was a more Machiavellian scheme behind the proposal and that it represented a trap for nationalists. Once more everything had to be judged by the standard of the national question:

> They had been invited to pay Mr Sexton a compliment of a particular kind, and they would find that they had simply made fools of themselves and they had given the opportunity to every Tory newspaper in England to parade the fact, as they would, of the decadence of the national spirit in the Dublin Corporation, as evidence by the fact that they had chosen a strong and consistent Conservative, a gentleman who had contested the city of Dublin in the Conservative interest [at a parliamentary election], and had rewarded him for his failure to become their parliamentary representative by making him high sheriff. There was no more earnest or hardworking member of the council than Mr Sexton and any gift in the disposal of the Corporation any member of the sixty would be only too glad to confer upon him, but at present local views and local matters were superseded and overshadowed by a very much greater matter – the national question. [2/3 Dec. 1888]

As if by way of corrective to this view Thomas Sexton began his second year as lord mayor with a speech in which he was very attentive to local matters. The list was a lengthy one: the borough surveyor, cleansing, markets, public health, the death rate, lighting, electric lighting, the organization of committees, public libraries, technical schools, open spaces, dwellings and lodgings, rates, the railway loop line, city expenditure, hospitals, industrial schools, city police, various financial matters and bills, the court of conscience and local government.[16] [1/2 Jan. 1889] As lord mayor he managed to attend to local issues, particularly Dublin's finances, at a time when the Corporation had been refocused on national concerns by the Irish Party.

Back on the national front Sexton had an easy publicity victory with a public altercation with the hated chief secretary, A.J. Balfour, over the welfare of William O'Brien, MP, who was then in jail. Sexton had a letter about the matter delivered to Balfour in the middle of the night. The latter was supposed to have responded to the messenger with, 'You are a ruffian and a cur, you're a cur, you're a cur.' Balfour went on to mock Sexton in a speech at the Liberal Union dinner and Sexton returned an invitation to a viceregal levee, refusing to attend 'whilst the government is insulting and torturing one of his parliamentary colleagues in prison for his political acts.' Once more the odium fell on the Dublin Conservative councillors who had been at the dinner. They claimed the criticism of their attendance had amounted to a call for them to be boycotted. Robert Sexton resigned in protest but stood at the by-election and was reelected. His decision was derided by nationalists. 'Mr Sexton had thought well to resign in a huff, and he did not think they ought to bewail that resignation. He could not support any gentleman of Mr Sexton's type who attended at a banquet and jeered and sneered with and supported the gentleman to whom that banquet was given [Balfour] (applause).' [1/2 Feb. 1889; 2/4 Feb. 1889; 4/5 Feb. 1889; 11/12 Feb. 1889; 4/5 Mar. 1889; 21 Mar. 1889]

But by the end of the year Thomas Sexton was trying to mollify the remaining five Conservatives, who were Sir George Owens, George Moyers, Sir Henry Cochrane, Robert Sexton and James Dobson. He asked them 'whether he had not always preserved the liberty of every member to be heard without distinction of party.' Perhaps some day each of them might become lord mayor 'if the present high tension and pressure in political matters were

**16** Cullen, 'Belfast and Dublin', p. 90. There were five rail terminals in Dublin; Broadstone, Kingsbridge and Amiens St, on the north side of the river; Westland Row and Harcourt St, on the south side. In 1891, the loop connecting line between Amiens St and Westland Row finally linked the two sides of the Liffey.

withdrawn from civic life.' Indeed, he noted that at that year's election the nationalists had decided not to oppose Sexton or Dobson. All in all the Conservatives now counted for little on the Corporation itself. Their treatment mattered, however, in terms of publicity in a hostile British press and in the townships, with their substantial Conservative populations and which the Corporation coveted. Nonetheless, the decade marked a remarkable change on the Corporation. The Dublin Liberals had come to an end and the Conservatives been much reduced. The beginnings of a politics representative of the working classes had been stymied in deference to the nationalist agenda. Nationalists dominated the Corporation but it had now lost its independence and was a creature of an external force, the Irish Parliamentary Party. The latter's political priorities were national ones and centred on home rule. Its economic priorities were those of rural Ireland, home of the vast majority of its supporters. The priorities of Dublin did not figure largely in its agenda. And yet, in Thomas Sexton, a national figure with a seat in parliament, the Corporation and city found a very effective lord mayor.[17] [20 Nov. 1889; 20/21 Nov. 1889]

17 The situation was thus the reverse of that of the late 1840s when the economic interests of the members of the Corporation and their electorate prevented the Corporation from becoming the focus for debate on how to tackle the Famine.

CHAPTER 12

# Division, 1890–3

THE YEAR 1890 BEGAN FOR THE Corporation, as it did for everyone in Ireland, with the recent news that Parnell had been named in the O'Shea divorce case, though the issue did not come to court until November 1890. After the divorce proceedings the Irish Parliamentary Party split over the question of Parnell's leadership. Parnell himself campaigned in Ireland at by-elections but died in October 1891. The early weeks of 1890, just after the initial news, saw meetings throughout the country in support of Parnell. In Dublin fifty members of the Corporation signed a requisition to hold a special meeting to pass a resolution to support him. Yet when the meeting was called only thirty-two members attended. [27 Jan. 1890; 29/30 Jan. 1890]

For the most part the Corporation was occupied in early 1890 with supporting a Dublin improvement bill in the Commons, one of whose most important provisions was that the townships would have to pay for the Blackrock Road. The Borough Funds (Ireland) Act of 1888 indemnified members of the Corporation from having to bear the cost of failed legislation they had promoted in parliament, if the legislation was supported by a ratepayers plebiscite. (Successful legislation always carried a clause covering the costs from Corporation funds.) A poll of the 8,300 Dublin burgesses had been taken and 4,000 had voted in favour of supporting the bill, with 1,300 against. [20 Jan. 1890; 5/6 Feb. 1890; 13/14 Jan. 1890] By September the bill had become law though T.D. Sullivan spoke with some bitterness of all the opposition it had received from the Corporation's old enemies, the chamber of commerce and the port and docks board, neither of whom, he warned darkly, had 'done all this at their own expense.' The opponents of the bill had alleged that the Corporation would disenfranchise Conservatives, or Unionists as they were now often called. 'But the opposition was in perfect keeping with similar proceedings which took place from time to time since the date of the reformation of the Dublin Corporation. From that time to this unhappily there had been in the city of Dublin a little party clique who looked upon the Corporation of Dublin with eyes of jealousy and entertained towards them feelings of distrust.' [1/2 Sept. 1890]

By December 1890, the Irish Parliamentary Party was in the process of splitting. A meeting of the Corporation was scheduled for 1 December but only the six Tories were present at the designated time as the nationalists were at a private meeting to discuss the Parnell crisis. Sir Henry Cochrane announced: 'Time is up. I beg to move that Alderman Robert Sexton take the chair. We are not going to wait for Mrs O'Shea or Parnell or anyone else.' However, the nationalists subsequently came in. [1/2 Dec. 1890] Parnell himself soon arrived in the city and dramatically captured the offices of the party newspaper, *United Ireland*, before campaigning in a series of by-elections in Ireland in the ten months up to his death in October 1891. Most of his leading followers opposed him, though John Redmond led his supporters. Tim Harrington, who had had such power over nationalist Corporation members, also remained loyal to Parnell. Over the following decade of division in Irish nationalism, the Parnellites were to receive strong support in Dublin, though they were to be in the minority more generally.

As early as March 1891 the lord mayor, J.M. Meade (1839–1900), a building contractor who had won the contract for the masonry for the loop line, helped establish a Parnell leadership fund. Many candidates for election to the Corporation would proclaim their loyalty. One wrote to the papers that 'I am a staunch follower and supporter of the leader of the Irish people, Charles S Parnell.' Yet when Parnell died once more the response on the Corporation was muted with only half the members of the Corporation turning up for a meeting to express its condolences. [10 Mar. 1891; 28 Mar. 1891; 8/9 Oct. 1891] When Meade was nominated for a second year in office, he was supported by the Conservatives, a sign of a new political fluidity which gave Conservatives renewed influence on the Corporation. This occasioned remarks from one member which though ostensibly in praise of them were in fact barbed references to the growing divisions within nationalism:

> In reference to the remarks of Alderman Sexton, he … hoped that the time was not far distant when gentlemen from the Conservative side of the house would be selected for the civic chair (hear, hear). They deserved some respect for their consistency. They were today what they were yesterday and twenty years ago; and twenty years ago they were what they could be while they lived. They did not take oaths of allegiance to an Irish Republic one day and swear oaths of allegiance to the crown and constitution on the next; they were Conservatives now and would always be Conservatives; and he hoped that the time was near at hand when no political opinions expressed by any gentleman would be a bar to his filling the civic chair (hear, hear). [6/7 July 1891]

An apparent warming towards Conservatives was in evidence again later in the year when some nationalists supported placing Robert Sexton at the top of the list of those nominated for high sheriff, though in the end he was voted down. Meade's attempts at getting a third term in office failed, even though some felt he might have succeeded through relying on the support of the Conservatives. James Shanks was nominated instead. He was a Protestant home ruler and his nomination drew on him the scorn of the Corporation Conservatives, who had proposed Sexton, but which he shrugged off. 'It is quite a popular and fashionable thing among the Tories of Dublin to throw dirty water on Protestant nationalists on every occasion (hear, hear).' Some felt that Meade should have been reelected in atonement for 'the stain of betrayal' because he had been beaten by a Catholic Unionist for the Dublin constituency of St Stephen's Green, at the 1892 general election. In general Conservatives/Unionists had done well in Dublin at that election, though, nevertheless, Dublin turned out to be one of the stronger areas for the Parnellites. Nationally, the Parnellites won only nine seats in parliament to the anti-Parnellites seventy-two.[1] As for the Dublin Conservatives they were gaining support under the changed political situation from wealthier Catholics, though in the end they failed to translate that support into anything lasting. [1/2 Dec. 1891; 3/4 June 1892; 8/9 Aug. 1892]

The new political divide brought with it shifting allegiances and the iron discipline that had once been the hallmark of the united Irish Parliamentary Party was less in evidence. One of the other features of the period was that nationalist newspapers themselves took sides. Under pressure from Tim Healy's *National Press*, the *Freeman's Journal* became anti-Parnellite.[2] In September 1892 at the start of Gladstone's final administration, a question arose as to whether the Corporation should present an address to the new lord lieutenant. Gladstone was pledged to bring in a new home rule bill, but he was unpopular with Parnellites as he had urged Parnell to step down as leader when the divorce issue arose, because many nonconformist Liberal supporters in Britain wished it. Parnellite feeling was thus against an address. However, the *Freeman's Journal*, in editorial comment, was delighted to report that, when the whole body of nationalists on the Corporation met to consider the matter, the motion in favour of an address was lost by only seventeen votes to sixteen. The minority included prominent Parnellites such as Meade and Shanks. Referring to the outgoing Conservative lord lieutenant (or viceroy) as well as the incoming one, the *Freeman's Journal* believed that their 'votes were a

1 Dickson, *Dublin*, p. 392; Patrick Maume, *The long gestation, Irish nationalist life, 1891–1918* (New York, 1999), p. 18. 2 Dickson, *Dublin*, p. 388; Maume, *Long gestation*, p. 19; Kelly, *Fenian ideal*, p. 44.

practical censure on the wild inanities of their organs in the press and of their unthinking orators, who maintain that a home rule viceroy and a coercionist should be similarly regarded by the people of Ireland.' There was a great backlash against the Parnellites who had voted for the address. Shanks wrote to the papers to defend himself. 'To judge by some of the newspaper comments and the speeches at ward meetings extensively reported, it would appear that a nationalist in Dublin may not aspire to win the confidence of his fellow nationalists and that when he occupies a representative positon he must endure the suspicions, misrepresentations and abuse of writers and speakers of his own party'. [24 Sept. 1892; 26 Sept. 1892; 27 Sept. 1892; 5/6 June 1893]

Controversy over addresses to the royal family dogged the Corporation the following year, with the intra-nationalist partisan press exercising an influence that some members of the Corporation found coercive. Over the question of a loyal address to the Queen on the approaching marriage of her grandson, the Corporation felt the sting of the Parnellite *Daily Irish Independent*. It was a paper controlled by John Redmond and Tim Harrington and even had a Fenian tinge.[3] As the lord mayor put it: 'there are some members of the council who think that the correct course is to give immediate information to the leader writers of the *Independent* newspaper in order that these gentlemen may lay down the law to us.' [5/6 June 1893]

In 1893, the Corporation promoted another Dublin bill in parliament as it was obliged to in order to extend borrowing powers as a result of accepting a sum of £109,000 from the treasury towards the main drainage scheme. [6/7 Feb. 1893] In the summer the lord mayor James Shanks ran into trouble and it scuppered his chances of a second year in office. He held a lunch in the Mansion House for the officers of the visiting USS *Chicago* but failed to invite the high sheriff and the former lord mayor, Joseph Michael Meade. An alternative banquet was held for the two snubbed men at which Tim Harrington, MP, was in attendance. Shanks was very repentant before the Corporation. 'That I should knowingly slight or offend this council, which only a week before the disturbing incident had paid me so high a compliment, is so absurd and foolish a proceeding that it would certainly show me to be unfit for the positon which I owe to your selection.' The debate descended into bickering about technicalities concerning whether various motions had been properly made before Shanks completely destroyed his own case. He accused Meade of having criticized his expenditure as lord mayor. When he would not withdraw he was shouted down by the Corporation and a motion to revoke

3 Maume, *Long gestation*, p. 16; Kelly, *Fenian ideal*, p. 76.

his nomination for a second term as lord mayor was passed. Nonetheless, the latter part of Shanks's one year in office was not unpleasant as he went to Chicago to represent Dublin at the Columbian exposition. A motion to allow the town clerk to go with him was defeated, however. Some believed it was from spite against Shanks. [22 July 1893; 25 July 1893; 7/8 Aug. 1893; 8/9 Aug. 1893; 11/12 Sept. 1893; 4 Nov. 1893]

Nationalists were not the only ones who could engage in internecine disputes, however. In November the Conservatives turned against one of their own, J.A. Walker. Allegedly, a number of fellow Conservatives had reported the fact that some of his municipal taxes had not been paid and he had been expunged from the roll of burgesses and would thus lose his seat. He told the Corporation that his colleagues had judged him too friendly with the non-Conservative member, Thomas Pile, and Sir Henry Cochrane had objected to the fact that he had voted for the reelection of the lord mayor. [6/7 Nov. 1893]

The nationalist division did not show itself to any great degree in the November 1891 municipal elections except in the Fitzwilliam ward where a Conservative won because a second nationalist stood. [20/21 Nov. 1891; 25/26 Nov. 1891] Divisions continued to be muted in 1892, mostly because of the *fait accompli* of Parnellite strength and because of a nationalist reluctance on both sides to allow Conservatives, who were now contesting more seats than hitherto, to benefit from nationalist divisions. Thomas Sexton, who was an anti-Parnellite and was the subject of repeated attacks by Parnellites, decided not to stand. At the election itself the positions of nine aldermen were in contention. Two Conservatives, Sir Robert Sexton and Sir Henry Cochrane, the mineral water manufacturer, were elected unopposed as were five Parnellites. In Royal Exchange a Conservative gained a seat from an agreed nationalist candidate. In Fitzwilliam ward Thomas Pile (1856–1931), a Protestant fish merchant and a supporter of home rule who, nonetheless, managed to appeal to Conservatives, retained the seat for the Parnellites in face of the opposition of a Conservative and anti-Parnellite candidate. In the fifteen councillor positions in contention nine candidates were elected unopposed, though not all of them were Parnellites. In Mountjoy ward a workingman's candidate was elected. The results in the contested seats changed little, except perhaps in the case of Fitzwilliam ward where a Parnellite beat a Conservative. This was, of course, the seat that had been held by Thomas Sexton and was thus considered a gain from the anti-Parnellites. Nonetheless, Tory numbers had now grown to nine members of the Corporation. [17 Nov. 1892; 26 Nov. 1892; 10/11 Apr. 1893]

In November 1893, fifteen councillor positions were available for election. Eight seats were uncontested. Parnellites stood under the banner of the

National League and nationalists who opposed them as candidates of the Registration Association. In the contested seats the Conservatives held one seat and gained another. The Conservative gain in Fitzwilliam was because candidates from these opposing nationalist groups stood against each other. In an indication of the growing power of the partisan press in an era of divided nationalism, it was alleged that the Parnellite candidate had been nominated by the editor of the *Independent*. The other five seats were held by nationalists though in at least one ward the Parnellite was unseated. [15 Nov. 1893; 16/17 Nov. 1893; 25/27 Nov. 1893; 6 Dec. 1893]

As far as the Corporation was concerned the early 1890s were like the reversal of the 1880s. In the 1880s the Corporation had come under the iron grip of a united Irish Parliamentary Party. The 1890s were more fissiparous years and the Corporation regained some of its independence. Nationalism was divided and lines of political demarcation were blurred in ways that surprisingly even opened the possibility of renewed Conservative (Unionist) influence if not a great increase in their numbers on the Corporation.

## CHAPTER 13

# Changed Corporation, new city, 1894–1901

DUBLIN CORPORATION HAD BEEN reformed on two occasions in the mid nineteenth century. The twentieth century would open with the city limits expanded by the incorporation of several of the townships and with an expanded municipal electorate. The 1890s, therefore, would be years of struggle towards those outcomes. But there were other matters, too, particularly financial matters that were not unrelated. In the sixty years between 1831 and 1891 the population of the suburbs rose from 12.4 per cent to 29.6 per cent of that of the city, as controlled by Dublin Corporation. Meanwhile, by 1880 the valuation of Rathmines, Pembroke and Kingstown, a measure on which local taxes could be levied, came to forty-two per cent of that of the historic city.[1] In 1888, Thomas Sexton as lord mayor had helped to restructure the Corporation's debts to the extent that some estimated that he had saved the city £70,000 a year. Yet within five years the Corporation's expenditure and indebtedness had increased to swallow up the savings. Much of this was designated for necessary capital expenditure such as the main drainage project. [2 Jan. 1894] But it highlighted the plight of the historical city, with its dwindling taxation base, and increased pressure for amalgamation with the townships, where two in seven of the city's effective population lived. [2 Jan. 1894; 31 Jan. 1894]

Matters of a more personal, but irritating, nature affected members of the Corporation in 1894, when as a result of a court ruling they were personally charged for the cost of the floral decoration of the Mansion House. This led to proposals that did not succeed to raise the lord mayor's salary to £5,000 so that he could meet such costs. [2 May 1894; 8/9 Aug. 1894; 13/14 Aug. 1894] There was little change at the November 1894 municipal elections apart from one Conservative loss. However, in Inns Quay ward the anti-Parnellite polled nearly twice as many votes as his Parnellite opponent, who had had the support of Tim Harrington. [11 Oct. 1894; 26/27 Nov. 1894] The year ended with Corporation support for the renewed amnesty movement. The movement had begun some years earlier with the aim of securing the release of those convicted of bombing outrages in Britain in the 1880s. The amnesty

1 Martin, 'Social geography', p. 179.

movement had since the days of the original Fenians been a means for constitutional and physical-force nationalists to find common ground.[2] This support, however, brought the Corporation into antagonistic contact with the Liberal government, though Gladstone was no longer prime minister. There were also proposals for a new Dublin improvement bill that might address water, sanitation and gas. Its most notable provision was to force Kingstown council to pay for the excess water it obtained from the Corporation. As time went on there were moves to extend the reforms proposed. Early in 1895 there was a row over whether the bill should also propose the extension of the municipal franchise, which was still around 8,000, to the higher level of the parliamentary franchise of 40,000. In fact, there was growing pressure from the Irish Trades Union Congress for an increase in the municipal franchise. Until the franchise was eventually reformed there were only one or two councillors who could be construed as representing the labour vote.[3] In March 1885, the secretary of the Trades Council was selected to stand in Fitzwilliam ward with some Parnellite support. In the event a Conservative won. To the charge that his standing had allowed this to happen the candidate said that he would not have stood except for the affront to working people given by the Corporation's refusal to support a strong measure of franchise reform. [5/6 Nov. 1894; 12/13 Nov. 1894; 26/27 Nov. 1894; 18/19 Feb. 1895; 3/4 Mar. 1895; 6/7 Mar. 1895]

Clearly there had been a fear of working-class voters by some in the Corporation and Shanks had been perhaps too honest when he had said that reform 'might bring in an undesirable class of voters.' In the end a rather general reference to a wider franchise was included. The row in the Corporation ended in some sour references about Shanks. 'He has come twice in my recollection [since ceasing to be lord mayor], and that with the object of either insulting members of the Corporation or making himself a specialist to plead a particular case that he had no interest in the world only for public show.' More generally working men felt let down by the Corporation, though Tim Healy was promoting what would turn out to be an unsuccessful municipal franchise bill for Ireland at the same time in parliament.[4] However, in a plebiscite, under the Borough Funds (Ireland) Act in which only a quarter of ratepapers took part, the proposal to promote the bill was defeated, with the ratepayers association, a surrogate for Conservatives, claiming the victory. The lord mayor certainly blamed the Unionist Registration Association. In view of the low turnout the Corporation decided to hold a second vote but a judge ruled this illegal. In the end the Corporation bill was withdrawn. The lord mayor, Valentine Blake Dillon, a cousin of John Dillon, was sardonic. 'The bill

2 Kelly, *Fenian ideal*, pp 77–8. 3 Daly, *Deposed capital*, p. 216. 4 Daly, *Deposed capital*, pp 215–16.

has now to be withdrawn, and it is withdrawn with the result that the shares of the gas company have gone up, I think £2 (hear, hear), and the Kingstown township, if it was a limited liability company, I suppose its shares would have gone up another £2.' Some felt the ratepayers' vote had been a protest against the Corporation's interest in national politics and neglect of immediate matters to do with public health. [18/19 Feb. 1895; 20 Feb. 1895; 21 Feb. 1895; 4/5 Mar. 1895; 8 Mar. 1895; 11/12 Mar. 1895; 23/25 Mar. 1895; 8/9 Apr. 1895]

In spite of this the Corporation decided to promote a new bill in 1896 that would once again deal with water payments from the townships and issues concerning gas, though some preferred to negotiate with the bodies in question. When the bill reached its committee stage in the House of Lords it faced titanic opposition from legal counsel for five townships, the gas company and the brewers Guinness. Meanwhile the anti-Parnellite leader, Tim Healy, announced he would scupper the bill unless it included clauses broadening the municipal franchise and changing the way in which councillors were elected. By the end of August, however, and after much wheeler-dealing in parliament the bill failed. There was considerable recrimination from Parnellites especially against Healy. [13/14 Jan. 1896; 5/6 Feb. 1896; 14 May 1896; 16 July 1896; 25/27 July 1896; 5/7 Sept. 1896]

Undaunted, the Corporation began 1897 by pushing a further improvement bill, this one dealing essentially only with the water issue. A poll of ratepayers supported it by 3,562 to 1,785. As the bill seemed to be moving forward successfully the townships began to take action. Blackrock which 'had for years been reveling in water for which they did not pay now proceeded to appoint inspectors and say that they would cut down expenses in every way.' [11/12 Jan. 1897; 2/3 Feb. 1897; 9/10 Aug. 1897]

As the decade wore on a number of anniversaries, particularly Queen Victoria's diamond jubilee in 1897 and the 1898 centenary of the 1798 rebellion, gave focus to the activities of new and more radical nationalist groups in Dublin, which were not reflected in the composition of the Corporation. It was predictable that Conservative attempts to have the Corporation present a loyal address to the Queen on her diamond jubilee would fail. [17/18 May 1897] On the streets of Dublin, however, the jubilee was the occasion for a riot.[5] One Conservative on the Corporation wanted to know why and how a black flag had been flown from City Hall on the night of the jubilee. He also wanted the permission for the Young Ireland League, a literary group with strong nationalist leanings run by the veteran

5 Murphy, *Abject loyalty*, pp 269–73.

Fenian, John O'Leary (1830–1907), to use the council chamber rescinded. [12/13 July 1897]

Attempts to have Conservatives elected as lord mayor did not succeed. In 1896 there was some support for Robert Sexton and this was reflected in the strength of the vote against giving the sitting lord mayor, Richard F. McCoy, a second term. McCoy was renominated by twenty-nine votes but twenty-three votes were cast against him. McCoy was not very popular and grumblings continued that it might be better to have a Conservative as lord mayor for the Queen's jubilee year. [6/7 July 1896; 30 Nov. 1896] Meanwhile, John Clancy was setting himself up as a spokesman for the new and more pronounced nationalism and republicanism of the times and was supporting the proposal of the 1798 centenary committee concerning the location of a statue of the United Irishman leader, Wolfe Tone (1763–98). This seems to have precipitated an onslaught of accusations of nepotism against him. When another veteran Fenian, Jeremiah O'Donovan Rossa (1831–1915), had supposedly wanted a position from the Corporation Clancy had allegedly replied, 'You stand in the way of a member of my family – my son wants this position.'[6] He decided to resign from the Corporation but defended himself at a meeting in his South Dock ward. 'He had occasionally been very badly slandered. It had been said that he, in his capacity as town councillor, crammed the Corporation with relatives of his own and put them into positions. Well that was – to put it mildly – not only untrue but there was not the semblance of truth in it.' His son had gotten a job but it had been paid for by 'the pawnbrokers of Ireland'. [6/7 Sept. 1897; 24 Sept. 1897; 4/5 Oct. 1897]

When McCoy was originally nominated for lord mayor, Clancy had accepted on his behalf. The suspicion of financial mismanagement would also fall on McCoy. In November 1897, he won a court case that had been taken against him over a coal contract. However, it raised the allegation that the firm of which McCoy was a partner had used another company as a cover for obtaining Corporation contracts. He denied it but it led to a heated debate in the Corporation. For some, his case, whether true or false, was symptomatic of a larger problem. 'There was in their midst a great mass of corruption. It was sought to make a hate of one man by people who held themselves up as being as pure and as innocent as the child unborn.' Accusations were made against other members. In the end though the Corporation expressed its strong disapproval of the actions of the lord mayor. A few weeks later the public had their say when McCoy's seat came up at the annual municipal election and he

**6** Several nationalists and republicans were given jobs by the Corporation during these years. The Fenian James Egan (1847–1909), for example, was appointed sword-bearer in 1898.

garnered only thirty-six votes as opposed to 274 for his opponent. The same election saw Tim Harrington, MP, standing for the Corporation for the first time and being defeated. His position as a leading Parnellite, particularly in Dublin, had been rather eclipsed by the rise of John Redmond, with whom he had fallen out over policy, and he was seeking to re-establish a power base in Dublin municipal politics without the support of the official Parnellites.[7] [1/2 July 1895; 4 Nov. 1897; 11/12 Nov. 1897; 17 Nov. 1897; 25/26 Nov. 1897]

The next lord mayor, Daniel Tallon (1836–1908), a leading wine and spirits merchant, ran into his own difficulties. There was trouble over outside organizations using rooms in the Mansion House as office space and he had also booked a military band for his inauguration. Later in the year he attended Gladstone's funeral which was controversial among certain Parnellites. There was also a row over the means of electing a new city marshal, in which contest Parnell's older brother got the job. [23 Dec. 1897; 31 Dec. 1897; 6/7 June 1898; 7/8 Mar. 1898] However, Tallon also managed to use the prestige of his office for political effect, something that Parnellites were keen on as they were in a strong position in Dublin, though in a minority in the country at large. Shortly after he assumed office he took up the cause of the deteriorating conditions in the west of Ireland, touring British cities for help and engaging in a fact-finding tour of the west, which garnered much publicity.[8]

The great event of the year was the Local Government (Ireland) Act. This set up a new and more democratic system of local government in the Irish counties but had some effect in urban areas, too, and increased pressure for reform in Dublin itself. The main actual change it brought about in Dublin was the increase in the municipal franchise from 8,000 to 38,000. Women ratepayers could now vote, though under the act women could be elected to urban and rural district councils but not to county or borough councils, such as Dublin. The act, however, resulted in a larger pool of working-class voters and increased opportunities for candidates linked with trade unions.[9] In Dublin Corporation there was bemusement at the pace of change and at this latest reform from a government pursuing constructive unionism. 'The bill was a democratic one, which some time ago they could scarcely conceive would come from a Conservative government.' The Corporation was consulted on whether triennial elections should replace their existing annual partial

7 Patrick Maume, 'Harrington, Timothy Charles' in *Dictionary of Irish biography*, accessed 10 November 2019. Harrington had retained control of the National League organization and of *United Ireland*, forcing Redmond's supporters to set up the Independent Irish League. After 1895 he called for reunion with the anti-Parnellites and supported the United Irish League, helping to push Redmond into reunion in 1900. **8** Patrick Maume, 'Tallon, Daniel' in *Dictionary of Irish biography*, accessed 10 November 2019. **9** Daly, *Deposed capital*, p. 216.

elections. There was support for this move and then a discussion on whether councillors should be elected every three years and the more senior category of member, aldermen, every six. Some wanted them, too, to be elected every three years. 'With a few exceptions the vast majority of the court of aldermen of the council went asleep and became fossilized for five years and then woke up the year they had to face their constituents (laughter).' Some even thought that the position of alderman should be abolished altogether. [22/23 June 1898]

When the issue of the lord mayoralty came up in July there was serious support among some nationalist members and some labour supporters for Sir Robert Sexton. Some felt it might soften the opposition of the more Unionist-minded townships to amalgamation with the city of Dublin if they had a Unionist mayor. Harrington, now at last a member of the Corporation, however, believed it would be a sign of weakness and the Unionists in the townships had shown no inclination to share power themselves. 'He would like to see those who were the opponents of the national party and who had the monopoly of power, commence by showing a lesson of tolerance (hear, hear).' He went on to accuse nationalists who supported Sexton of being renegades, though in return his own nationalist credentials were questioned and he was accused of being a detached maverick. Thomas Pile quoted John Redmond against Harrington. 'He told them that their only hope of getting home rule was by showing tolerance all round and using every possible effort to induce their Conservative friends to see the necessity of it.' Sexton was duly nominated for the position. The nomination of a Unionist, however, immediately became a matter of intra-nationalist party politics. The anti-Parnellite leader, John Dillon, MP, wrote to North City ward approving of their determination to support 'candidates for the coming election in January pledged not to support any Tory for the positon of lord mayor.' This would be 'a conspiracy to inflict a most dangerous blow on the Irish national cause by handing over the mayoralty of the Mansion House of Dublin to the Unionists at a period so critical as the present is.' At a meeting in Fitzwilliam ward Pile was shouted down with cries of 'No Pile drivers' and 'No Tory lord mayor.' All of this was taking place at a time of realignment among nationalists with several factions coalescing around the United Irish League, under William O'Brien, though the eventual reunification of the Irish Parliamentary Party under John Redmond in 1900 was still a little way off. In December 1898 the Corporation itself debated the issue of reunification. [4/5 July 1898; 9/10 Nov. 1898; 18/19 Nov. 1898; 5/6 Dec. 1898]

In January 1899 an election of all the seats of the existing Corporation took place under the new franchise with those at the head of the poll named as aldermen and with the plan to revert thereafter to partial elections of the Corporation on a yearly basis as heretofore. Nearly 120 candidates stood for the sixty seats, including eighty-eight nationalists, eighteen Unionists, ten Labour candidates and one socialist republican. Nationalists were keen, where possible, to maintain the porous boundary between them and Labour supporters that had been evident for some time and thus to soften the effects of a labour vote both by expressing sympathy themselves for working men's interests and even by facilitating the election of friendly Labour candidates.[10] [9/10 Dec. 1898] This was the analysis of the anti-Parnellite *Freeman's Journal* before the election:

> There is not much likelihood of a revolutionary change in the composition of Dublin council. With the practical consent of all parties the artisan and working population are being given what they regard as a fair representation; and the only contests of interest are those that take their rise in the recent mayoral controversy. It will be unfortunate, however, if every member of the council who was led to vote for a Tory mayoralty by Mr John Redmond's appeals for a one-sided 'toleration' should be driven from the service of the city. They have given pledges, now that Mr Redmond has explained his meaning to be the toleration of the Tories where no Redmondite could hope to be returned, not to repeat the blunder. [5/6 Jan. 1899]

Thirty incumbents were reelected, twenty-four nationalists and six Unionists, almost halving the Unionist numbers. Overall forty-five nationalists were elected to the Corporation, eighteen Parnellites and twenty-seven supporters of the United Irish League. Seven Unionists were elected as were eight Labour candidates, three of whom topped the poll and thus became aldermen.[11] Support for Sir Robert Sexton as lord mayor had evaporated amid internecine nationalist conflict and at the first meeting of the new Corporation on 23 January 1899 Tallon was duly reelected for a second term as lord mayor. The old line that the absence of home rule excluded Conservatives from office was invoked by one of the speakers. 'Had this council met under a measure of home rule instead of under a limited measure of local government none would rejoice more than they would that the necessity no longer existed for the exclusion from offices of honour in this Corporation men who differed in political opinions and that the time had come when the men of all sections could work harmoniously for the common good.' He proposed a home rule

10 Joseph V. O'Brien, *Dear dirty Dublin: a city in distress, 1899–1916* (Berkeley, 1982), pp 78, 80.
11 O'Brien, *Dirty Dublin*, p. 79.

resolution as the first act of the new, more democratic Corporation and it was seconded by William Redmond (1861–1917), John Redmond's brother, who was now a member. Sexton was rather sour about the Redmonds' *volte face* on his candidature under pressure from the criticism of rival nationalists. He had been referred to as 'the bitterest Conservative in the city' by William Redmond when addressing a group of working men. 'He very much regretted the apple of discord should be thrown into this council because Mr Redmond and his brother had said very often that they would not introduce anything like a party spirit.' Redmond's defence was that because some in England thought local government reform a substitute for home rule 'this was not a party matter but an Irish nationalist matter.' For the Labour group, Joseph P. Nannetti pledged to support Tallon as lord mayor but was keen to assert that his members were acting independently. There then followed much acrimony over nominations for several other posts including first position on the list for high sheriff, with Thomas Lenehan, who eventually won, pitted against William Redmond. When Lenehan was accused of making shovels a supporter answered, 'Alderman Lenehan was not ashamed to make shovels.' Redmond became almost histrionic, 'If they voted him down they voted down Parnell's flag (noise and interruption and general uproar). If he, Parnell's friend and follower, was beaten he would be beaten by the Unionists of Dublin (applause).' To this Lenehan replied 'with great vehemence' and that 'if Redmond is beaten it will be by him (Lenehan).' Referring to the fact that Redmond had once served in the army, he went on: 'I was serving my country when Willie Redmond wore a British coat.' [23/24 Jan. 1899]

The achievement of an extended franchise was a victory in half of the battle for a new city. Boundary extension was the other half and the Corporation lost no time in pressing for it. A poll of electors duly took place in which 20,498 voted in favour of the Corporation promoting a boundary extension bill in parliament and only 3,116 voted against. [18/20 Feb. 1899]

In the autumn there was a debate over who should be lord mayor in 1900 with Pile being narrowly nominated. His higher social position and greater wealth were adduced as reasons why he might be an improvement on Tallon. But the debate also raised issues to do with boundary extension. He was praised as a positive force for extension as he owned property in areas that were likely to be absorbed and was still in favour of the move. There was criticism, however, of the Labour group for having the temerity to propose a candidate of their own for lord mayor. One speaker remarked that 'if he were a member of the township bodies he certainly would oppose the annexation when he saw the Labour party within six months trying to thrust one of their men into the position of lord mayor and attempting to grasp everything.'

Nannetti apologetically claimed that some nationalists had proposed it to them. The Unionists argued that electing Sexton would be a good signal to the townships and that the Labour members should support him. Yet this was to be only the beginning of a time of difficulty for the Labour party on the Corporation as it faced charges of corruption. It was alleged that several of its members accepted bribes in order to promote the bid of the Municipal Industries Syndicate Ltd to take over the electric lighting of the city. [4/5 Sept. 1899; 2/3 Oct. 1899; 20/21 Nov. 1899]

Prospects for a boundary extension were not helped in the early part of 1900 by popular nationalist support for the Boers who were then at war with Britain in southern Africa and by the visit of Queen Victoria to Dublin in April. It was her first in nearly four decades and was in part the result of the fact that Britain's then unpopularity in Europe because of the war meant she could not travel to the Continent as was her annual custom. Tallon had stymied a pro-Boer resolution in the Corporation so as not to endanger the boundaries bill. The announcement of the royal visit took nationalists off guard. Initial hostility was mitigated by a guarded welcome from John Redmond. But then he changed his mind and came out against gestures of welcome. As far as Dublin Corporation was concerned matters centred on whether to make a loyal address to the Queen. In the light of Redmond's initial welcome of the visit nationalist members of the Corporation voted forty-three to three in a private meeting at the Mansion House in favour of an address. But when it came to debating it at the Corporation a little later William Redmond, consonant with his brother's changed position, opposed it, as did Tim Harrington who had disapproved all along. Nonetheless, there was a momentum in favour and with the support of the lord mayor, Thomas Pile, it was agreed, with a significant though not overwhelming majority of thirty to twenty-two. Pile was duly created a baronet for his trouble. Harrington lamented that the address had been seen in the British press as an 'abandonment of our claim for national self-government.'[12] [14/15 Mar. 1900; 31 Mar. 1900]

The boundary issue came to a conclusion late in 1900 after much toing and froing between Commons and Lords, with each reversing the other's decision on the degree of annexation. Eventually the bill was referred to a joint parliamentary committee. The result was a compromise in which Dublin annexed the contingMuous townships of Clontarf and Drumcondra to the north and the working-class township of Kilmainham to the south-west. Pembroke (modern day Ballsbridge) and Rathmines, the redoubts of Unionist power to

**12** Murphy, *Abject loyalty*, pp 279–89.

a degree, escaped annexation until 1929 though they had to pay for joint costs with the Corporation as the price for not being absorbed with the other townships at the beginning of the century. Land in Crumlin in the south and in Cabra in the north that had not been part of a township was also added. The city increased its size by 4,125 acres, its valuation by £100,000 and its population by 26,000. A general revaluation took place in Dublin to ensure fairness for the newly annexed suburbs. This was not welcomed among certain interest groups as it greatly increased the valuation of public houses, for example.[13] [13/14 Aug. 1900]

Five new wards were added to the Corporation bringing the number of members up to eighty. In January 1901, complete elections were held in these new wards and rotational elections in the other wards. Pile, a Protestant nationalist, albeit one who was close to Unionists, was returned with a large majority in Fitzwilliam ward, which had once been a Unionist stronghold. Nine Unionists were returned for the four new northern wards.[14] [17 Jan. 1901]

Victorian Dublin, the Dublin between the first reform of the Corporation and the extension of the franchise and boundaries of the city, has had its defenders in terms of infrastructure. As one author has written:

> The establishment by the 1850s of five separate railway companies each with its own elaborate central terminal; the achievement of the much-celebrated Vartry water scheme, bringing an abundant supply of fresh water to the city in 1867; land reclamation and improvement works undertaken in the port including the construction in the 1870s of a new deep-water basin providing accommodation for the largest steam vessels; and the establishment by the end of the 1880s of a growing network of telephone lines connecting many public offices in the city with a central exchange can hardly be described as indicators of decline.[15]

Yet, of these four achievements two were the work of private enterprise, one of a public body other than the Corporation and only one, Vartry, the work of the Corporation itself. In fairness, though, the provision of a new system of markets should also be considered as an achievement and this was one in which the Corporation had played a large part.

**13** Daly, *Deposed capital*, pp 234–9; Dickson, *Dublin*, p. 417; Ciarán Wallace, 'Fighting for Unionist home rule: competing identities in Dublin, 1880–1929', *Journal of Urban History*, 38:5 (2012), 932–49. **14** Dickson, *Dublin*, p. 475. **15** Cullen, 'Belfast and Dublin', p. 5.

In many ways the Dublin that emerged between 1898 and 1901 was a new city, new in terms of its geographical extent and new in terms of its electorate. Yet the Dublin that was to face the early twentieth century was, in spite of the improvement of its infrastructure, to have the same old problems as it had been noted for in the nineteenth century. It would be a city notorious for its poor housing conditions and high rate of contagious disease, especially among the poorer classes.

Mary Daly has blamed this situation in the early twentieth century on the dominance of publicans and landlords on the Corporation of the time. It was 'a Corporation whose actions were unchecked by any viable political alternative and a body whose dominance by drink sellers and tenement landlords did little to articulate any broader goals for municipal government, other than narrow political gain and survival in office.' More generally, and looking back on the nineteenth century, she is critical of the nationalist focus on anti-British politics, which she sees as a way of hiding failure to deal with the city's dire social problems. 'The evils of British rule became a regular theme in the increasingly nationalist Corporation, a convenient scapegoat for a body which proved singularly unsuccessful in tackling the city's numerous health and sanitation problems.' And there was little protest against this from below. Popular engagement over national aspirations by groups such as the Fenians certainly stunted organization, analysis and agitation by groups lower down the social scale.

Daly further blames both nationalists and Conservatives for the growth of sectarian tensions and for the Protestant withdrawal to the townships.[16] It was certainly the case that some of the few actual achievements of the Corporation such as the Vartry water scheme were won when members of the Corporation from different backgrounds were able to work together. Equally, though, it was a nationalist lord mayor, Thomas Sexton, during a time of intense politics, who was able to effect significant fiscal reform. A move to the new suburbs would have in any event been inevitable with the coming of suburban railways and trams.

Conservatism generally tends to be faced with the choice of focusing on its core support or reaching out to win over new adherents. Disraeli had successfully managed the latter strategy during his time as British prime minister. Though often toying with the idea of broadening their appeal, through the notion of improvement for example, Dublin Conservatives had

**16** Daly, *Deposed capital*, pp 219, 17. Tenement landlords figured prominently on the Corporation in the early twentieth century.

tended to revert to their base, with its hankering after the ascendancy past, just at the time when that base was shrinking with the flight to the suburbs.

*Pace* talk of the Corporation being a civic parliament not a lot of time was in practice spent discussing national politics. It was rather that the national divisions that ran so deep over Ireland's constitutional position and over religion soured local politics. Perhaps, though, it might be truer to say that Dublin, with its own long and particular history, was itself both a microcosm of those national divisions and a site for peculiar local conflicts between a recessional Protestant and Conservative establishment and what was eventually to become its Catholic, lower-middle-class, nationalist replacement.

Because there was no common social establishment no forward-looking civic vision emerged for Dublin, as it did in British industrial cities such as Leeds and Birmingham. The Corporation certainly produced some extraordinary individuals such as John Reynolds, Francis Codd and John McEvoy. It was only occasionally though, as with the case of Sir John Gray and his colleagues, that an individual or group garnered enough authority to push through significant change. The Corporation certainly never lived up to the much-vaunted aspiration of some that it would prove to be Ireland's civic parliament and thus a harbinger for Irish self-rule.

# Individuals mentioned in the text

**Albert, Prince Consort** (1819–61), spouse of Queen Victoria, the location of a posthumous statue of whom in Dublin proved controversial in the 1860s.

**Arabin, John L.**, Protestant Liberal member of Dublin Corporation who was lord mayor in 1845. He was subject to charges concerning his domestic life in 1846, which were withdrawn and he was appointed a stipendiary magistrate.

**Atkinson, Richard**, Conservative lord mayor in 1857 and 1861. He was criticized for the large number of freemen he admitted to the parliamentary franchise.

**Aylward, Margaret** (1810–89), foundress of the Holy Faith sisters, imprisoned over a custody case.

**Balfour, Arthur** (1848–1930), Conservative chief secretary for Ireland (1887–91), who relied on coercion legislation but also effected reforms. He was later prime minister (1902–5).

**Balfour, Gerald** (1853–1945), brother of Arthur Balfour and chief secretary for Ireland (1895–1900). He pursued a policy of reform.

**Barrington, Sir John**, Conservative lord mayor in 1865 and 1879. He lost his seat on the Corporation to resurgent nationalism in 1884.

**Barry, QC, Charles Robert** (1823–97), the subject of controversy in the Corporation in 1864 over whether he had been paid for helping it with a matter before parliament.

**Bazelgette, Sir Joseph** (1819–91), a civil engineer who oversaw the creation of a sewer network for central London and consulted on similar plans for Dublin.

**'Bomba', King Ferdinand II** (1810–59) of the Two Sicilies, unpopular in Liberal circles in Britain because of his treatment of his people.

**Bonsall, Onseley**, a Conservative candidate in 1860 for lord mayor in 1861 but his role in a controversy concerning the South Dublin Union damaged his chances.

**Boyce, John Tandy**, Conservative alderman in the 1840s.

**Boyce, Joseph**, Conservative alderman in the 1840s and 1850s.

**Brooks, Maurice**, lord mayor in 1874, MP for Dublin City, 1874–85, Protestant Liberal and moderate nationalist.

**Burke, T.H.** (1829–82), under-secretary for Ireland, assassinated in the Phoenix Park, Dublin.

**Burroughs, Sir Edward**, a Conservative who stood against O'Connell for lord mayor in 1841.

**Butt, QC, Isaac** (1813–79), defended the unreformed Corporation before parliament and, as a member of the reformed Corporation, debated against O'Connell over repeal in 1843. In the 1870s as an MP he headed the movement for home rule.

**Byrne, John**, a Conservative member of the Corporation in the 1860s and 1870s.

**Callaghan, Ignatius**, elected to the reformed Corporation in 1841 as a Liberal supporter of O'Connell but clashed with O'Connell over the latter's influence.

**Cameron, Dr (later Sir) Charles** (1830–1921), public analyst for Dublin in 1862; chief medical officer for Dublin from 1876.

**Carey, James** (1845–83), informant against the Phoenix Park murderers. He was elected to the Corporation in 1882 but was assassinated the following year.

**Carroll, Dr (later Sir) William**, Liberal lord mayor in 1868. He managed, as a non-nationalist Liberal, to retain his seat on the Corporation in 1884 in spite of the rise of Parnellism.

**Cavendish, Lord Frederick** (1836–82), chief secretary for Ireland, assassinated in the Phoenix Park, Dublin, on the evening of his arrival in the city.

**Chamberlain, Joseph** (1836–1914), mayor of Birmingham, 1873–6, and later MP as Liberal, Liberal-Unionist and Conservative opponent of Irish home rule.

**Clancy, John** (1844–1915), ex-Fenian and independent-minded member of the Corporation in the 1880s and 1890s who served as sub-sheriff of Dublin from 1885. In 1886 the Parnellites contrived to have him lose his seat. In the late 1890s he was an advocate for republicans.

**Clarendon, Lord** (1800–70), Whig lord lieutenant between 1847 and 1852.

**Cochrane, Sir Henry**, mineral water manufacturer and Conservative member of the Corporation in the 1880s and 1890s.

**Codd, Francis** (*c.*1808–67), a Catholic merchant and secretary of the Dublin chamber of commerce, he served on the Corporation between 1850 and 1860, presenting himself as an independent though mostly siding with the Conservatives. He often clashed with John Reynolds but cooperated with Dr John Gray and Robert Kinahan on the Vartry water scheme.

**Costigan, Denis**, a candidate for Dublin city treasurer in 1843 after James Finn absconded. He managed to frustrate the candidacy of Robert Guinness.

**Cotton, Thomas J.**, appointed as Dublin Corporation gas inspector in 1888. He was a brother of W.F. Cotton.

**Cotton, William Francis** (1841?–1917), worked for Dublin Corporation as a lighting and gas examiner in the 1860s and 1870s. From the 1880s he was employed by the Alliance and Dublin Gas Consumers company.

**Cullen, Paul Cardinal** (1803–78), Catholic archbishop of Dublin, 1852–78.

**Dargan, William** (1799–1867), Irish railway pioneer and sponsor of the great Dublin exhibition of 1853.

**Davitt, Michael** (1846–1906), Land League leader and member of the Corporation in 1886.

**Dawson, MP, Charles** (1842–1917), lord mayor of Dublin in 1882 and 1883 when the Corporation became more nationalist in outlook.

**De Grey, Lord** (1781–1859), Conservative lord lieutenant of Ireland, 1841–4.

**Dennehy, Cornelius**, member of the Corporation at various times from the mid-1850s to the mid-1880s. He was independent-minded, often to the annoyance of others, and became more pronouncedly nationalist over time.

**Derby, Lord** (1799–1869), Conservative prime minister, 1852, 1858–9 and 1866–8.

**Dickinson, Sir Drury Jones**, Dublin city accountant in early 1840s.

**Dillon, MP, John** (1851–1927), conferred with the freedom of the city of Dublin in 1882 and anti-Parnellite leader in the 1890s.

**Dillon, John Blake** (1814–66), former Young Ireland leader and member of the Corporation, 1863–6.

**Dillon, Valentine Blake**, cousin of John Dillon and lord mayor, 1894–5.

**Disraeli, Benjamin** (1804–81), Conservative prime minister, 1868 and 1874–80.

**Dobson, James**, Conservative member of the Corporation at the end of the nineteenth century.

**Drummond, Alderman**, member of the unreformed Corporation who came in for Tory criticism for temporizing with O'Connell over reform, thus losing his chance of becoming lord mayor.

**Duffy, Charles Gavan** (1816–1903), Young Ireland leader and member of the Corporation in the late 1840s.

**Dunne, Jeremiah**, lord mayor in 1848, defeating John Reynolds for the position.

**Fagan, James**, Liberal member of the Corporation; unsuccessful candidate for lord mayor for 1844.

**Finn, James**, Dublin city treasurer appointed under the reformed Corporation. He absconded to America with Corporation funds in 1843.

**Fitzgibbon, QC, Gerald**, serjeant-at-law who opposed plans for a new Dublin water supply in 1860–1.

**Ford, William**, town clerk for Dublin from 1842. In 1849, John Reynolds made an unsuccessful attempt to censure him at the Corporation.

**French, John**, independent-minded Protestant member of the Corporation, from the late 1850s until his death in 1880. Initially an ally of John Reynolds, he was identified as a Conservative by the late 1860s.

**Giffard, John** (1745–1819), member of unreformed Corporation who coined the term 'Protestant ascendancy.'

**Gill, Henry J.** (1836–1903), publisher, MP in the 1880s, member of the Corporation in the 1880s and 1890s, he was subject to orchestrated public pressure to withdraw when he wanted to stand for lord mayor in 1887 against Thomas Sexton.

**Gladstone, William Ewart** (1809–98), Liberal prime minister, 1868–74, 1880–5, 1886, 1892–4.

**Gough, Field Marshal Lord** (1779–1869), Irish-born general. In 1879, there was controversy over erecting a statue to him in Dublin.

**Gray, MP, Edmund Dwyer** (1845–88), proprietor of the *Freeman's Journal*, son of Sir John Gray and lord mayor of Dublin in 1880, he was seen as ambivalent about nationalism. He was appointed high sheriff of Dublin but imprisoned in 1882 for publishing rather than reporting irregularities in a legal case.

**Gray, MP, Dr (later Sir) John** (1815–75), proprietor of the *Freeman's Journal* and an ally of O'Connell, the erection of whose statue in Dublin he later promoted, was a repeal and then Liberal member of the Corporation in the mid-1840s and then from 1852 onwards. During 1859–61 he and others pressed for the adoption of the Vartry water scheme and he subsequently helped oversee its implementation. As MP for Kilkenny City, 1865–75, he campaigned for Irish church disestablishment.

**Gregg, Revd Tresham Dames** (1800–91), Protestant controversialist active in Dublin in the 1840s and early 1850s.

**Gregory, William** (1816–92), Conservative MP for Dublin City, 1842–7.

**Grogan, Sir Edward** (1802–91), Conservative MP for Dublin City, 1841–65.

**Guinness, Sir Arthur** (1840–1915, later Lord Ardilaun), Conservative MP for Dublin City, 1868–70 and 1874–80.

**Guinness, Benjamin Lee** (1798–1868), Conservative MP for Dublin City, 1865–8.

**Guinness, Robert**, banker and member of the Corporation in the early 1840s. His offer to become treasurer in the aftermath of the disappearance of James Finn was rebuffed.

**Harrington, MP, Tim** (1851/2–1910), lord mayor of Dublin in the early twentieth century. On behalf of the Irish Parliamentary Party in the 1880s he directed the nationalists on the Corporation though he did not become a member until the late 1890s. He was a Parnellite after the split in the party though an isolated one.

**Harris, Alfred Wormser**, Jewish Conservative member of the Corporation in the late nineteenth century.

**Healy, MP, Tim** (1855–1931), anti-Parnellite leader in the 1890s.

**Hudson, Edward**, Conservative member of the Corporation from the 1840s to the mid-1860s.

**Jackson, Frederick**, Dublin solicitor who promoted a parliamentary bill in the late 1840s to replace Dublin Corporation by a commission.

**James, Sir John Kingston**, last lord mayor of the unreformed Corporation and briefly treasurer of the city after the reform.

**Jameson, John**, whiskey distiller, elected alderman for Arran Quay ward in 1871.

**Keogh, William** (1817–78), discredited leader of the Independent Irish Party in the 1850s; later, controversial judge in the Galway petition case, 1872.

**Kimberley, Lord** (1826–1902), lord lieutenant of Ireland, 1864–6.

**Kinahan, Robert H.**, Tory member of the Corporation from the mid-1840s until his death in 1861, he was lord mayor in 1853. Very partisan during the first reform of the Corporation, he became more accommodating during the second, cooperating with Gray and Codd on the Vartry water scheme.

**Knox, Captain Laurence**, owner of the newly established *Irish Times* and Conservative member of the Corporation in the early 1860s. He clashed with Sir John Gray and his fellow Tory John Martin, causing Knox to resign from the Corporation.

**Kossuth, Lajos** (1802–94), Hungarian political leader.

**Lambert, James**, Conservative member of the Corporation from 1848 to 1862, lord mayor in 1859, having refused to attend a banquet for a cardinal at the Mansion House the year before.

**Lane-Joynt, William** (1824–95), Protestant Liberal lord mayor in 1867, his election, contrived by John Reynolds, interrupted the alteration of Liberal and Conservative since the second reform of the Corporation. His appointment to the port and docks board in 1879, when he was no longer a member of the Corporation, caused controversy.

**Lenehan, Thomas**, nationalist member of the Corporation from 1887, he successfully defeated William Redmond for the position of high sheriff in 1899.

**Lyndhurst, Lord** (1772–1863), Tory leader in the House of Lords in the 1830s who was prepared to countenance some reform to Irish municipal Corporations.

**McCarthy, M.J.F.** (1864–1928), ex-Catholic Unionist and political commentator.

**McClelland, Robert**, Presbyterian repeal member of the Corporation in the early 1840s.

**McCoy, Richard F.**, nationalist member of the Corporation, 1888–97, Redmondite lord mayor in 1896 and 1897, he lost his seat after a court case involving corruption which he won.

**McCullagh, William** (1813–94, later William Torrens McCullagh Torrens), Protestant Liberal barrister and member of the Corporation in the early 1840s, he became disillusioned with the repeal movement after the treatment of Robert Guinness and resigned in 1844. Between 1848 and 1885 he was a Liberal MP for English constituencies.

**McDonnell, Sir Edward**, Liberal lord mayor in 1854 who tried to reform the markets.

**McEvoy, John**, outspoken, independent member of the Corporation from the late 1870s until 1887, though close to the Conservatives and later identified as such.

**MacManus, Terence Bellew** (1823–61), Young Ireland leader whose Dublin funeral was a harbinger of Fenianism.

**McSwiney, Peter Paul** (1810–84), merchant and political ally of Cardinal Cullen. Liberal member of the Corporation and lord mayor in 1864 and 1875.

**Mackay, John**, outspoken Tory member of the reformed Corporation until he lost his seat in 1842.

**Mackey, James Vokes**, unsuccessful Conservative candidate for lord mayor for 1868.

**Mackey, James William**, Liberal lord mayor in 1866.

**Magee, William** (1766–1831), established church archbishop of Dublin, 1822–31, who called for the conversion of Catholics.

**Mapother, Dr Edward**, medical officer for health for the Corporation from 1864.

**Marlborough, Frances Anne, Duchess of** (1822–99), lady lieutenant of Ireland, 1876–80, who established a relief committee in 1879 for rural distress.

**Marlborough, John, Duke of** (1822–83), Conservative lord lieutenant of Ireland, 1876–80, who refused to attend the lord mayor's banquet in 1880.

**Martin, John** (Fitzwilliam ward), Conservative member of the Corporation from the late-1850s until his death in 1864, who failed to be elected as lord mayor for 1863 on account of his alleged anti-Catholicism. He also came into conflict with fellow Conservative Captain Knox.

**Martin, John** (Trinity ward), Liberal member of the Corporation in the 1850s.

**Maturin, Revd Charles Robert** (1782–1824), novelist and clergyman of the established church.

**Maunsell, George Woods**, Tory member of the Corporation from 1850 to 1860 who was often in conflict with John Reynolds.

**Maunsell, Dr Henry** (1806–79), Tory member of the Corporation in the 1840s and owner of the *Dublin Evening Mail.*

**Maximilian**, Emperor of Mexico (1832–67).

**Mayne, Thomas**, merchant, nationalist member of the Corporation in the 1880s and 1890s and an MP between 1883 and 1890.

**Meade, Joseph Michael** (1839–1900), building contractor and Parnellite lord mayor, 1891–2.

**Meagher, William**, nationalist lord mayor in 1884.

**Meath, Lord** (1803–87), received compensation because of the Vartry water scheme.

**Morgan, Frank**, Corporation law agent at the time of the Vartry water scheme.

**Moyers, George**, final Conservative lord mayor in 1881 under the rotation arrangement. He vetoed the first attempt at awarding the freedom of the city to Parnell and John Dillon.

**Murphy, Christopher**, a 'very dirty specimen of a Dublin porter' who gave evidence in 1849 that John Reynolds was not a burgess (municipal elector) of Dublin city.

**Murphy, William Martin** (1845–1919), businessman and nationalist MP (1885–92).

**Nannetti, Joseph P.** (1851–1915), nationalist and Labour politician and leader of the Labour group on the Corporation, following the election of 1899 under the wider franchise.

**Napoleon III**, Emperor of the French (Louis Napoleon) (1808–73).

**Naas, Lord** (1822–72, later **Lord Mayo**), Conservative chief secretary for Ireland, 1852, 1858–9, 1866–8, later assassinated while viceroy of India.

**Neville, Parke** (1812–86), Dublin city engineer from 1851.

**Nicholas I** (1796–1855), Emperor and Autocrat of All the Russias.

**O'Brien, MP, Sir Timothy**, Liberal and repeal lord mayor in 1844 and 1849. He lost his seat to a Conservative in 1856.

**O'Brien, MP, William** (1852–1928), nationalist and land-war activist and later founder of the United Irish League.

**O'Brien, William Smith** (1803–64), Young Ireland leader, sentenced to death but transported to Van Diemen's Land (Tasmania).

**O'Connell, Daniel** (1775–1847), nationalist leader, first lord mayor of Dublin in 1842 under the first reformed Corporation and dominant figure on the Corporation until his death.

**O'Connell, MP, John** (1810–58), son of Daniel O'Connell, dubbed 'the young Liberator'.

**O'Connor, John**, lord mayor in 1885 during the royal visit, MP for Kerry, 1885–7, owner of public houses and supportive of the interests of vintners.

**O'Donovan Rossa, Jeremiah** (1831–1915), Fenian leader.

**O'Leary, John** (1830–1907), Fenian leader.

**O'Shea, Mrs Katharine** (1846–1921), partner and later wife of C.S. Parnell.

**Owens, Sir George**, Conservative member of the Corporation, 1881–90.

**Parnell, Charles Stewart** (1846–91), leader of the Irish Parliamentary Party.

**Peel, Sir Robert** (1788–1850), Tory leader and prime minister, 1834–5 and 1841–6.

**Pile, Sir Thomas Devereux** (1856–1931), Protestant fish merchant and home rule supporter with an appeal for some Conservatives, who was lord mayor in 1900 during the visit of Queen Victoria and was created a baronet thereafter.

**Power, Sir John**, Liberal member of the reformed Corporation in the early 1840s who did not support O'Connell's motion on repeal in the Corporation in 1843.

**Purcell, Peter**, mail coach proprietor and non-repeal Liberal member of the Corporation in the early 1840s, who clashed with O'Connell and lost his seat in 1844 as a result.

**Quinton, Thomas James**, Tory member of the unreformed Corporation who warned that reform would mean the end of Protestant ascendancy.

**Redmond, MP, John** (1856–1918), leader of the Parnellite faction and of the reunited Irish Party after 1900.

**Redmond, MP, William** (1861–1917), brother of John Redmond, elected to the Corporation in 1899 but failed to be elected as high sheriff of Dublin in that year.

**Reilly, John**, repeal member of the Corporation in the early 1840s.

**Reynolds, John** (1794–1868), pugnacious repeal and later Liberal member of the Corporation who clashed with O'Connell over Corporation finances and later targeted ministers' money and the freeman parliamentary franchise for removal. In 1850 he was a controversial and undignified lord mayor.

**Roe, George**, distiller and Protestant, irenic, non-repeal Liberal who was lord mayor in 1843 but disapproved of O'Connell's use of the Corporation to promote repeal and resigned in 1844. He returned to the Corporation in 1851 under the second reform and supported the Vartry water scheme but resigned again in 1862 due to pressure from John Reynolds.

**Russell, T.W.**, unsuccessful temperance candidate for the Corporation in 1883.

**Sadlier, John** (1813–56), discredited leader of the Independent Irish Party in the 1850s.

**Salisbury, Lord** (1830–1902), Conservative prime minister, 1885–6, 1886–92, 1895–1902.

**Sexton, Sir Robert**, Conservative member of the Corporation in the 1880s and 1890s. In 1898, he was nominated as lord mayor for 1899 but after the municipal election under the new franchise he was not elected to the position.

**Sexton, MP, Thomas** (1848–1932), nationalist member of the Corporation from 1886 to 1892, lord mayor in 1888 and 1889, he helped to restructure the Corporation's debts.

**Shackleton, Abraham**, Quaker miller and nationalist member of the Corporation, from which he resigned when it was taken over by the Irish Parliamentary Party in the early 1880s.

**Shanks, James**, Protestant home rule lord mayor in 1893, he scuppered his chances of a second year in office by snubbing some other nationalists.

**Shaw, Frederick** (1799–1857), recorder of Dublin and Tory ally of Sir Robert Peel who was open to the reform of the Corporation.

**Smyth, John**, law agent for the Corporation who was unsuccessfully scrutinized by John Reynolds over a railway scheme in 1864.

**Staunton, Michael**, newspaper proprietor and repeal member of the Corporation in the 1840s.

**Stephens, James** (1825–1901), Fenian leader whose escape from the Richmond bridewell in Dublin in 1865 caused difficulties for the Corporation.

**Sullivan, MP, A.M.** (1829–84), member of the Corporation from 1862 until his defeat in 1870, proprietor of the *Nation* newspaper, jailed for seditious libel for supporting the 'Manchester martyrs' in 1868. He promoted the erection of a statue to Henry Grattan in Dublin.

**Sullivan, MP, T.D.** (1827–1914), brother of A.M. Sullivan and nationalist member of the Corporation from 1881 to 1893, lord mayor in 1886 and 1887. At the end of the latter year he was imprisoned on account of his political activity.

**Sweetman, Patrick**, stood unsuccessfully against John Reynolds for the position of alderman in Merchant's Quay ward in 1851.

**Symes, Thomas R.**, Protestant, non-repeal Liberal who was a member of the Corporation, 1842–3.

**Tallon, Daniel** (1836–1908), wine and spirits manufacturer and lord mayor, 1898 and 1899, he campaigned in Britain concerning distress in the west of Ireland and muted Corporation support for the Boers so as not to endanger the extension of the city's boundaries by parliament.

**Vance, John** (1808–75), Tory MP for Dublin City, 1852–65.

**Vereker, John Prendergast**, Conservative lord mayor in 1863, he was elected in spite of opposition from John Reynolds.

**Victoria, Queen** (1819–1901), monarch of the United Kingdom of Great Britain and Ireland and Empress of India.

**Wales, Edward Albert, Prince of** (1841–1910), heir apparent to the British throne to which he succeeded as King Edward VII.

**Walker, J.A.**, Conservative member of the Corporation in the early 1890s who was unpopular with his colleagues and lost his seat on the Corporation. He claimed it was because he was too friendly with some non-Conservative members.

**Walker, Richard**, Tory member of the Corporation in the late 1840s.

**Wellington, Field Marshal, the Duke of** (1769–1852), prime minister, 1828–30 and 1834, Tory leader in the House of Lords and ally of Sir Robert Peel.

**Winstanley, James**, nationalist candidate for lord mayor against Thomas Sexton in 1887.

**Wolseley, General Sir Garnet** (later **Lord Wolseley**) (1833–1913), was proposed, unsuccessfully, for freedom of the city of Dublin in 1882 by the Conservatives on the Corporation.

# Bibliography

## DUBLIN CITY ARCHIVES

City council minute books, 12. C2/A1/12 (Dec. 1842 to May 1844).
*Minutes of the municipal council of the city of Dublin from the 1st of January to 31st of December, 1881* (Dublin, 1882).

## NEWSPAPERS

*Dublin Evening Mail.*
*Freeman's Journal.*
*Irish Times.*

## SECONDARY READING

Barber, B.J., 'Aspects of municipal government, 1835–1914' in Derek Fraser (ed.), *A history of modern Leeds* (Manchester, 1980), pp 301–26.
Brewer, James Norris, *History of Leinster* (London, 1829).
Carroll, Denis J., 'Waste disposal and waste management in Dublin, 1850–1922' (PhD, Maynooth University, 2005).
Carroll, Lydia, *In the fever king's preserves: Sir Charles Cameron and the Dublin slums* (Dublin, 2011).
Clare, Liam, 'The Dublin Cattle Market', *Dublin Historical Review*, 55:2 (2002), 166–80.
Corcoran, Michael, *Our good health: a history of Dublin's water and drainage* (Dublin, 2005).
Crossman, Virginia, *Local government in nineteenth-century Ireland* (Belfast, 1994).
Cullen, Francis J., 'Local government and the management of urban space: a comparative study of Belfast and Dublin, 1830–1922' (PhD, Maynooth University, 2005).
Cullen, L.M., *Princes and pirates: the Dublin chamber of commerce, 1783–1983* (Dublin, 1983).
Daly, Mary E., *Dublin, the deposed capital: a social and economic history, 1860–1914* (Cork, 1984).
Dempsey, Pauric J., 'Cotton, William Francis' in James McGuire and James Quinn (eds), *Cambridge dictionary of Irish biography*, https://dib-cambridge-org, accessed 10 November 2019.
Dickson, David, *Dublin: the making of a capital city* (London, 2014).
Fraser, Derek, *Urban politics in Victorian England: the structure of politics in Victorian cities* (Leicester, 1976).

Geoghegan, Patrick M., *Liberator: the life and death of Daniel O'Connell, 1830–1847* (Dublin, 2010).

—, 'The impact of O'Connell, 1815–50' in Kelly (ed.), *Cambridge histroy of Ireland, iii*, pp 102–27.

Hill, J.R., *Patriots to Unionists: Dublin civic politics and Irish Protestant patriotism, 1660–1840* (Oxford, 1997).

—, 'The 1847 general election in Dublin city' in Alan Blackstock and Eoin Magennis (eds), *Politics and political culture in Britain and Ireland, 1750–1850* (Belfast, 2007), pp 41–64.

Hourican, Bridget, 'Reynolds, John' in James McGuire and James Quinn (eds), *Dictionary of Irish biography* (Cambridge, 2009), *9 Patterson to Stag*, pp 458–9.

Jefferies, Henry Alan (ed.), *Cork: historical perspectives* (Dublin, 2004).

Jones, Stefanie, 'Dublin reformed: the transformation of the municipal governance of a Victorian city, 1840–1860', 2 vols (PhD, TCD, 2001).

Kanter, Douglas, 'Post-famine politics, 1850–1879' in Kelly (ed.), *Cambridge history of Ireland, iii*, pp 688–715.

Kelly, James (ed.), *The Cambridge history of Ireland, iii (1730–1888)* (Cambridge, 2018).

Kelly, M.J., *The Fenian ideal and Irish nationalism, 1882–1916* (Woodbridge, 2006).

McCarthy, Michael J.F., *The Irish revolution, 1. The murdering time, from the Land League to the first home rule bill* (Edinburgh, 1912),

McManus, Ruth, and Lisa-Marie Griffin (eds), *Leaders of the city: Dublin's first citizens, 1500–1950* (Dublin, 2013).

Maguire, Martin, 'The organization and activism of Dublin's Protestant working class, 1883–1935', *Irish Historical Studies*, 29:113 (1994), 65–87.

Martin, J.H., 'The social geography of mid-nineteenth-century Dublin city' in W.J. Smith and Kevin Whelan (eds), *Common ground: essays on the historical geography of Ireland, presented to T. Jones Hughes, MA MRIA* (Cork, 1988), pp 173–88.

Maume, Patrick, *The long gestation, Irish nationalist life, 1891–1918* (New York, 1999).

—, 'Charles Dawson and the public sphere in late Victorian and Edwardian Dublin', *Éire-Ireland*, 50:3 (2015), 113–32.

—, 'Harrington, Timothy Charles' in *Dictionary of Irish biography*, https://dib-cambridge.org, accessed 10 November 2019.

—, 'Tallon, Daniel' in *Dictionary of Irish Biography*, accessed 10 November 2019.

Morton, Graeme, *Unionist-nationalism: governing urban Scotland, 1830–1860* (East Lothian, 1999).

Murphy, James H., *Abject loyalty: nationalism and monarchy in Ireland during the reign of Queen Victoria* (Washington, 2001).

—, *Ireland's czar: Gladstonian government and the lord lieutenancies of the red Earl Spencer, 1868–86* (Dublin, 2014).

Ó Maitiú, Séamas, *Dublin: suburban towns, 1834–1930: governing Clontarf, Drumcondra, Dalkey, Killiney, Kilmainham, Pembroke, Kingstown, Blackrock, Rathmines and Rathgar* (Dublin, 2003).

Prunty, Jacinta, *Dublin slums, 1800–1922: a study of urban geography* (Dublin, 1998).

—, 'Improving the urban environment: public health and housing in nineteenth-century Dublin' in Joseph Brady and Anngret Simms (eds), *Dublin through space and time* (Dublin, 2001), pp 166–220.

Royle, Stephen A., 'Workshop of the empire, 1820–1914' in S.J. Connolly, *Belfast 400: people, place and history* (Liverpool, 2012), pp 199–236.
Stack, Ellis, 'Victorian Cork' in Jefferies (ed.), *Cork: historical perspectives*, pp 172–91.
Takagami, Shin-ichi, 'The Dublin Fenians, 1858–79' (PhD, TCD, 1990).
Wallace, Ciarán, 'Fighting for unionist home rule: competing identities in Dublin, 1880–1929', *Journal of Urban History*, 38:5 (2012), 932–49.
Ward, Roger, *City-state and nation: Birmingham's political history,* c.*1830–1940* (Chichester, 2005).

# Index